WOMAN OF TOMORROW

WOMAN OF
TOMORROW

KATHY KEETON

WITH
YVONNE BASKIN

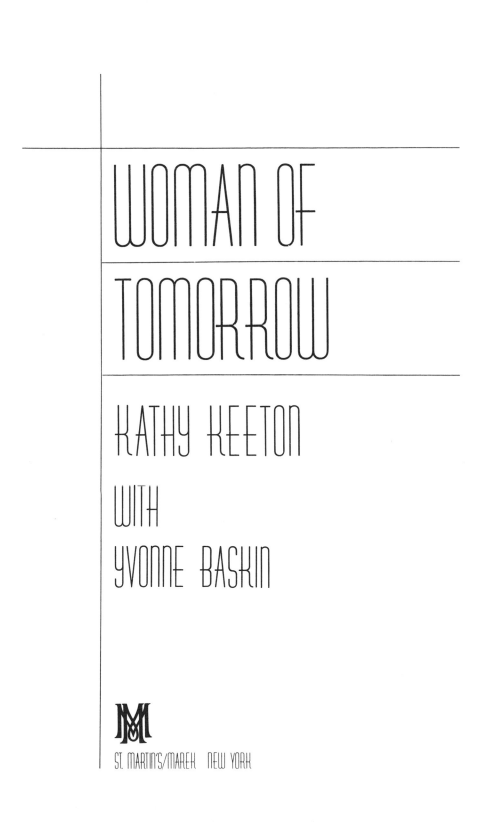

ST. MARTIN'S/MAREK NEW YORK

Grateful acknowledgment is made for permission to reprint from the following:

In a Different Voice by Carol Gilligan. Copyright © 1982 by Carol Gilligan. Reprinted by permission of Harvard University Press.
Sexual Behavior in the Human Female by A. C. Kinsey et al. Copyright © 1953 by A. C. Kinsey et al. Published by the W. B. Saunders Co. Reprinted by permission of the Kinsey Institute for Research in Sex, Gender & Reproduction, Inc.
Megatrends by John Naisbitt. Copyright © 1982 by John Naisbitt. Reprinted by permission of Warner Books.
2081: A Hopeful View of the Human Future by Gerard K. O'Neill. Copyright © 1981 by Gerard K. O'Neill. Reprinted by permission of Simon and Schuster.
Women in Science by Vivan Gornick. Copyright © 1983 by Vivan Gornick. Reprinted by permission of Simon and Schuster.
"The Mechanization of Woman's Work" by Joan Wallach Scott. Copyright © 1982 by *Scientific American.* All rights reserved.
"What's a Parent to Do?" Copyright © 1984 by *Psychology Today.* All rights reserved.

Design by Joe Marc Freedman

Library of Congress Cataloging in Publication Data
Keeton, Kathy.
 Woman of tomorrow.
  1. Women—United States. 2. Women—United States—
Attitudes. 3. Women—United States—Psychology.
I. Baskin, Yvonne. II. Title.
HQ1426.K43 1985   305.4'0973   85–12403
ISBN 0-312-88652-7

First Edition
10 9 8 7 6 5 4 3 2 1

TO BOB
WITH ALL MY LOVE,
RESPECT, AND
ADMIRATION

CONTENTS

ACKNOWLEDGMENTS

Woman of Tomorrow is an enormously complex book that required the cooperation of thousands of women not only throughout America, but also in countries as far-flung as Japan, South Africa, and England. All of them, those anonymous women who gave their valuable time in completing surveys, deserve a very special thank you.

Others contributed their time and insights, and need to be mentioned specifically by name: Eileen Koslow and Roni Stein, who supervised the collation and interpretation of material from abroad; Beverly Wardale, Molly McKeller, Elska Keeton, my cousins Shannon and Greer Keeton, James Odate and Eiji Nakayama of the Nippon Business School, and Kanae Takeda of Bancho Media, who all proved to be invaluable in gathering information in various localities. Also deserving of thanks are Chikako Lorenzetti, who painstakingly translated the Japanese questionnaires, and last but not least, Florence Skelly and the staff at Yankelovich, Skelly and White, who launched and conducted the major U.S. survey.

I would also like to thank in particular Bob Weil, the editor of the *Omni* Book Division, without whose help and encouragement over the past three years this book would never have been written; Marcia Potash, who provided all the essential public-relations planning and organization so vital to the success of any book; to everyone at *Omni* who has given me support over the years, including my assistant, Gerry Ryan; to Ted Hannah, who first told me to write a book; to my agent, Barbara Lowenstein; to the entire staff of St. Martin's for their dedication, including Richard Marek and especially Joyce Engelson, who as my editor was wonderful to work with; and to my collaborator, Yvonne Baskin, whose efforts throughout the course of this book have been greatly appreciated. The real heroine, however, is my mother, who always encouraged me to be ambitious and without whose love and support I would never have been able to be a woman of tomorrow.

A WOMAN'S TIMELINE
OF TOMORROW

No one knows what sort of lives we will create for ourselves in the future. The decisions are still there for us to make. But experts in biomedicine, space sciences, engineering, and computer technology can forecast the trends and breakthroughs that will shape our choices. Here, then, is a very possible timeline of tomorrow:

1986–1990

- Test-tube fertilization and embryo transfer techniques become socially accepted, and thousands of women use them to overcome infertility.

- The first successful gene transplants are performed to cure an inherited disease.

- The first truly effective metabolism-boosting pills to help with weight loss become available by prescription.

- Sex selection of children becomes a real alternative through use of new sperm-separation techniques.

- More men and women spend part time working at home and telecommuting to the office.

- A safe, implantable, five-year contraceptive is made available to women world-wide.

1991–2000

- Women and men born in this decade could witness the turn of the twenty-second century because of advanced life-extension practices.

- Energy-boosting pills, memory-enhancers, intelligence-builders, and anti-aging drugs become available.

- Videotex networks bring computerized banking, bill-paying, and shopping services into millions of homes, reducing the time spent running errands and writing checks.

- The burden of preventing pregnancy is shared increasingly by men after the introduction of effective male contraceptives.

- A woman runner sets a world record in the 100-mile ultramarathon, beating the best men's times.

- The first automated systems to screen fetal DNA for genetic defects are made available to hospitals.

- A man married to a professional woman is elected president of the United States.

2001–2010

- Home robots come into wide use for housecleaning, cooking, laundering, and babysitting.

- The workweek drops to twenty-five hours.

- Women can have embryos stored using cryogenic freezing techniques in order to beat the biological clock as they build their careers.

· Women make up half the crew on the first manned mission to Mars.

· The first woman is elected president of the United States.

· Pressures on working parents ease as a new kind of extended family becomes more common, in which close friends as well as relatives share in family life.

· Keyboards and typing become obsolete as advanced voice recognition techniques and artificial intelligence make computers easy to talk to.

· Each individual's nutrient requirements can be precisely calculated down to the molecular level and an optimum diet prescribed.

BEYOND 2010

· Advanced genetic engineering techniques allow parents to shape their unborn child's intelligence, personality, appearance, and athletic and artistic ability.

· The first "spacelings" are born aboard an orbiting space station.

· Artificial wombs are used to incubate babies to term for women who cannot carry a pregnancy.

· The first male pregnancies are attempted.

· Human children are born and raised in large settlements on Mars' and Jupiter's moons.

· Fusion-fueled ships shuttle workers and tourists to space stations and planets throughout the solar system.

· The first starship begins its journey to Alpha Centauri.

FIRST WORD

I like the dreams of the future better than the history of the past
—Thomas Jefferson

The most fundamental experience we can have is the mysterious. It is the
fundamental emotion that stands at the cradle of true art and true science.
—Albert Einstein

This is a book about our future. Women's future. It's a book not of predictions but of possibilities, because our opportunities today are better than they've ever been. It's a book about the things we women care so deeply about—health, sex, men, careers, babies, families, and homes. But, it's also about matters too many of us tend to ignore because, historically, they have been the province of men—the science and technology of radical individual and social change through bionics, computers, genetic engineering, space travel, psychobiology, and all the related wonders and promise of the next millennium.

There's no question that science and technology are the most powerful forces for change in the world today. They already have transformed and will continue to transform our lives in the most fundamental and personal ways even if we try to ignore them. After you have read this book, I hope you'll want to learn more about science and that you will understand that if you want to be involved in shaping your own future instead of simply being swept *along by the tide of technological change, you must have at least some understanding of what is going on.*

Perhaps some of you will even take up the challenge and get involved yourselves. If enough of us women do, I predict a marvelous future indeed.

Today's technological advances may seem less remote and impenetrable to me than to many of you because practically all my life, I have been fascinated with science. Many of the things that have already happened were once my childhood fantasies. I used to gaze at the skies above the vast South African veldt and dream of spaceships plying the thin air of Mars, carrying Princess Thuvia over ruined seas and scarlet swards. I read of positronic brains that mimicked human intelligence, robots created to serve humanity, astronauts living on space stations, and travelling to the stars. It was all pure science fiction then, the imaginings of men like Edgar Rice Burroughs, Isaac Asimov, and Arthur C. Clarke. I'm sure it seemed to others a most unlikely preoccupation for a farmer's daughter.

If all of it were only science fiction, I wouldn't wish my visions on anyone; but Asimov's positronic brains are today's computers, and Clarke's communications satellites serve us daily.

Scientists everywhere are in a high-stakes race to create the fifth generation computer, a machine as "smart" as we are. Industrial robots are already at work designing and building cars, homes, and jet engines, and even aiding in delicate brain surgery. Work on America's first permanent space station has begun, and as for Mars, planning is underway in the Soviet Union and the United States to land on the Red Planet as early as 2001. Does that still seem remote to you? It's only a few years away. Sputnik 1 was launched twenty-eight years ago, and John Glenn flew the Friendship 7 twenty-three years ago. It's sixteen years since we went to the moon.

Our minds can stretch easily into the past, much farther than our lives. Schools require that we study history, but they treat the study of the future as frivolous. I could never have guessed from what I was taught in school how quickly science was catching up with fiction. And I certainly wasn't encouraged to think that a mere girl could participate in bringing dreams like these to reality.

But my early interest in science never waned, and in 1965 when I found someone who shared it, I was thrilled. My friend Bob Guccione and I spent many hours, usually late at night, speculating on everything from the origin of the universe to the possibility of faster-than-light speeds. By 1974, we began to convert this idiosyncratic passion into a realistic enterprise. The debut of Omni magazine in 1978 was our dream come true. It was a business as well as a psychological triumph when you consider that the so-called experts and pundits in the publishing industry categorically predicted that there was insufficient interest in science, technology, and the future to support a national magazine devoted to the subject.

Well, Omni *disproved all that. It operated in the black within its first year and was quickly acknowledged as one of the most successful magazines in the history of publishing, fostering a whole new generation of would-be imitators. Today,* Omni *is the world's leading consumer-science magazine with readers in fifty-six countries, five million in the United States and Canada alone. Our books and television specials reach millions more, celebrating our collective vision of a better world and a better life.*

As president of Omni, *I enjoy the privilege of mingling daily with some of the best scientists, writers, educators, high-tech entrepreneurs, and researchers in the world. They've impressed on me not just the global implications of technology—for world food production, health, communications, energy, and so on—but the many personal ones, the human ones. I've learned firsthand about the revolution happening in the workplace, where machismo and muscle are rapidly giving way to mind, and where test tubes and silicon chips are creating thousands of new, well-paid, and personally rewarding jobs for people who excel mentally instead of physically. I've listened with wonder to accounts of new birth techniques, from genetic screening to test-tube fertilization that make it safe for women to delay bearing children until later in life, when their careers are solidly established. I've seen how electronic networks and satellite relay stations can bring vital medical information to even the most primitive areas of the world as well as every kind of information from "specials" at the supermarket to stock market quotes into our homes, allowing us to pay bills, order goods, or scan an encyclopedia with the push of a button.*

My job also allows me to invest time, energy, and money supporting important research projects from robotics and space science to the March of Dimes' battle against birth defects. I travel extensively and have developed an interest in art, for art and science are two sides of the same coin. A fundamental relationship exists between the two, something too few people in either art or science seem to appreciate. Unquestionably, that unique understanding has been an important reason why Omni *is so popular. "I love the art" is a universal comment from readers.*

But one thing that's become obvious to me during the past seven years greatly disturbs me. I meet so few women who share my enthusiasm. *Only 30 percent of* Omni's *readers are women. Relatively few women turn up among the thousands of men I see at computer fairs, electronic shows, and robotics and astronautics meetings. Only 13 percent of all the scientists and* engineers in the United States are women. Evidence everywhere says that large numbers of us sidestep math and science, ignoring the job boom in technical fields, sending sons, but not daughters, to computer camps.

Even though I've often disagreed with feminists, I must agree with Gloria Steinem's assessment: we women are "a Third World Country, wherever we are. We're low on capital, low on technology, and labor-intensive." **Others have called us "technopeasants"—as ignorant of technology as medieval serfs, overwhelmed by the changes taking place around us, and helpless to direct our own future. If we are ever to realize our full potential, I think women must take it upon themselves to reverse this trend; and do it now.**

Before I sat down to write this book, I decided to find out more reliably, through a survey, how other women feel about all this, and to get a look at what kind of world women really want.

What specific scientific and medical breakthroughs would be most important to you? What kind of career interests do you have? Whom do you want your daughters to emulate? What style of family life do you prefer? What do you expect from men? Do you want children, and if so, by what method, when, and with what sort of man (or sperm donor)? How do you rate yourself—do you have sufficient self-esteem, enough ambition? Can you adapt to change? (I've included a copy of the full questionnaire in this book in case you want to see how your answers fit with the results of our survey.)

I called my friend Florence Skelly, who is president of one of the country's most prestigious research firms, Yankelovich, Skelly and White, Inc. Florence, a true woman of the future, is also on the Advisory Board for NASA. Using our questionnaire, the research firm surveyed a representative sample of American women between the ages of twenty-five and forty-four, who had at least some college education and a household income of $15,000 a year or more. The researchers first telephoned a randomly selected national sample of women in order to identify ones who met our guidelines. Ninety percent of the women they identified in this way agreed to fill out a mail questionnaire. Questionnaires were mailed during July and August of 1984; 71 percent were returned, an unusually good response.

While that research was underway, I recruited staff, friends, and family to help conduct mini surveys in Japan, South Africa, and England, and among the women at our headquarters in New York. These responses, of course, can't be considered representative, but they do give some provocative insights into how other groups of women view the future.

As we approach the year 2000, I sincerely hope women everywhere will *rise to the challenge of the future and actively participate in helping to shape the twenty-first century into a world of peace and prosperity for all. It is perhaps an idealistic vision—but one that is well within our grasp as intelligent, caring beings.*

—KATHY KEETON
New York

PROFILES AND POSSIBILITIES

WOMAN OF TOMORROW

I am vitally interested in the future because I am going to spend the rest of my life there.

—Charles F. Kettering

Life is either a daring adventure or nothing.

—Helen Keller

New ages don't arrive with dramatic flourish, appearing overnight. They accrete in bits and pieces until one day we look around our homes and offices and realize the world has changed around us.

We're in the midst of such a transformation right now, hurtling into what various prophets have called the electronic age, the information age, the postindustrial society, or the superindustrial society. I know you've seen the bits and pieces that mark the arrival of this new age: satellite dishes sprouting on rooftops, computers in homes and schools, microchip-controlled microwave ovens in your kitchen, automated teller machines at the local bank, secretaries "processing" words instead of typing. And along with the advances in electronics have come even more dramatic breakthroughs in science and medicine: artificial hearts, test-tube babies, genetic engineering.

I'm sure all of you have been touched in some small way by this scientific and technological transformation. But I can tell from the results of our survey that few of you have cast a long look toward the future and prepared yourselves to take full advantage of the forces now reshaping our society. And believe me, *these forces will alter every aspect of our lives, and women's lives most intimately and dramatically of all.* I believe this new age, by whatever name it comes to be known, holds astounding promise for women who, as C. P. Snow says, have "the future in [their] bones."

Because of technology, tomorrow's most plentiful, challenging, and rewarding careers will require the powers of mind, not muscle. And psychology and brain research are making it clear, despite all of yesterday's clichés, that women have all the intellect and ambition needed to go after these jobs. Science is also relieving us from the tyranny of the biological clock, allowing us the freedom to delay bearing children until our late thirties or even forties while we concentrate on our careers. And soon into our fifties and sixties!

The changes in work and reproductive choices are, in turn, revamping our family lives, encouraging "parallel" marriages in which husband and wife both share the work within and outside the home. Innovative home technologies also promise to lighten the load of housework and errands, releasing women of tomorrow from the double workload most career women now bear (in spite of more helpful husbands, as you'll see).

From press reports, you might get the idea that people are frightened by these changes sweeping our society. The media, sadly ill-informed and often scientifically illiterate, perpetuate the belief that our future is one of irrevocable doom and gloom: disintegrating families, people thrown out of work by machines, cities eventually vaporized through atomic conflagrations and earth devastated by nuclear winter.

These dismal portraits of the future disturb me immensely. I'm bothered that talented journalists virtually ignore the positive accomplishments of science in favor of "monster-in-the-lab" type sensationalism. And also that they have so little faith in our ability to make technology our servant rather than our master. I've learned, however, that news accounts aren't always in synch with the real mood of a people. And this was hearteningly confirmed by the results of our survey.

I was delighted to find that 63 percent of American women rate themselves as generally optimistic about the future. Only 3 percent consider themselves generally pessimistic, and the other 34 percent rate themselves "some place in between." *The biggest optimists are women without children.* Some 73 percent of them are generally optimistic, compared to only 54 percent of the working mothers with children under ten at home.

Overall, 65 percent of the American women think the world will be a better place in the year 2000. Of the rest, 18 percent don't expect the world to improve in the next fifteen years, and 17 percent aren't sure. In contrast, the women we talked to in England, Japan, and South Africa were markedly more pessimistic. At least a third of them don't expect the world to be any better, and nearly half are uncertain. Almost two-thirds of the English women are uncertain.

When we asked American women how interested they were in the future, 38 percent said they're fascinated, 55 percent said mildly intrigued, and only 5 percent claimed to be basically indifferent. But when we asked them about science and technology—the fields that will have the biggest impacts on our future—few women claimed to know much. I expected that, but I was really discouraged to find that the majority aren't even interested in learning more, except about computers.

Only 6 percent of those women surveyed claim to have some familiarity with robotics, and only 27 percent say they want to learn more. (And yet, as you'll see later, two-thirds of women say they'd like to own a home robot that could help with the housecleaning.) Fourteen percent of women say they have some familiarity with genetic engineering, and only 33 percent want to learn more. A mere 10 percent claim some knowledge about bionics, and only 27 percent want to know more. Eighteen percent have some familiarity with molecular biology, and 28 percent want to learn more. Eighteen percent of women also have some knowledge of astronomy and 34 percent want to know more. Only a third of women have any familiarity with infertility and test-tube baby research, and about the same proportion want to learn more.

The exception came in the field of computers. Almost two-thirds of women—64 percent—say they have some familiarity with computers, and 63 percent want to learn more. I'm sure much of this reflects the impact of advertising, which diligently drives home the economic perils of computer illiteracy. Just owning a computer isn't enough to remedy this, however. Only 71 percent of the women who already have personal computers at home claim to have some familiarity with the machines.

Eighteen percent of these educated American women say they aren't familiar with any of these fields, from computers to test-tube baby research. That includes 23 percent of housewives, 22 percent of all the mothers, working or nonworking, and 21 percent of women who don't have personal computers in their homes.

Imagine my surprise, then, to find that three-quarters of women think we're just as prepared for the future as men, or more so. Only 25 percent think men are more prepared for the future, 38 percent say women are more prepared, and 36 percent believe the sexes are equal. That puzzled me until I read some of the responses that women on my staff wrote to that question: Women are "more flexible and more adaptable," "more eager for change," and "stronger emotionally," some of them wrote. We "have had to deal with more setbacks," "have been the underdog, which gives us the edge," and we "always see the alternatives in everything."

One of our advertising assistants wrote, "I believe that women are better prepared for the future. They're used to change. They've changed in the last hundred years. I'm not saying that men don't change, but women have gone through much more. We don't have as much to lose as men do. The future holds promise for women. I believe they're looking forward to the new changes in favor of women." A department manager noted that women today "have had to deal with changes all their lives. Men are just beginning to deal with the changes in society's structure, and the consequences can be seen. They don't like it. They're having a hard time adjusting. If I was pampered all my life I wouldn't want to give that up either."

What I read here is that *women simply think we're better survivors than men, whatever happens, and that we don't have as much to lose even if society is turned on its head. I agree. But women today have the opportunity to face the future armed with so much more than this hardy old stoicism. We can do more than cope. We can participate, and even lead.*

I believe women owe it to themselves, to their families, and to society to be informed enough to be active in matters that affect our future. You may not mastermind a communications satellite that brings educational programming to remote villages of the world, but you may have to help decide whether the PTA should spend its money on science lab equipment or on a new football stadium. You can certainly tell your representatives what you think of the lack of funds for research on test-tube fertilization or aging or alternative energy sources. You have the opportunity to speak when the local utility company is deciding whether to invest in solar technologies or strip mining. You bring video recorders, "smart" telephones, digital TVs, and computers into your home, and you have the power to use them in ways that strengthen your family and contribute to a fair division of labor around the house.

I certainly consider myself an activist, and I've become one without any special schooling or encouragement. Too many women believe that they need a Ph.D. in astrophysics to care about science. I have to disagree. All my early training was directed toward dance and theater, although that was more a consequence of fate than choice. Actually, it was the same fate that led me to my first science fiction books. Let me explain. When I was quite young, I suffered a case of polio that left my back and leg considerably weakened. Doctors prescribed ballet and swimming as therapy, and I turned to reading about distant times and places to lift my spirits. By the time I was twelve, my dancing had won me a scholarship to study at The Royal Ballet School in London. Off I went to a distant land, always keeping my science fiction books for company in this alien city. I learned more by visiting the museums in London so that I could better understand what I read. In fact, I learned more that way than in any school I had previously attended.

Only later, after I turned from show business to magazine publishing did I find a way to make a career out of my passion for science and the future. I'm certainly no expert even now, but before I go off to lunch with a Nobel prize–winning DNA scientist I *know* how to turn to my personal computer and retrieve my file on molecular biology.

Women in all walks of life need to move beyond technopeasantry. But more than that, women need to carve out careers in scientific and technical fields. It's not enough for women to want to be lawyers, executives, and politicians. The future is shaped by those who generate new knowledge, create new products, and find new options for solving the problems of humanity—hunger, overpopulation, energy and other resource shortages, and even the dangers caused by unwise use of technology itself. That's one reason I hope the women who *do* go into business and politics will be more technologically savvy than some of the technologically ignorant men we have in government and business today.

In a nation faced with increasing scientific illiteracy, we women contribute more than our share to the problem. There's no biological reason for it, and today no longer as much social or legal discrimination. As you'll see later in this book, the few social obstacles that remain are highly surmountable. The doors of the nation's science and engineering programs are wide open to us. I have to agree with Samuel Florman's assessment that feminists are sometimes "more concerned about battering on closed doors than they are about walking through those that are open."

In his book *Blaming Technology,* he suggests that women have until now been more interested in claiming the privileges than taking on the responsibilities of full participation in society. "But the ultimate feminist dream will never be realized as long as women would rather supervise the world than help build it," Florman concludes.

Look at how the dictionary defines technology: It is "the system by which a society provides its members with those things needed or desired." Too much female energy is wasted, in my own judgment, on side issues that will not really help the woman of tomorrow. *I think women of the future will be prepared to take a full role in deciding just what it is that humanity needs and desires and in guiding the technology that provides it.* I'm speaking not of hard-edged female technocrats, but of confident, feminine women contributing their intellect and their unique sensibilities to the twenty-first century, on earth and in space.

Perhaps it would help for me to show you a few of these women of tomorrow. In the time machine of my own imagination, I've often visited the twenty-first century and envisioned the women of that new age. True, they've grown away from us, but they are not aliens. You'd find them as bright and caring and witty as your favorite women friends today. But I think you'd see, too, a new spirit of boldness, of fulfillment, of optimism that most women of our generation have only begun to sense. Join my imaginings for a moment then and let me introduce you to them. They are being born among us right now. You'll find, in fact, that they are *our daughters.*

o   o   o

The year is 2025, the twenty-first century one-quarter past. Sitting in front of the small computer console in her den, Kelly leans back from her work and closes her eyes for a few minutes, shutting out the image of a Degas pastel glowing with rich warmth from the wall screen opposite her. A call from her mother, a fortieth birthday greeting from a cruise ship somewhere off the Chinese Riviera, had broken Kelly's concentration. She had to smile. She could remember a time when her mother had never vacationed farther from home than Atlantic City. But then Kelly had to admit that only twenty years ago she herself had actually been wary of computers. Late bloomers, she and her mother. But they were both flourishing now.

Kelly had been born in 1985 to what history books call a "blue-collar" family. Her parents' only interest in technology had been the purchase of a big-screen TV with a projection system that took up half the living room. When she was fourteen her father had celebrated the turn of the century by getting a small satellite receiver for the family camper so he wouldn't have to miss football games during fishing trips. He hadn't even let her and her younger brothers stay up to watch the spectacle of Earthlight 2000 that New Year's Eve. Craziness, he said.

Her mother had never worked while Kelly was growing up, and Kelly couldn't remember anyone ever mentioning that work would be anything but a temporary stop on the road to marriage for her, either. In fact, it wasn't that first time around. Graduating from high school in 2003, she had taken a sales job in a department store. It had taken about five seconds to learn to whisk the wand of a computerized scanner across the digital price tags, and Kelly had never asked what was happening at the other end of the cable. In school she had practiced her math drills on the class computer occasionally, but the teacher hadn't been too comfortable with the machine and had made only a half-hearted attempt to teach her what else could be done with it.

The same year she graduated from high school, Kelly had got married. Two kids and five years later, she had divorced. It had been a rude awakening, and thinking back on it now she found it hard to believe she had ever been so out of touch with her own generation. She had always assumed, deep down, that she would somehow be taken care of. When her parents had split up in 2006, after twenty-five years of marriage, reality had begun to sink in. Kelly was determined, when she divorced, in 2008, not to fall apart the way her mother had.

(Of course, her mother was hardly an object of pity today. She had pulled herself together a few years after the divorce, taken some classes, and after a series of resort jobs ended up as recreation director aboard the *Atlantis*. The cruise business, like the rest of the leisure industries, had really begun to flourish after the twenty-five-hour work week became the norm.)

Kelly had moved with her children that year to a newly built townhouse complex that offered daycare on site and schools nearby. She'd been able to attend college part time and begin teaching art history. In 2015 she had married again, to a computer systems analyst with a three-year-old daughter. With three children between them, they came to appreciate the support of other working couples, single parents, and retirees in the complex. The place had the feeling of a large extended family, with numerous aunts and uncles and companions available to every child.

In college, Kelly had been reintroduced to computers and video technology and holography, this time by teachers who understood their potential. She had delighted in being able to see the art treasures of the world in all their rich detail and true color and in "walking" around great sculptures, looking at them from all sides without ever leaving her chair. With the help of her second husband, she had used the interactive video to build an independent business that let her spend a lot of time at home with the children.

Turning back to her console now, Kelly speaks to the computer, and the digitized image of Degas's pastels begin to grow on her wall until they softly fill the whole screen. She gives more commands to sync this video close-up with a section of her lecture on Impressionism that's already entered in memory. She moves on through the lecture, cuing in pastels by Degas as ballerinas glowingly fill her wall, then taking a video tour through a nineteenth-century theater.

Next week, when her lecture is made available, the students will be able to listen to audio or read it as text while they watch the stunning video presentation, either alone at home or in class groups. They might interrupt or freeze the presentation while they call up additional material from databanks, discuss it among themselves, or record opinions for her to critique later. Today, of course, classroom teachers serve mostly as guides and counselors, leaving the course development to professionals in each field like Kelly. Teachers see their students a few times a week when they gather for sports and assemblies or take lessons together as some children still prefer to do. The job of the teacher is more that of social director—cum—guidance counselor.

Kelly finishes transmitting her lesson to the school system's databank just as her stepdaughter, Pamela, races through the door, calls out a greeting, and heads straight for the food preparation unit.

Pamela is thirteen now and quite independent. Just as the other two children did when they were younger, she has traveled extensively with her parents, visiting museums and cultural festivals around the world, making video recordings, and talking to art experts. When it's not convenient for her to travel with Kelly and her father, Pamela enjoys staying with her favorite "aunt and uncle" at the complex, Adrian and Mike.

o   o   o

Driving toward home, Adrian waves at Pamela speeding past on her bicycle. It's late afternoon, much later than Adrian usually arrives home. She wishes Pamela were on foot so she could offer her a ride and announce her triumph to someone. After a nerve-wracking series of auditions, she's just been offered the chance to play Desdemona in the amateur theater's production of *Othello*. Her first starring role, and she's bursting to tell Mike. And whomever else will listen.

For two people born in the same year, Kelly and Adrian's childhoods could hardly have been more different. Both of Adrian's parents were business executives, and she grew up ambitious to follow them. When she was thirteen her parents had turned the family accounts over to her for bill-paying and cash management. She had taken a lot of pride in sitting at the kitchen computer after school on Wednesdays, transferring money from the bank account to the grocery store, utility company, laundry, and other services by telephone hookup, then balancing the electronic ledger and moving the surplus funds into designated investment and savings accounts. Her parents had always checked the printouts and complimented her on her work.

Her brother, a chemistry nut from the time he was small, had been assigned to the terminal on Monday nights to put together menu plans from the family's list of favorite dishes. After analyzing the nutritional content of the meals and checking them against each individual's require-ments, he had made adjustments and then printed out a grocery list. (It had always seemed to include his favorite snacks, but not hers, unless she was especially nice to him.) He'd also managed to use the computer time to tally up the stats for his football team.

Both children had grown up feeling like important parts of the family, and dividing up the workload had taken a lot of pressure off their parents. Adrian found it hard to believe that her mother had once had to run the household alone after work, and without a computer. (Her father always claimed that he had taken out the garbage and loaded the dishwasher from the time they were married in 1976.)

Today, of course, Adrian and Mike let their "smart" computer do the meal planning, investments, and bill-paying automatically, just as it controls the temperature and humidity of each room, sends the remote vacuum unit across the floors on schedule, and heats the family's dinner on week nights just before six. They simply keep an eye on the computer/robot and every now and then revise the premises on which it makes its decisions to suit their changing lifestyle.

When she was fourteen, Adrian had rung in the new century partying on the beach with her family and friends, watching the night sky pulse and glow with the worldwide spectacle of Earthlight 2000. Orbiting mirrors and clouds of charged gases released by artists and technicians aboard dozens of spacecraft from many nations turned the night into a brilliant, man-made dawn. What began as a party became the mystical touchstone of a generation. Her parents compared it to a mid-twentieth-century event called Woodstock, but she didn't believe an old-fashioned rock festival could have matched the hope and joy of Earthlight. Even now, twenty-five years later, she would sometimes rise to watch the dawn and recapture some of the spiritual energy of that time. Not until Mike introduced her to acting had she found a really satisfying way to express that energy in her own life.

Through her mother's contacts, Adrian had landed a very lowly job in a real estate office after high school to help her pay her way through college. She'd stayed with the company while she completed a bachelor's and a master's degree in business, moving up to agent and then to office systems manager. She'd moved on to two other agencies, then a few years ago opened her own. And in all that time, she'd never seriously thought of doing anything else. She loves meeting new people, moving around the city, visiting homes, and having a flexible schedule.

Besides, the holographic images—three-dimensional images produced by laser light—she uses in the office to let people "walk through" and preview homes appeal to her sense of the dramatic. It still seems a little bit like magic to her, but she was delighted when the Multiple Listing Service began to offer holographic images on videodisc to go along with its sterile, computerized listings of homes. It saved a lot of time for her and her clients because she had to take them out to see only homes they were already interested in buying. And that left time for the little extras she really enjoyed—introducing the new family to the neighbors, the schools, her favorite restaurants, shops, and parks. And, of course, "her" theater. (Since she began the audition two weeks ago, her clients actually haven't heard about much else!)

It was through one of her clients that she'd met Mike, a psychologist and "human factors" specialist who helps in the design of industrial systems where people and robots work together. He'd also turned out to be an amateur actor, and his passion for classical theater had been infectious. Today they devote much of their free time to the local theater, acting, raising money, doing whatever needs to be done. Mike will be elated at her first big stage success.

They had moved into the townhouse complex together in search of a place within short commute of the city that had a real community feeling. Neither Adrian nor Mike want children of their own, or marriage, right now, but they do enjoy having children around and feeling like part of an extended family.

They had met Kelly and her family—especially Pamela—the first day they moved in. Pamela was only five then, and it hadn't been the happiest day of her life. Or Kelly's. Adrian had first spotted her neighbor on hands and knees in the living room, trying to scrape up the crushed remains of the crayons Pamela had left in the Butlerbot's path as the blind, primitive little machine was vacuuming. Kelly had asked Mike then to help her teach Pamela about personal responsibility in living with machines. Pamela had been their "niece" ever since.

No, kids aren't easy to raise, even with all the support that's available today, she muses as she reaches her tree-shaded front porch. She and Mike both have too many other dreams to work on. And besides, Nina and Paul are about to provide them with another niece or nephew after so many years of trying.

o   o   o

Nina's shuttle flight is about to touch down at Earthport 3. After an intense two weeks spent setting up experiments at one of the orbiting industrial parks, she's always ready for a break, and home is only a short jet ride away. Her husband should be home already, probably scurrying around with Maxwell III to get the place cleaned up for her return. She smiles as she imagines them. He never made that robot lift a finger when she was away. Tonight she'd get Max to set a fire in the fireplace before he shut off to recharge. She and her husband have some very special plans to talk about

Nina, too, had been born in 1985. When she was in grade school, her mother had bought her a computer and taught her to program butterflies that would flutter across the screen. Her father, with whom she stayed on weekends, was proud of her creative graphics but encouraged her to learn word processing "just in case." She had watched in fascination in the 1990s as television reporters aboard the early space shuttles beamed live coverage of the construction of America's first space station back into her home. Space became to her a neighboring country, like England or Japan, a place she resolved to visit when she was old enough.

In her high school, computers had replaced blackboards in most classes, from English to math to future studies. Even her basketball coach had used a computer to analyze player assignments and plan game strategies. At home, Nina had been forced to hone her own programming skills just to keep her computer-nerd brother from cracking the code to her diary. Farsighted teachers and counselors had encouraged her to pursue a broad range of studies so she'd be well prepared to shift career directions throughout her life. Today the prospect of change is not novel or frightening to her. Change has become part of the rhythm of twenty-first-century life, and Nina is well prepared. She feels in control.

Like many of the Earthlight generation, she had signed on for a tour of duty in the new Youth Service Corps after getting her first college degree. Her major in biology had landed her a post as a lab technician. She was sent to help an international relief agency manufacture vaccines against parasitic diseases that still plagued some of the developing nations. As she tended the computer-controlled fermentation tanks where genetically engineered microbes turned out vaccines, she had developed a fascination for microbiology that eventually led her back to college for a Ph.D.

Even as Nina probed the life processes of bacteria, the lure of space had never been far from her mind. Of course, with her training, she could have applied for a job in one of the orbital drug-manufacturing complexes. One of her closest friends from high school was already doing construction on solar power satellites at one of the European space stations. But that was technician work, and she knew even the heady adventure of space wouldn't be enough to keep her from getting bored with a job like that. She had been looking for a bigger challenge. When the president of the United States had announced her determination to establish a permanent base on the moon by 2019, Nina was ready.

Having got a Ph.D., Nina had won a slot on a NASA/industry task force planning for possible biomining operations on the moon. Since before she was born, genetic engineers had been modifying microbes to make them more efficient at leaching metals from low-grade ores and mining rare elements from the earth. New modifications would be needed if bacteria were to be of practical use in the harsh lunar environment.

A grander dream lay behind the immediate goal of mining and processing lunar materials. For three decades, work stations had been proliferating in earth-orbit–like frontier outposts. But permanent colonies, with families, homes, schools, and parks, were long overdue. The cost of launching the needed raw materials from the earth was just too great. Moon resources would finally make the settlement of space a reality. Nina, caught up in the momentum of the mission with a mystical fervor she hadn't felt since Earthlight, had embraced her job with the task force. The start of the twenty-first century had brought on a euphoria unseen in years. Now, with plans for the colony reaching their conclusion, a similar enthusiasm could be felt.

The camaraderie of her project team had extended beyond the research lab to evening soccer games and weekend parties. Most of the other team members had been in their thirties and single, too. Young people caught up in a goal. Colleagues had become close friends and work had merged into play. All of this had helped to keep Nina's spirits up even as the romance of her graduate school days was fading through the electronic mail. Not that she hadn't expected it. They had talked at the start and agreed it wouldn't be forever. Now he was halfway around the world producing a holographic documentary on another drought in the sub-Sahara. Still, they had been good lovers and close friends, and she couldn't talk herself out of that hollow feeling of loss. After six months on the team, however, she'd met a lawyer working on treaties and legal codes for the moon base. The rapport was instant, and she'd known from the start that this one wasn't going to be temporary, if she could help it.

Nina shakes her head when she looks back now at the apartment they had moved into that year, in the fall of 2016. The old structure had been put up before intelligent buildings became standard. The walls had contained no built-in sensors or microprocessors to control temperature, lighting, or security. They hadn't even contained hookups for telecommunications systems. (She had always been secretly pleased with one thing: this primitive arrangement had made a videophone too expensive to install. His mother was a dear lady, but nosy. She called at all hours and was constantly annoyed that she couldn't peek around the apartment electronically while they talked.)

The real disaster, though, had been the early-model maintenance robot that came with the apartment. Its vision and touch sensors were so unsophisticated it had quickly banged up the charming old 1960s blond Scandinavian furniture she'd inherited from her grandmother. But she and Paul had been younger then, still used to living like students. They hung their favorite Moondance Theater posters and felt perfectly at home.

Two years later Nina had got her first assignment in space, a month-long experiment with her microbes aboard a moon-simulation station, its gravity designed to be one-sixth that of earth. Her mother and a small group of friends had flown down to the earthport to see her off. The following year she had made two more flights. Busy as she'd been on those flights, she'd found time to linger at the viewports and watch the distant earth. For the first time since adolescence she had begun to write poetry again.

Nina had been finishing up her third tour on the moon-simulation station when the Armstrong I team, launched from another earth-orbiting platform, completed its history-making descent to the moon. Half a century after the Apollo astronauts first set foot on the moon, humans had returned to stay.

In the years since then, as the moon base had grown, the research task forces had been gradually replaced by engineering teams assembled by private industries. It would be years before anyone with her background was needed at the base. Nina had begun to grow restless to get on to something new. In addition to her research, she had started building up a consulting business based on her expertise in biomining and microbe husbandry in harsh environments. But she and Paul had decided they were ready for even bigger changes. In 2022, they had married and begun trying to have a family.

Leaving Earthport 3 now aboard a homebound jet, Nina recalls that for the first year or two, when she hadn't become pregnant, they hadn't worried a great deal about it. Perhaps their busy schedules had kept them apart at critical times, they'd figured. So they took vacations in Majorca and redoubled their efforts. It was fun, but it hadn't worked. Then medical tests had shown her Fallopian tubes were partially blocked, making it difficult for eggs to get to her womb.

Slowly her infertility had begun to eat at her self-confidence. After all, it was the first thing in life she'd ever failed at, and such a simple thing, too. She'd never thought she'd have to turn to technology for help just to have a baby, even though lots of women did.

But she'd been pleasantly surprised at how easy the test-tube fertilization process had been: just a scanner wand held over her abdomen to locate her ovaries and the developing eggs inside them, then a hollow needle punched through the skin and into the ovaries to retrieve them. In a petri dish, a lab technician had done then what she and Paul had been unable to do naturally—get sperm and eggs together. Twice she'd gone through this and had the tiny embryos deposited in her womb through a catheter. The second time had worked. Now she's four months pregnant, quite a welcome fortieth birthday present.

As soon as they married, Nina and Paul had moved into the same townhouse complex Adrian and Kelly lived in. Max had quickly become the star of the complex's traditional Sunday brunch on the green when, after weeks of tinkering with his programming, Nina had taught him to flip an omelet. At first she and Paul had balked at the cost of him, debating whether to settle for a simple maintenance robot or pay the price for hearing and speech synthesis capabilities and logic systems that would allow the machine to make some independent decisions.

Fortunately they had gone the whole way, and less than a year later Nina couldn't imagine life without Max. He's become a favorite of the neighborhood children, patiently answering their endless questions, often with riddles and puzzles, and tirelessly swinging his end of the jump rope. He also recognizes the voice prints of everyone in the complex and sets off quite a noise when strangers try to talk to the children.

As the plane touches down, Nina remembers that next month's trip may be her last space voyage for a few years. Soon she will be leaving NASA to go into business for herself. Paul recently accepted a law school teaching post that will allow him time to write a book on the fast-changing specialty of space law. Both of them want to have flexible schedules while their child is young. And they plan to make more time for their shared hobby of wilderness trekking.

By the time the child is in grade school, the first space colony should be ready for settlement. Paul has a good chance to be named as a magistrate and administrator of the colony, and both of them are looking forward to the chance to be among the first pioneers of family life in space. Being based in the colony will be convenient for her, too, since consulting opportunities will be available at the moon base by then. The moon. Another childhood dream almost in reach. As the electric cab nears the village, Nina leans back with a feeling of tired euphoria. The year 2025 will be full of new beginnings, and the decades ahead hold delicious promise.

o   o   o

I feel that no book has yet provided a *bridge* to tell women how we'll move from what we are now to what Kelly, Adrian, and Nina will be in the twenty-first century. This is what I hope to give you in the chapters that follow: an exciting, challenging, and optimistic look at what science tells us about ourselves and the needs, strategies, and sensibilities we carry with us into the future.

I'll explore how our brains are formed, what values and talents we specialize in, why some of us live longer and healthier lives than others, how our sexual styles are changing, which family patterns make us happiest, what our children need and don't need from us, how technology is freeing childbirth from the biological clock, what changes we can expect in our home life and on the job, and why more women should be planning careers in science and technology, helping to guide the forces that are reshaping our world.

We women have been claiming the *rights* of full citizenship for more than half a century, and in the near future we're going to be called upon to take our full share of the *responsibilities*, too.

I think the more we understand about *who* we are, the more confidence we'll have in facing the new century, not as resigned survivors but as take-charge, enthusiastic, happy women of tomorrow.

THE FEMALE BIRTHRIGHT

2
EVE'S RIB

At various times in human history, it was felt that the entire fabric of human society would be destroyed if more than some fixed number of planets were observed, if the universe were not geocentric, if the biblical account of creation were not literally true, if heretics and witches were not burned at the stake, if women did not abhor sexual activity, and if Freud were not wrong. We have survived our increasing understanding of the universe, and history has repeatedly demonstrated that knowledge serves human welfare far better than false beliefs.

—Dr. Jerre Levy, biopsychologist

What are little girls made of?
Sugar and spice, and everything nice;
That's what little girls are made of.

—Nursery rhyme

Chances are very good that the first thing anyone ever wanted to know about you was your sex. Boy or girl? For most of us, it's the first question that comes to mind when we hear of a pregnancy. After all, we need to know so we can tell what color crib sheets and sleepers to buy as gifts—or the value and type of fruit, jewels, or livestock to give, depending on your culture. But there's more to it than that. The very fact that we consider different gifts appropriate for boys and girls is a clue to our deeper purpose in asking the question. We expect the answer to temper our behavior and attitudes toward the child and our expectations of it.

I sense that a warning click sounded in some of your minds just then. Different expectations. Sexism, you're probably thinking. And you're partly right, because that's half the story. Every human culture fosters myths and attitudes about men and women that reinforce the status quo and help to mold individuals into roles that in the past served to keep the society stable.

Obviously, many of these roles are outmoded today and long overdue for change. The range of human possibilities they tap is much too narrow for a world caught up in rapid technological advance. We as women are already challenging the status quo at home and at work, breaching some of the barriers that have kept us out of traditionally male domains like law and finance. In the chapters ahead I'll be urging that we push even harder to make a place for ourselves in fields such as science and engineering that will have the biggest impact on our future.

As we break away from the old stereotypes, the attitudes and expectations we bring to the birth of a boy or girl in the future will undoubtedly change. But I want you to understand that even when all the social and professional barriers have fallen, the question "boy or girl?" will still have meaning. Our expectations, as I pointed out, are only half the story. *Babies, male and female, arrive in the world with built-in differences that go beyond genitalia. Sex, even in the absence of sexism, affects the way each of us perceives the world and behaves in it.* That's basic biology, not sexism, and biology is what this chapter is all about.

Women of tomorrow, women like Adrian and Nina, will possess the kind of boldness and secure confidence that comes from self-understanding. I think this understanding can only begin with an appreciation of our own biology, and that's what I hope you'll gain from this chapter.

The study of biological and other sex differences is being carried out on many fronts by anthropologists and psychologists, who catalog human behavior, neuroscientists, who probe the brain, and endocrinologists, who trace the action of hormones in the body. It's still a very young science; its findings are often controversial. But in the past two decades, a clear theme has emerged: *Every child is born with innate biases or preferences, predisposed to pay more attention to some sights and sounds than to others, to react to certain happenings more strongly, to learn some things more easily.* And we can spot these biases even before babies outgrow their cribs.

My friend Candace Pert, who discovered the brain's opiate receptor as a graduate student in the 1970s, is today one of America's most accomplished neuroscientists. She's also a mother of three children, and her observations about childrearing do much to underscore the role of genetics and biology in determining the behavior of a child.

"When we were first married," says Pert, "my husband was a graduate student in learning theory, and we believed in John Watson. We believed that a child was a tabula rasa, that learning was everything. I can remember our son crying and my husband saying, 'Is he diapered? Is he fed? Then everything is fine. Don't go in.' We waited outside the door, and the baby fell asleep. We did it, we thought—brilliant, rational parents of the twentieth century, using behavioral principles. Then nine years later we had our little girl, and we couldn't do anything with her. She slept with us until she was five years old. So we've come to believe that the brain unfolds as a flower unfolds. Of course it's nice if the flower grows in a supportive environment, with rain, good soil, and sun."

Some of these differences are split along sexual lines. By the time he's four to six months old, a boy baby is more interested in looking at objects, geometric patterns, and blinking lights than at people's faces. He may smile for you when you coo and grin at him, but he'll smile just as readily at a brightly patterned mobile hanging over his crib. In contrast, a girl baby saves most of her smiles and baby noises for faces that smile and make noises back to her. By about four months of age she can tell one person's face from another. (These are statistical averages. Few babies are going to fit these averages in all respects).

As their senses mature, boys and girls begin to experience the same world in quite different terms. The same sounds appear much louder to her than to him, and she's more sensitive to touch, odors, and, possibly, taste. His eyesight is sharper in the light, while hers is more sensitive in the dark.

No infant, boy or girl, is independent enough to like being left alone. But in the secure presence of a parent or sitter, boys and girls do behave differently. The average girl spends more time smiling, playing, and interacting with the adult while the average boys crawls off to explore. As they get older, she talks more, and he makes more noise. He spends more time roughhousing and trying to dominate other boys. If new children join the playgroup, she's more likely to take an interest in them. He develops better mechanical and spatial skills, but she learns to read more quickly and speak more fluently.

As they grow, of course, children also get feedback from their parents and from the larger world. This is where those attitudes and expectations I mentioned earlier come in. And this socialization process, as psychologists call it, can exert quite different pressures on girls and boys. Every woman I know can remember hearing "that's a boy's toy" and "girls don't . . ." pronouncements. I certainly did. I know some of you must feel that your life has been shaped more by such influences than by your own inclinations. But it's important to understand that you *did* come into the world with a unique agenda. Every child does. That's why boys and girls don't necessarily respond to social influences in the way we might expect.

Infant boys, for instance, get a lot more attention from their mothers than do baby girls. They get held, played with, talked to, and smiled at more than girls. So why do boys like objects more than faces? Why aren't *they* the ones who develop the more fluent speech?

Each child prefers certain responses from the world and quickly learns how to elicit them. Just think of the absurd antics you've probably put yourself through at some point trying to make an unhappy baby smile— making faces, cooing, jumping about. When the baby finally gets the response she's looking for and rewards you with a smile, she's also training you in what to do the next time she fusses.

Every child sets up a novel pattern of interactions with the world. Each response she receives is filtered back through her perceptions, and classified and stored. The process is what we call *learning,* and it indelibly alters her growing brain, revamping nerve connections, adjusting chemistry, further biasing her future perceptions, values, sensibilities, thoughts, and behaviors.

The end result of this interaction for any child is a uniquely individual brain. And if the child is a girl, the result is a female brain that, on average, will be quite distinct from its male counterparts.

Once again, I sense shudders among some of you reading this. Female brain. Female nature. I'll admit these concepts have been abused all too often, and we don't have to go far back in history for examples. The nineteenth-century craniologists and phrenologists collected human brains and measured them meticulously in their ludicrous efforts to prove the common wisdom that men were smarter than women (and European gentlemen smartest of all, of course). Much of this flourishing science of the Victorian era was pressed into questionable service to justify keeping women in their traditional places. Women's biology, it was said, made them too emotional and suggestible to vote or hold office, too delicate to partici- pate in vigorous sports, and too frail of nerve to attend medical schools.

(Amazingly enough, there are still some pathetic survivors of that era in the halls of science. In 1982, Vivian Gornick interviewed the distinguished nuclear physicist I. I. Rabi, then eighty-four, for her book *Women in Science.* He told her that "women were temperamentally unsuited to science. He confided in me that it was a matter of the nervous system. 'It's simply different,' he said. 'It makes it impossible for them to stay with the thing. I'm afraid there's no use quarreling with it, that's the way it is.' ")

These abuses of science make it easier to understand why early twen- tieth-century reformers abandoned biology altogether and embraced the notion that society alone makes us what we are. In emotion, intellect, temperament, and behavior, they declared, we arrive in this world empty, all with the same capacity to be filled by education and training. It was a heady, progressive notion, and in practice I'm sure it was far more humane than the extreme and misguided version of biological determinism that preceded it. *The early women's movement picked up the same theme: men and women want, need, and value the same things. Give us the same opportunities and we'll make the same choices in work and lifestyle and accomplish the same things that men do.*

The trouble with this idea is that it's wrong. It assumes that men and the institutions they've created are the human norm that women, once "liberated," will rise up to. It implies, for instance, that the legion of women now marching out of business schools should put on dress-for-success suits and fit right into the male corporate structure without making changes or disrupting business as usual. And it says that once the paths men have followed into science, math, and engineering careers are fully opened to women, equal numbers of women will flock at men's heels, settling into traditionally male jobs without causing a ripple.

But presenting our sons and daughters with exactly the same experiences —computer or piano lessons, soccer or ballet practice, astronomy clubs or babysitting—will not necessarily cause them to value and pursue the same careers, or to behave alike even if they enter the same fields. As we'll see later in this book, getting girls interested in computer programming often requires a very different approach than the one that captures boys' interests. Schoolgirls often take the same advanced math courses as boys, excel in them, get plenty of encouragement, and still opt out of math-oriented careers. It's time we recognize that girls and boys do *not* come into the world empty. They bring their unique abilities, or agenda. *And if we want girls to enter eagerly into fields now dominated by men, we have to make it clear that they can manage corporations, manipulate genes, or design interplanetary space probes without mimicking the style or sensibilities of the men who preceded them.*

Male and female brains—they are different, although not in ways that would support most of the sex stereotypes of the past. The distinction is certainly not one of intelligence, for the average female brain is as smart as the average male brain by whatever test we use to measure it. The difference lies in questions of values, interests, style, and motivation. Scientists have barely begun to figure out how and why, but throughout your lifetime you're going to hear a lot more about this research. I hope as you read these accounts of genes and hormones, brain circuitry and behavior, here and in the future, you won't fall into the old trap of thinking that "different" is a value judgment. "Different" does not mean "superior" or "inferior," and denying biology is not the way to shake off the myths that have accumulated about female nature. (In his brilliant book *Frames of Mind,* Howard Gardner argues that the human intellect is not a single entity anyway. Multiple forms of intelligence exist, including musical, linguistic, spatial, logical-mathematical, interpersonal, and bodily kines-thetic intelligences. *All* individuals, except the rare idiot savants in whom a single talent flourishes, have an intellectual mix that includes all these types in varying proportions. And the mix may be weighted differently in each sex, too.)

I believe it's vital for those of us who are sincerely committed to expand-ing women's options to begin to understand the agenda that we as women are born with and how our sensibilities are then shaped by our experiences in the world. *My dream for tomorrow's woman is not that she become like man but that she influence the future with her own intellect, values, and perceptions.* I'm firmly convinced that the female has singular strengths to contribute to endeavors that have until now been primarily male. Self-understanding must be a first step to self-respect as women of tomorrow.

o   o   o

If you were raised with the biblical myth of Adam's rib you might still have the impression that women are afterthoughts, or variations recast from an original male theme. But the Bible got the story backward. *The original human plan, body and brain, is female. Males are actually the makeovers.* All mammalian life begins as female. Let me take you through the process and show you what we know about how an embryo—from its sex organs to its brain—ends up feminine or masculine.

It hasn't been that long since we figured out how babies are made. A little over 150 years ago, scholars, all men of course, still believed that men made them. Their theory was that each male sperm was actually a complete little person—a homunculus. Unseen within the glands of each tiny male homunculus were even smaller homunculi, and so on—all future genera-tions of man packaged like Chinese nested boxes within boxes and waiting to be deposited in a womb to grow. Women served only to incubate the little male-begotten creatures to birth. ("Male pregnancy envy" is how researcher John Money characterizes the theory.)

In the 1820s, scientists using microscopes discovered the female egg and set that theory to rest. So sperm fertilizes egg to create an embryo. But that didn't provide any clues as to why some embryos turn out female and some male. The answer to that came in 1902, with the discovery of the X and Y sex chromosomes. Two X chromosomes cause an embryo to begin developing as a female. An X and Y set in motion the development of a male. The egg always carries an X, so it's the X or Y contributed by the sperm that makes the difference. Notice how tentatively I said "set in motion the development of a male." The pairing of X or Y chromosomes is only the first step in a chain of events that has to go off smoothly in order to produce an individual we'd recognize as male or female.

Every embryo starts life prepared to develop into a female. Within it are two clusters of cells that, left to themselves, will develop into ovaries. The job of the Y chromosome is to interfere with this feminine development plan and cause the embryonic clusters to develop into testicles. (It wasn't until 1976 that researchers discovered how. They found that a gene carried by the Y chromosome sets up production of a substance called H–Y antigen. This antigen coats the clusters, and by the sixth week of fetal life begins to virilize their development.) Once testicles have formed, they take charge of the masculinizing process, blocking development of another embryonic structure that would have become the womb and turning out testosterone, which spurs the development of sperm ducts and male sex organs.

So it takes a nine-month remodeling effort to make a male. Scientists call this the Adam principle—although it reverses the Adam and Eve tale. If anything interferes with the work of the H–Y antigen or the testosterone, the fetus reverts to its original female development pattern.

Now, all kinds of things can go wrong, with chromosomes, or the H–Y antigen, or hormones. An embryo may end up with only one sex chromosome, or multiple Xs or Ys. (An embryo with a single X can live, but a single Y cannot—another sign that the Xs carry the essential core of the human being.) Any one of tens of thousands of genes carried by the chromosomes may be defective, leaving the embryo with too much or not enough of various hormones, or even unable to use the hormones it makes. Sometimes the problem is not in the embryo itself. The mother may use hormones or drugs that leave their mark on her growing child.

As a result, experts like John Money, of Johns Hopkins University, who directs one of the world's top centers for studying such problems, find it hard to think of sex as a strict dichotomy, male and female. Sex is a range of possibilities, a whole medical textbook of in-betweens with various combinations of chromosomes, physical appearance, behavior, and internal and external organs: XX individuals with fertile ovaries and a penis of sorts, who may never question their maleness until they fail to father children; XY individuals who live unsuspectingly as women but never menstruate or get pregnant; even XY men, with fully formed wombs in addition to all the normal male parts. One of every 500 or so men you see on the street is XXY and probably doesn't know it, although the extra chromosome is likely to have left him sterile.

But that's not the part of maleness and femaleness I want to spend time on. There's much more going on here than who gets a penis or a womb. During the first few months of embryonic life a whole marvelous choreography commences as the heart begins to beat, the brain forms, nerve cells reach out for connections, tiny shoots stretch into limbs, and a recognizably human face takes shape.

The testosterone that begins to flood the male fetus at this stage stamps its mark not only on the reproductive organs but also on the developing brain. It may bias how belligerent the child will be, what hand he'll write with, how easily he learns to read, perhaps even whether he'll be attracted to male or female sex partners when he grows up. *(Bias, remember, not preordain.)*

Only twenty years ago those statements would have brought outraged cries of heresy from many scientists. Today, the evidence is overwhelming. That surge of testosterone during fetal life, and perhaps even in the first three months after birth, virilizes certain pathways in the brain as it develops. If the hormone isn't there in sufficient proportions, the female plan reasserts itself over body and brain. Testosterone can actually be picked up by nerve cells and carried inside, where it may influence which genes are turned on, what proteins are produced, and thus perhaps how the cells grow and make connections. *The issue that's still controversial is exactly what impact this hormonal stamping has on attitudes and behavior.*

I'll tell you a little bit about animals first, because that's where the research began and it's also where the most dramatic evidence for inborn sex differences comes from. The links between hormones and behavior in animals have been growing stronger since the early part of this century, even before we began looking into the brain itself for physical clues. The strongest evidence comes from the fact that we can take female animals such as rats, guinea pigs, dogs, sheep, or monkeys and cause them to behave, sexually and otherwise, like males simply by injecting testosterone into them while still in the womb or during a critical period soon after birth. Males, likewise, can be made to act like females by castration before or shortly after birth.

If you inject testosterone into a pregnant rat or monkey early, while the external sex organs of the offspring are forming, you'll get hermaphrodites —chromosomal females with male sex organs and behavior. (This happens to some human females, too, and shortly I'm going to talk about what it does to them.) Later in the pregnancy or shortly after birth, the hormone injections will affect only behavior, not appearance. So what does a hermaphrodite or a "tomboy" rat or monkey act like? The most obvious change is in sexual behavior: these virilized females tend to position themselves for mounting, as males do, rather than crouching and presenting, as their sisters do.

But the hormone effects also show up in nonsexual behaviors, too. Perhaps it's hard for you to imagine that male and female rats have different personality traits and abilities that can be measured, but they do. Males are generally better at learning to run mazes. Females learn more quickly how to heed a warning signal that allows them to avoid electric shocks by running from one enclosure to another. And when you put female rats into large open spaces, they're more active and exploratory, less fearful than males. Hormones can cause shifts in all these behaviors. Female monkeys given testosterone before birth are judged tomboyish because they engage in more chasing, threatening, and rough-and-tumble play than do other females.

Now for the brain itself. *The strongest connections between prenatal hormones, the brain, and behavior have been found in an area of the brain where you might expect males and females to differ—the hypothalamus, a part of the limbic system or "emotional brain," which we share with all mammals.*

The hypothalamus is the master controller of our hormones. It stimulates the pituitary gland at the base of the brain to release hormones that regulate sperm or egg production, menstruation in women, sex hormone production, and sexual arousal. The hypothalamus also regulates body temperature, blood pressure, and appetite. This is the part of your brain responsible for that speechless, sweaty, heart-fluttering feeling of love at first sight or the adrenaline surge and rising blood pressure of fear or stress.

Some of the effects of testosterone on this part of the brain are hard to dispute, since they're necessary to run the different reproductive machinery of males and females. *Before birth, for instance, testosterone resets the biological clock of the hypothalamus so that it will regulate hormone flows along a male schedule instead of in the cycling pattern of females. Testosterone also seems to affect nearby brain pathways that bias our sexual and courtship behaviors. And some scientists now believe it also biases our attentions, perceptions, aggression levels, social styles, and parenting tendencies.* But we'll get back to this shortly.

Not until the 1950s did scientists begin to find evidence of physical differences in the hypothalamus and other brain regions of male and female animals. (I'm not talking about anything so crude as comparing the average size of whole male and female brains, as the nineteenth-century craniologists did. Total brain size has more to do with body size than with behavior or intelligence.) And the first *direct* linkages between hormone exposure, brain differences, and behavior have come only in the past decade. Researchers are now able to alter *both* the physical structures of the brain and an animal's behavior by hormone injections. In even more dramatic experiments, they can make the same behavioral changes by transplanting parts of male brains into females.

For example, in the forward part of the hypothalamus in rats is an area called the "sexually dimorphic nucleus," or, more popularly, the "gonads of the brain." It's three to six times larger in males than in females. (And Dutch scientists have just reported finding a similar difference in male and female human brains.) Castrating a male rat or giving testosterone to a female before or just after birth will reverse this structural pattern as well as the animal's behavior. And when Roger Gorski, of the University of California, Los Angeles, transplants these regions from the brains of young male rats into the brains of their female litter mates, the females take on some of the mating behaviors of their brothers.

So that's the hypothalamus. *But what about the "higher" parts of the brain, the cerebral cortex, where learning and memory take place?* Well, some of the most dramatic work that's happened there has been done with canaries. Now I realize the canary is even more removed from us on the evolutionary tree than are rats and other mammals, but it has a forebrain that's equivalent to our cortex. Only male canaries are supposed to sing, and males have clusters of nerve cells in their forebrains that are three to four times larger than the ones in females. But, as one may suspect, a dose of hormones will enlarge the clusters in the female's brain and suddenly she sings too.

A structural difference has also been found in the rat cortex, although it produces nothing as splendid as song. In rats, just as in humans, the cortex is divided into two hemispheres, right and left. The right hemisphere is thicker in males, the left in females. And this sex difference in the cortex can be altered with the same hormone doses that alter the hypothalamus.

I'm going to turn now to our own brains. Obviously it would be unthinkable to do these sorts of experimental hormone injections and brain transplants on human babies, so, as a consequence, our knowledge about *direct* links among hormones, brain structure or function, and our own behavior is more limited. *What we do know can be divided into three categories:* First, we know some connections between prenatal hormone exposure and later behavior, without knowing the parts of the brain involved. Second, we know some actual physical differences between male and female brains, without knowing how the differences got there and what impact they have on behavior. We also have evidence that male and female brains process the same input through different pathways and with different efficiencies. And third, we've found some universally observed differences in the way men and women, on average, think and behave.

We don't yet know how prenatal hormones leave their mark on the hypothalamus, or cortex, or any other region of our brains. And we don't know precisely how any of these brain circuits affect our behavior. *The human brain is still one of our greatest frontiers, and I expect in my lifetime we're going to discover a great deal more about how genes, hormones, wiring, and neurochemistry set the stage upon which we play out our lives. There may come a time in the not too distant future when we know enough to intervene, if we choose.* By sometime early in the next century, if not sooner, I predict we'll have discovered drugs that will make schizophrenia, depression, and other mental illnesses successfully treatable. Later, through genetic or hormonal engineering we may be able to influence the personalities or talents of our children before they're born. (I can tell you that when this option becomes available, there'll definitely be a market for it. As you'll see in a later chapter, *one of every ten American women we surveyed, and slightly greater proportions of women in the other countries, said she'd consider making genetic changes in the intelligence, personality, or emotional traits of her child if it were possible.*) Farther on the horizon there exists the possibility of "biochips," tiny organic computers that can be inserted into our brains, perhaps making the wealth of all the world's libraries instantly available to our memory circuits. But that's tomorrow. Let's look at what we know now, one area at a time.

First, how does our exposure to hormones in the womb influence our behavior? Since we wouldn't think of experimenting directly on people to find the answers, scientists have studied instead some of nature's own experiments—those in-between individuals we discussed earlier for whom fetal life didn't go normally.

The most valuable insights have come from girls with a genetic defect called adrenogenital syndrome that causes their own adrenal glands to churn out abnormally high levels of testosterone. Their exposure to this testosterone begins early in fetal life, so the girls are physically virilized to some degree. They usually have an incomplete penis or else very ambiguous sex organs. Money and Anke Ehrhardt, a clinical psychologist who is now at Columbia College of Physicians and Surgeons, wondered whether this unusual exposure also influenced the girls' attitudes and behavior. (By the way, I'd better clarify here that *all* women produce testosterone, just as *all* men produce estrogen. The sex hormones were labeled male and female when they were first isolated in the 1920s, but it's quite misleading. The difference between normal men and women is not *which* hormones they secrete, but the ratios.)

Before 1950, the kind of behavioral study Money and Ehrhardt wanted to do wasn't possible. There was no treatment for these girls. The flood of testosterone continued to masculinize and distort their bodies, sometimes bringing them to puberty as early as three years of age. Since they couldn't grow up being treated like normal girls, it was meaningless to compare their attitudes and behavior with that of the other girls around them. In the United States today, however, such girls are usually diagnosed at birth. Drug treatments are available to prevent further virilization, their genitals are surgically feminized if necessary, and they're raised as normal girls. *But their brains retain the testosterone imprint.*

The result, Money and Ehrhardt found, was a group of girls who proudly regarded themselves as tomboys and were regarded as such by friends and families. They preferred athletic, outdoor play and competitive team sports that, until recently, were still considered the domain of boys. "They liked boys to permit them to play on their baseball, football, and other teams, but they did not become dominant or assertive to an extent that would not be tolerated by boys," Money wrote. They were not "assaultive or violent" but they weren't "timid in self-defense," either. They preferred jeans to dresses. "They neglected the dolls they possessed or else gave them away," he noted. They were either indifferent about or actively avoided "rehearsing parentalism in doll play and playing house with friends . . . and when they became older, baby-sitting." They envisioned themselves growing up to have independent careers, with roles as wives and mothers secondary. "In teenage they reached the dating and romantic stage three to nine years later than their age mates," Money found.

June Reinisch, now head of the prestigious Kinsey Institute, in Bloomington, Indiana, has played a seminal role over the last decade in the study of sex role differences in boys and girls. Like Money, Reinisch found similar dispositions in girls whose mothers had taken synthetic progestogens during pregnancy (usually to try to prevent a threatened miscarriage). Progestogens are in the same family as testosterone. And boys who had received this added hormone exposure while still in the womb were rated more energetic and aggressive than average boys.

While Reinisch's professional career is interesting, so is her personal story. I came to know her in 1984, when she already had been appointed to the Kinsey Institute for Research in Sex, Gender, and Reproduction, but her life story, in my opinion, reflects that of a real "woman of tomorrow." In the 1960s, June was enormously successful as a rock promoter, booking such groups as Sly and the Family Stone, as well as concerts like Woodstock. Although she was already at the top of her profession, she decided that she would never be taken seriously, as a woman, if she remained attached to the world of rock.

"I was a woman, and there *weren't* any women in the record business then, except for the secretaries and a couple in the art department, maybe. So there was only one thing to do. And that was to get a master's degree in psychology, earn myself a little respect, get taken on in a record company's personnel division, and then be switched, with the help of friends, to A & R, y'know, 'Artists and Repertoire.' "

Reinisch, in attaining her Ph.D. from Columbia University in biological psychology, became a trendsetter for her generation, a woman who immersed herself rigorously in science in order to be taken seriously as a professional and as a woman.

Along the way, Reinisch became fascinated by the existence of a group of young girls and women who had been exposed in utero to high concentrations of male hormones. It was a subject that drew a response from her past. "I was a horrendous tomboy. I looked like one. I behaved like one. There was little feminine about me," June today recalls.

I cite Reinisch's story in some detail because I want to say something about the word *tomboy*. I'm using it for the same reason John Money used it in this context. People know what you're talking about when you say it. But it's a misleading word. It implies there are exclusively male traits and exclusively female traits, and girls who display male traits are tomboys. That's a false dichotomy. As Money says, the only noninterchangeable abilities are that males can impregnate and that females can menstruate, gestate, and lactate. And you don't even have to do any of those to qualify as a man or woman. (Money thinks science will make even these roles interchangeable by end of century.) The traits we call tomboyish are really part of the normal range of female characteristics, and most of us who grew up that way suffered no disease. (I was one of those proud tomboys who trooped around at the head of a pack of little boys, shooting peaches and apricots off fruit trees with my catapult. The best peaches were at the top of the tree.) Adrenogenital children have a disease, but their preference for jeans and sports is not pathological. In fact, since every baby develops under the influence of a slightly different mix of hormones, that in itself may be the source of a lot of the individual variations in temperament we see in both men and women.

But the question remains, just what do prenatal hormones do to our behavior? They certainly don't turn us into robots with preset responses to life. Life experiences may even erase their impact entirely. Ehrhardt has pointed out that some adrenogenital girls aren't tomboyish at all. Here's how Money and many others in the field of sex differences have come to think about hormones: *Certain capacities such as the ability to learn a language, nurture our young, or fight when our life is endangered are wired into all humans as part of our genetic legacy. What hormones do is to adjust the "biostat," the thresholds at which some behaviors will be triggered in each individual.* A key difference between the sexes is therefore the way similar behaviors are organized and elicited—for example, what catches our attention, what we respond to most, the range of our response, and its intensity, what we learn most easily.

We already know that prenatal hormones organize and sensitize our sex-related traits, the ones that are activated at puberty by a new surge of hormones. For instance, biological events that take place at the beginning of the second trimester of pregnancy determine whether you grow a beard or start to menstruate when you reach puberty. It's probable that some of our most fundamental behavioral traits are organized in the same way.

Money has come up with a list of *nine basic kinds of behavior* that can be related to hormonal changes. The list isn't set in concrete, and he's the first to say it may need to be revised as more research is done on us and our fellow primates:

1. High activity levels and expenditure of energy, especially in athletics and muscular work
2. Competitive rivalry and assertiveness, especially for "a higher rank in the dominance hierarchy of childhood"
3. Roaming and territory- or boundary-mapping or marking (perhaps seen in the way boy babies crawl off to explore)
4. Defense against intruders and predators

These first four are more prevalent or more easily triggered in males.

5. Guarding and defense of the young
6. Nesting or homemaking
7. Parental care of the young

These second three are more prevalent or more easily triggered in females.

8. Male or female style of sexual rehearsal play
9. Method of sexual arousal (Dependence on erotic images is most prevalent in men, dependence on touch and physical stimulation in women.)

This is a much more realistic way of looking at human nature than is dividing all our traits into two separate camps. Aggression, for instance, used to be considered a male trait (and by default women were considered passive). There's no question that men commit most of the mayhem in any culture, no matter what other nontraditional division of labors they've adopted. Even among the Tchambuli people of New Guinea, where anthropologist Margaret Mead found that the women fished and conducted business while their men danced, adorned themselves, and gossiped, men were still the headhunters. Men everywhere fight most of the wars, commit most of the murders.

Now we realize, however, that aggression is a potential the sexes share. What makes men and women different is the sort of provocation they'll respond to, and the intensity and duration of their rage. Men are much more likely than women to get worked up to fighting level over honor, tradition, or territory. Start a far-off war or invoke the honor of long-dead patriots, and young men will flock to recruiting stations to get their share of the glory. Make the threat personal, to child or loved one, and a woman can react with violence as fierce as any man's. Culture, too, influences how people respond to provocations. Some societies wink at adultery. Others require that it be avenged by blood. Women in cultures that live by war and violence may be more ferocious than most men in more peaceful cultures.

And speaking of violence, there's a possible spin-off of number nine on Money's list that's provoking fierce and impassioned debate among otherwise calm people. It has to do with homosexuality. Very few researchers today think a person is born with predetermined sexual preferences. ***But there may well be some differences in the way the hypothalamic-pituitary pathway is programmed before birth that "expedites, though does not preordain" the development of a homosexual, bisexual, or heterosexual, Money says.*** Such programming may make it "either easy or difficult to conform to one or the other of the strict gender stereotypes," he says, leaving some children more or less "versatile" than others—or "vulnerable" if you think of homosexuality as pathological.

Some researchers have found a biological difference between straight men and *some* gay men that could reflect the influence of prenatal hormones on their brains. The experiments involve the way the men's bodies respond to injections of estrogen, a response that's ultimately regulated by the hypothalamus. Some of the homosexuals had response patterns that were halfway between those of heterosexual men and heterosexual women. Similar results were found both in West Germany, during the 1970s, and more recently at the State University of New York at Stony Brook. (Nobody seems to have done such research on gay women.) Money notes that if hormones are a factor, they must do their work in prenatal life because therapists who have tried to "cure" adult homosexuals by altering their testosterone levels have failed completely.

Again, inborn biases don't assure that a person will grow up to be bisexual or homosexual. And the social factors that tip the final balance during childhood are even more obscure than the biological ones. Perhaps subtle distortions in family roles and relationships may send mixed signals to a child about what's expected, Money says. The father may "covertly court his son's allegiance, in place of what he finds missing in his wife," and the son "may solicit his father's allegiance as a formula for keeping him in the household, and for preventing a parental separation." Money also notes that in a society like ours that hasn't learned to deal with normal childhood sexuality, it's no wonder that healthy masculinity or femininity sometimes ends up "misrepresented or transposed in the brain."

Now the second area we know something about is actual physical differences between men's and women's brains. There are structural differences, although we don't know how they develop. And there are also differences in the ways male and female brains function. *Circumstantial evidence seems to point to these differences to account for women's advantage in verbal ability, social savvy, and intuition, and for men's superior mechanical and spatial skills.*

I am referring to the largest portion of our brains, the cerebral cortex. This is the "thinking" part of the brain, the seat of mind and consciousness. The cerebrum is divided into two hemispheres, right and left, connected by a large bundle of nerves called the corpus callosum. *I'm quite sure you've heard popular accounts about right brain/left brain differences; that is, men are right-brained, women, left-brained. Well, it's not that simple at all. The package just doesn't fit together that way.* Every normal person uses both sides of the brain for almost every intellectual or perceptual process. (Jerre Levy, who's been in the forefront of this work for many years, says that the "reality of the human brain . . . is contentious, mislead-ing, complex, and flirtatious." I think she said it with more awe than frustration because it's a marvelous puzzle on which to spend a lifetime.)

Neuroscientists like Levy are still trying to sort out exactly what the capabilities and specialties of the right and left hemispheres are. They are also still trying to pin down what's different about how the hemispheres operate in men and women. And they're not sure yet how these differences in men and women develop. I'll start at the beginning because this is a fascinating quest that you will hear a lot more about in the future.

Our basic understanding of how the right and left brain operate came out of the work of Nobel Laureate Roger Sperry and his group, including Levy, at the California Institute of Technology in the 1960s. To test the competencies of each hemisphere, the team used a machine that separated the field of vision so that the left eye was presented with a different image than the right. The left eye sends its input to the right hemisphere, the right eye to the left. To make sure they were testing the talents of each side of the brain individually, the researchers worked with so-called split-brain patients. These were people whose corpus callosa had been surgically severed in a last-ditch effort to relieve devastating epileptic seizures. Their hemispheres couldn't "talk" to one another, so during the test each side of the brain was on its own.

From the results a *basic theory* emerged: In almost all right-handers and two-thirds of left-handers, the left brain specializes in speech and language, the understanding of symbols and abstract complexities. It is rational, analytical, and attentive to detail. The right brain specializes in visual-spatial tasks, including rapid pattern analysis, but it's also good at recogniz-ing melodies, interpreting tone of voice, recognizing faces, "getting" jokes, and appreciating metaphor. It is intuitive and holistic, specializing in syn-thesizing things into global form.

Much has been learned since then, especially from newer tests using normal individuals whose right and left brains interact. Levy, who is now at the University of Chicago, says that *it now seems possible that each hemisphere may have both analytic and synthetic skills. The two sides of the brain may split up the work based on the nature of the task at hand.* Under this theory, the work of detailed analysis would be assigned to the hemisphere that's not able to put together the big picture. For instance, when Levy used verbal test material, no matter which side of the brain received it, "it was the normal left hemisphere that manifested holistic processing. The right hemisphere exhibited feature-by-feature analysis." If the incoming information were spatial, then presumably the left side would pick apart the details while the right side put together "the emergent synthesis."

A further complexity is suggested by the work of Polly Henninger, who once worked with Sperry and is now at Pitzer College. Her work suggests "that each hemisphere may itself house a hemisphere—a secondary center that to an as yet undetermined degree mimics the role and functions of the opposite half of the brain." Other researchers suggest a division of labor that makes the right side of the brain a "jack-of-all-trades, a generalist" that tackles novel problems. The left side under this scheme is a specialist, making quick work of familiar problems. So while a musical novice would put her right brain to work trying to name a tune, a professional musician would leave such a routine task to her left hemisphere.

When we try to figure out the differences in how male and female hemispheres operate, the puzzle becomes even more complex. Sex differences do show up in the kinds of experiments I've just described. *The pattern of electrical activity and blood flowing through the brain while a man or woman is performing various tasks is different.* The results could reflect variations on how specialized each hemisphere is, what functions each side is best at, the speed with which each side processes information, or how closely the right and left hemispheres work together in men and women.

Levy proposed more than a decade ago that *a woman's brain may be less "lateralized," less tightly organized than a man's.* In other words, verbal functions like speaking and understanding what others say aren't centralized in a single area of women's brains the way they are in men's. This could explain why men are more likely than women to lose their ability to speak coherently after a stroke on the left side of the brain, or to suffer deficits in spatial ability after the right side is damaged.

The major sex difference that's been found in the structure of the human brain also fits nicely with the possibility that women's brains are less specialized and have greater integration and communication between the two sides than men's brains. A team of scientists reported just three years ago that the back end of the corpus callosum is broader and larger in women than in men, even before birth. The greater size of this nerve cable could indicate that women have more pathways for interaction between the hemispheres.

More recently, Levy has also suggested that *men and women may use the same sides of their brains for different purposes.* Each hemisphere may specialize in different skills for each sex. Men, for instance, excel at spatial tasks like rotating three-dimensional images in their heads and picturing what they look like on all sides. That's considered a right hemisphere specialty. Women's right hemispheres apparently aren't as specialized in this skill, but they appear to be more highly specialized than men's in understanding emotion and discerning the meaning of facial expressions. (Martin Safer, at Catholic University, suggests we may have another advantage in understanding emotion, too, because after our right brain has interpreted the image, it gets better help from our left side in putting a verbal label on it—happy, sad, angry. Perhaps this is why we're better able to put our own emotions into words, too.)

Even some of the disabilities men and women suffer seem linked to hemispheric differences in the brain. For instance, autistic, reading-disabled, and mathematically *gifted* children, and their relatives, are much more likely than other people to be left-handed and to suffer from immune disorders, including allergies. And these children are also more likely to be male.

All of this gets us back to those floods of testosterone that wash through the male embryo and the notion of just how chancy the making of a male is. *Perhaps only a small shift in the hormone mix is all that lies between prodigy and learning disability. Males are subject to greater hormonal reshaping in the womb, and thus more men than women end up at each extreme.* Norman Geschwind, at Harvard, proposed that the testosterone levels males are exposed to slow the development of the left side of the brain, allowing the right side to become relatively more dominant. (The effect of hormones on the cortex gets support from those rat experiments I talked about earlier. Remember, the right side of the cortex is larger in male rats, the left side in females. But testosterone reverses the female pattern and enlarges the right brain.)

Because the left hemisphere has the most direct control in regulating the immune system, retarding its development could chance leaving the child vulnerable to immune disorders. (In fact, men in general have weaker immune systems than women, as you'll see in a later chapter.) And retarding the left side could also leave them susceptible to verbal disabilities. Reading problems and speech problems like stuttering are by far more prevalent among boys. If the balance is just right, though, the child may retain his left hemisphere functions and get better than average right-side abilities, too, including spatial skills. (And, as you'll also see later, this may form the basis for high mathematical reasoning ability.)

Levy, too, believes hormone exposure during fetal life enhances the "cognitive capacity" of the right hemisphere, and also that this exposure promotes a high degree of specialization on both sides.

Not everyone agrees, however, that the difference in men's and women's cerebral hemispheres takes place this early. If brain development continues throughout childhood, then the fact that girls reach puberty about a year earlier than boys could mean that their right and left hemispheres have less time to specialize.

Another possibility is that the differences in our right and left brains may be the result of our experiences in the world. Of course that doesn't rule out the likelihood that prenatal hormones influence this process in an indirect way. Diane McGuinness, of Stanford University, proposes that inborn sex differences in the hypothalamus and the rest of the "emotional brain" bias our perceptions and the things that grab our attention, and thus influence what we learn.

"One of the functions of the brain is to sift out from all of the possible signals impinging on the senses those events that are most meaningful and useful," she says. "Therefore, if males and females have different inherent tendencies, or predispositions, they will pay attention to different events." And this takes us all the way back to babies in their cribs, the way they respond to people and objects, the way they perceive sound, touch, and odor, the way they choose to spend their time. *I mentioned earlier that there's a third category of male/female differences we know something about but can't yet link directly to genes, hormones, or brain structures. I'm talking about widely observable differences in the values and interests of girls and boys, men and women—the kind that seem to start in the crib.*

We don't even know what makes human beings social animals, so we certainly don't know where to look in the brain yet to see why girls enter the world more interested in people and social situations than are boys. "Where," McGuinness asks, "do we find the object/person distinction in the brain? Nobody can answer that question. What makes dogs, wolves, people, and chimpanzees need to live in social groups and develop complex structures of mutual aid and support? And leopards or solitary orangutans —why don't they like to live in groups? Where is that going on in the brain?"

This question is complicated by the fact that being "social" isn't a category of things that girls are and boys aren't. "Men need the buffering of the group, but they prefer to act somewhat more independently as long as that stability is in place," McGuinness notes. "Men *are* vulnerable. You take the support and the structure away and they seem to fall apart. They fall apart from divorce and bereavement more than women do. But once the social structure is in place they seem to have much less talent for really being in tune. For empathy. And we don't know why that is."

These apparently inborn differences in social style and interests may set the stage for a phenomenon that you can see in any playground: young girls and boys form separate playgroups. And it's the influence of these groups, perhaps more than that of parents and teachers, that will shape their later interactions with the world. Stanford psychologist Eleanor Maccoby believes the differences between men in groups and women in groups are much greater than individual differences between the sexes.

"If you look at the characteristics of the playgroups that the two sexes spend most of their time in outside the classroom during the years six to twelve, they're very different," she told us. "During that age period sex segregation is enormous. There *are* certain contacts between the groups. Like the boys will occasionally raid through the girls' jumprope, for instance, tear the rope out of the hands of whoever's turning it, and run off shrieking. The girls may chase them a little, or vice versa. This is what one sociologist called 'border work.' You have two cultures that are side by side, and every once in a while they intersect."

Maccoby finds that the way these "two cultures" deal with each other is utterly different from the way they deal with peers of their own sex in their own playgroups. "Girls do tend to have more intimate friendships. The breaking up of a friendship in girls is a much more emotional, intense process than the breaking up of boys' friendships. Boys' friendships are more oriented around enjoying the same activities. 'He's my friend because he's a good first baseman and I'm a good second baseman and we're on the same team.' For girls, friendship has to do with deeper, shared interests. It's more that you've revealed secrets to each other. And so, when you break up a friendship, this other person is in a position to jeopardize you, almost because she knows too much about you.

"And even in conversations, apparently the function of talking is different in girls' groups. Girls try to give everybody in the group a chance to speak. When they start talking, they more often refer to what the other person just said and build on it. In boys' groups, you try to take the floor away from the other guy. You try to hold it as long as you can. You do it by joking or telling stories. You interrupt. You put the other person down; almost never refer to what the other person said when you make your own statement," Maccoby says.

"It makes for a very interesting set of questions about what happens when people growing up in these two cultures begin to encounter each other in a dating way as they get into adolescence," she adds. (Amen. I think we've all been through that culture shock. One of the divorced

women on my staff wrote on her survey form: "I love men, but I wouldn't want to be one of them. They fascinate me. They don't think at all like women. Our thought processes are different . . . What's amazing is that we've accomplished reproduction at all. That we haven't become extinct.")

"When I look at the quality of these two cultures and the extent to which they're really separate in those middle childhood years, I think we've underestimated their importance as a socializing environment," Maccoby says.

"We find, for example, that the little girls who play exclusively with other little girls when they're in preschool are rated by their teachers as more cooperative and helpful and prosocial (behaving for the benefit of others) in a variety of ways than the little girls who have not played exclusively with girls. Boys who choose early to play in same-sex groups aren't later rated by their teachers as more prosocial. They're not rated more antisocial, either. But a girls' group, in other words, has a socializing effect. It's kind of curious. I don't know why, but it's the antecedent fact to this communicative and mutually supportive style that girls have in their groups. And it's very different from the boys' groups.

"Now, you may ask," she adds, "why do the kids go into same-sex groups? What is it that determines the quality of the communicative style that develops in these two kinds of groups?

o   o   o

And indeed, she and other researchers are continuing to ask questions like these as they probe our brains and our behavior and examine anew questions like how our inherent emotions, including empathy, affect the development of our moral behavior. I'm excited by this work. I foresee great payoffs in terms of our self-understanding and self-respect.

We women do have unique strengths that can be as valuable aboard a space shuttle or in a genetic engineering lab as they have been in the nursery. Probably more so. I hope the kind of knowledge that's coming from science will give women now and in the future the confidence to apply their own intellect and their unique sensibilities to the task of creating a better future.

3 | THINKING LIKE A WOMAN

Although women are gaining access to power individually, the very nature of power will change as their numbers mount. A synergy of male and female leadership qualities will emerge, a new combination that is to everyone's advantage.

—John Naisbitt, author of *Megatrends*

want you to think for a minute about the women and men around you. Whether you spend your days shuttling children to school and Little League or running a corporation (or both), you're likely to deal with a great variety of people every week. Garage mechanics, stockbrokers, mail carriers, teachers, lawyers, grocery clerks, accountants, and doctors. Try to put their job titles and backgrounds aside and divide them mentally into two groups, male and female: women mechanics, clerks, and doctors mingled together, male teachers, CPAs, and lawyers. Now, once you've done this, could you make any generalizations about each group? Is there something besides gender that sets this diverse group of women apart from an equally various group of men?

This is what we asked the women in our survey. After genes and hormones, perceptions and lessons, parents and playmates have all worked their influence on us, how is the average woman different from the average man? How do the sexes compare in self-esteem, professional ambition, and motivation? Who, if anyone, has the advantage in sports and physical skills, mathematics, social skills, verbal and communicative skills, nurturing ability?

The results tell me that we women still cling to a lot of misinformation about our own abilities and motivations. It's not just men or tradition that limit us. Perhaps the biggest obstacle we have to overcome in carving out a full role for ourselves in the world is our own sense of limitation.

First, only 54 percent of the women in our survey said that women are just as ambitious and self-confident as men, or more so. That percentage ought to be much higher, and I think it will be in the future. But let's take a closer look:

Self-Esteem—When we asked women which sex has the highest self-esteem, 46 percent gave the edge to men, 41 percent said it's equal, and only 13 percent answered women. Surprisingly, it's professional and managerial women who give men the highest marks for self-esteem. Some 52 percent of them think men have the advantage. Only 42 percent of unemployed housewives think so.

If what these professional women observe is accurate, then something must be going on in their labs or offices to dampen their self-esteem. Contrary to old stereotypes, girls aren't born feeling meek and inferior. Psychologists haven't found any sex differences in self-confidence or self-satisfaction among children or adolescents.

Professional Ambition/Motivation—Overall, 48 percent of our respondents said the sexes are equal in professional ambition, 46 percent gave the advantage to men, and only 6 percent said women. That same majority of housewives who pronounced women equal or better on self-esteem don't feel as strongly about ambition. Fifty-one percent of them said men have the most professional ambition. In contrast, only 37 percent of working mothers gave men the edge, and nearly two-thirds said women are just as ambitious or more so.

The working mothers were right on the money. When psychologists Eleanor Maccoby and Carol Jacklin pulled together all the research that had been done on "achievement strivings" in boys and girls, the studies either reported no difference or rated girls superior. Getting boys to show the same motivation as girls required "appeals to ego or competitive motivation."

Somewhere along the line large numbers of women still seem to be suppressing their native self-confidence and ambition. Perhaps they've been told it's unfeminine, or they fear it will drive away the men in their lives. Or perhaps these women have simply lost their spirit after running into too many obstacles. Obviously, however, obstacles serve as a challenge to some of us, and these seem to be the women in the survey who believe our own sex has the strongest drive and self-esteem. "I think women have more ambition because they have to fight harder to prove themselves these days," one of our young clerical workers told me. And an executive put it this way: "Women have to have high self-esteem or we wouldn't be fighting our second-class citizenship status."

Few women in our survey seemed to be under any illusions about men's social or communicative skills. Ninety-five percent gave women equal or better marks on verbal and communicative skills, and an overwhelming 98 percent felt we have equal or superior social skills. My question is why so many women only find us equal when we clearly start with an advantage in this area? Here's what we found:

Verbal/Communicative Skills—Fifty-four percent of women surveyed believe men and women are equal in this area, 41 percent said women have the advantage, and only 5 percent find men superior. Women in professional and managerial jobs are most certain of our superiority in these matters, voting 49 percent for women, 48 percent for equal competence, and only 3 percent for men.

So, about half of our respondents seem to feel that the men around them are as fluent and communicative as the women. Yet research clearly shows men don't grow up this way. Women have a strong advantage starting in childhood. From infancy, as we saw earlier, girl babies show more interest in communicating with people than do boys. Young girls have an easier time producing accurate speech sounds, they put together longer sentences, they learn to read more easily. Boys are much more likely to suffer reading disabilities. Girls also excel at creative writing and verbal reasoning tasks like drawing analogies. Our early advantage increases from puberty through at least high school.

Social Skills—Overall, 57 percent of our respondents gave women the edge in social skills, 41 percent called it a draw, and only 2 percent think men are superior. I was surprised to see that more housewives (62 percent) than working women (54 percent) say we have the advantage in this area.

Again, psychologists rate women higher than men on "behavioral intelligence." We're more emotionally expressive and more intuitive, better at reading nonverbal cues like facial expression, stance, and tone of voice. (This doesn't mean women are more "social" as in "sociable" or that men are antisocial. Men need the company of others as much as women—and fall apart more quickly without it, as we'll see later—but they just aren't generally as adept at sizing up social situations and responding appropriately. And it doesn't mean men don't have intuition or make decisions based on hunches.)

Why do so many women rate the sexes equal instead of embracing what should be one of the strong points of female nature? Perhaps by adulthood these women have internalized one of those social myths that tell us it's unladylike to press the advantage, or that no one will love us and take care of us if we show too much competence and intelligence. Or perhaps not enough of us have been able to carve out a place in the larger society where we can use our strengths and talents in ways that bring status and respect. Biology isn't destiny. Early advantages can slip away from us if they're not developed and put to use.

Almost three-quarters of women surveyed feel we're more competent at nurturing than men. That's a pretty dismal attitude for women who, as you'll see later, expect men to take an equal role in caring for children.

Nurturing Ability—We found that 71 percent of our respondents think women are superior at this, another 28 percent feel the sexes are equal, and only 1 percent give the edge to men. The split was essentially the same across age and income levels, and among women with children and those without, housewives or professionals.

Let's take a closer look at this, because these are the attitudes that will shape our home life in the future. Now it's a fact that nowhere in the world, in any human culture, do men spend as much time as women caring for babies and children. With few exceptions, the same thing can be said of most mammals. But is this an indication that some strong and immutable "maternal instinct" is at work, an innate drive that makes women seek this role and fill it better than men ever could? If that's so, there's no evidence for it. *Parental behavior is one of those sex-shared abilities where the triggers simply seem to be set at different levels in males and females.*

That's true even among our nonhuman cousins. For instance, when a researcher puts a female monkey into a cage with an infant monkey, it doesn't take the female long to begin comforting and caring for it. Adult male monkeys put in the same situation are at first a little more awkward. They don't get the point as quickly. They'll just ignore the infant, or maybe even abuse it. But leave the pair together and the bond strengthens. The male not only learns to take care of the infant, he may also become so attached he turns violent when they are separated.

"Women are more nurturing because society has made them that way," one of our young secretaries said. "Men haven't been taught to be nurturers." I agree. But instead of "taught" I might have said "required." Or perhaps even "allowed," because we've jealously guarded some of those motherhood myths that we now find so burdensome when we try to juggle career and family. Think about it. Women who bear children have a nine-month head start on developing an attachment to them—"bonding" is the popular jargon now. But as a father holds and cares for his child in the first few weeks after birth, all indications are that his bond can become quite strong.

Until women—and even the law—accept the equal competence of men, and encourage the development of new traditions of fatherhood in our culture, women's options in the world will remain limited. Men often want children, as much as women, but for different reasons, and when push comes to shove, they can take care of them just as well. They can also learn to fill the jobs in the traditionally female "helping" professions that open up as we spread our talents to other arenas. (I wish we'd guard our head starts in language and social skills and fight against the erosion of our confidence and ambition as fiercely as we cling to our edge at nurturing. Once men get involved, you can bet salaries will increase in these fields!)

Sports Ability/Physical Skills—For some reason, 44 percent of women think the sexes are equal in sports ability and other physical skills. Perhaps this reflects the uniformed fears of some feminists that we have to claim full equality in all things or else go back to the kitchen.

It's futile and unrealistic to try to prove ourselves equal to men in muscular strength and sheer physical power. That's really biology, and you're going to hear more about it in this book. In any event, it doesn't really matter. Brute strength is not where the opportunities for the future lie. Physical strength equates with political power today only in a few primitive tribes, in some Middle-Eastern countries, and in the Third World, and it has little economic value except in professional football and boxing or on the loading dock. Women don't have to try to defy biology or be "more like men" in any way to compete successfully for tomorrow's top jobs or share in shaping the future.

Math Ability—Just over half the women surveyed believe we have mathematical ability that is equal to or greater than men's. This is where simplistic news accounts of the past few years have taken their toll on our self-confidence. And this, not physical ability, is the area we should be worrying about if we want to help make the world go round.

This is a subject I'm going to spend some time on because our feelings about math greatly limit our career horizons. *The facts about women and math are hardly in dispute, although there's bitter disagreement about the causes:*

- It's a fact that adolescent boys in the United States and many other countries consistently score higher than girls on math achievement tests. The average differences aren't large, usually in the 3-percent-to-5-percent range.
- Girls, however, make slightly higher grades in math than boys and excel at basic arithmetic.
- Boys typically score higher on mechanical-spatial tests. (You remember those tests where you had to imagine folding paper diagrams into three-dimensional objects, rotate them in your mind, and describe what they would look like from various sides.) Most people think spatial ability has something to do with aptitude for the kinds of math that come after arithmetic, like algebra, geometry, and calculus.
- It's also true that boys take more math courses than girls, get more attention from their math teachers, more often pursue technical hobbies and play with scientific toys, and are more likely to choose careers that require math skills. Teenage girls face a lot of peer pressure not to excel in things like math, and school counselors often steer them away from the math background needed for technical careers. (I still get furious when I think of my visit to one of the best private schools in New York where I heard a male counselor try to give this sort of drivel to a girl in my own family.) Only 5 percent of the Ph.D.s in math are awarded to women.

So what's cause and effect here? Do boys have some natural ability and interest in higher math, once they've managed to pass arithmetic, that teachers just can't help but recognize and try to foster? Do girls lack this? I certainly don't believe it. *A large part of the problem is that our schools teach math as though we were still in the nineteenth century.* Remember, it wasn't that long ago that girls were schooled only in domestic arts because that's all society wanted us to concern ourselves with. At the opening of the twentieth century, respected educators were still debating whether women's delicate nervous systems could handle the strain of coeducation without risk of hysteria and reproductive failure. Now we have finally been allowed into schools, but in many cases we're still being handed a curriculum that was designed for males.

Math and science were all-male professions then, and both their social structure and the training for them reflected male values and interests. *It's appalling to see that in some classrooms today math is still taught as though it were the province of solitary scholars pondering abstract con-*

cepts that have no application to human life or needs. That lifestyle may still appeal to some boys—you can see the shadow of such reclusive scholars in today's more obsessive computer hackers—but few girls would choose it. *The truth—a truth that not enough schoolgirls get told—is that that's not what most careers in science or math are like today. In our technological age, these are mainstream professions, full of human contact and vitally concerned with real life issues.*

For more than a decade, a few educators interested in getting more women into science and engineering—or just turning more girls into fully informed citizens—have been trying to spread this word. Today, all over the United States, new programs are beginning to spring up to overcome the barriers for girls: peer pressure, lack of role models, lack of encouragement and support from teachers, counselors, and parents.

But in 1980 a notion that had been pushed into the background suddenly became hot news: perhaps boys *are* innately superior at math.

You've probably seen newspaper headlines like these over the past few years: "Are Boys Better at Math?" "Do Males Have a Math Gene?" "Boys Have Superior Math Ability, Study Says." Most of the headlines were generated by the work of two psychologists, Camilla Benbow and Julian Stanley, of Johns Hopkins University. Bitter controversy still surrounds their studies. *I think you should know some of the details because I'd hate to see your expectations of yourself or your daughters lowered by simplistic accounts of this work that you may have seen on TV or in the press.*

First, Benbow and Stanley don't work with ordinary kids—they work with the cream of the crop. Since 1972, the researchers have identified about 85,000 gifted adolescents through their talent searches, about an even number of girls and boys. These are self-selected, highly motivated, straight-A seventh- and eighth-graders. One thing they asked these students to do was take the SAT math test designed for college-bound high school seniors.

The result: The boys as a group scored better than the girls by a mean difference of about thirty points. But the greatest differences came at the extreme upper ends of the scale. Among the seventh- and eighth-graders scoring over 500—which is the average for college-bound twelfth-grade males— there were two boys for every girl. At 600 or above the ratio went to four boys to every girl. At scores of 700 or more they found thirteen boys for each girl.

These results weren't startling by themselves. As I mentioned before, boys usually average higher scores on achievement tests. But Benbow and Stanley claimed their tests hadn't measured achievement. Their studies had measured inherent mathematical reasoning ability, they said, and thus the results indicated boys might be naturally superior at math. That's what set off the headlines about "math genes."

Benbow and Stanley's reasoning went this way: The SAT math exam includes algebra and other high school math, which these seventh- and eighth-graders haven't studied yet. Therefore, a twelve- or thirteen-year-old who scores high must be using innate abilities, not learned skills. Other researchers vehemently disagree. *The SAT test was never designed to measure innate ability,* and there's no proof that it does, they say. Just because these youngsters haven't sat through algebra classes is no indication they haven't picked up the concepts elsewhere. Remember, these are the exceptional kids, the ones who teach themselves computer programming, skip grades, or go off to college when their friends are still thinking about the junior prom. Other critics reinforce that by saying "no one short of Einstein would be able to reason these [math principles] out on their own during the tests." Benbow and Stanley stand behind their interpretation, and to date the issue is unresolved.

As for all those social factors I listed before, the different messages that girls and boys get from parents, teachers, and friends about math, only limited studies were done on these 85,000 students. Some of the youngsters were asked to fill out questionnaires about how their families had trained or encouraged them, and little evidence of sex differences was found. But even Benbow admits such influences may be too subtle for girls to recall and list on a questionnaire years later. All the students said they liked math, and at that age slightly more girls than boys were planning to major in it in college.

But there's evidence that these girls had already received a social "message" about math. Every summer Benbow and Stanley offered accelerated math courses for these gifted students at Johns Hopkins. They found it much harder to attract girls than boys. And the girls who enrolled tended to drop out. Researcher Lynn Fox, who studied these gifted girls, found many opted out of the summer programs because they didn't want to be labeled "different" by their friends. And they thought of the boys they'd meet there as "little creeps." (Here's that persistent image of mathematicians as "nerds" and hackers casting a shadow again.)

When these gifted kids went on to high school, the boys took more math and science courses than the girls, although the girls made better grades in the courses they did take. When they entered college, the boys went in with more background in math and science, better SAT scores, and better marks on math and science advanced placement exams. Since the oldest students in Benbow and Stanley's program are only in their mid-twenties now, no one really knows yet what those 500, 600, or 700 SAT scores mean in terms of college performance or creative professional achievement.

Another question still hanging is what all of this has to do with boys and girls in general. (Many of the newspaper accounts didn't even mention that these studies dealt only with exceptional students.) Even though Benbow discounts the influence of social forces on the gifted students' SAT scores, she admits such factors "undoubtedly . . . are important in determining sex differences in mathematics in the average population."

I'm willing to keep an open mind about the possibility that some innate factor is involved in the performance of these precocious kids. (After all, Howard Gardner's theory of "multiple intelligences" predicts that some children will inherit a greater dose of math talent than others, just as some will start with better musical or language talents.) Benbow and Stanley have recently found that in addition to high math ability, these youngsters have higher rates of left-handedness, immune disorders, and nearsightedness than other kids their age. As we saw in the last chapter, all of these traits seem to cluster together in a way that links them to brain lateralization— the way the right and left hemispheres of the brain develop, specialize, and interact.

There's another possible biological explanation for the difference in male and female math scores that has nothing to do with innate ability. The sexes may simply be biased toward two different problem-solving strategies, one of them more effective than the other for certain types of math. I hope to see more work done on this theory because it implies that we need to make even more radical changes in the way we teach math than just introducing girls to women mathematicians and showing them how challenging and socially useful a math career can be.

This theory has two variations. One says that girls are forced by their inferior or less-well-developed spatial ability to apply verbal strategies to math problems. The other variation says that, even if girls' spatial abilities are just as keen, they have a preference for using their highly developed verbal skills. And verbal strategies are thought to be inadequate once you move beyond arithmetic into "spacy" abstract math like calculus, analytical geometry, and differential equations.

"It really seems as if girls start off with a missing strategy," Stanford research psychologist Diane McGuinness notes. "You can do arithmetic by memorizing the rules and the counting system. You don't really recognize what a base-ten number system is, how it's structured, and how you can play around with base tens in multiples and groups and make patterns. You just memorize your multiplication tables; the rules that are designated by signs like multiply, divide, subtract, and add; place values so you can carry one or carry five . . .

"And you can go all the way through to algebra and do perfectly well on the basis of being fairly bright and having good rote memory skills and being good at managing symbols, which are essentially verbal," McGuinness says. "Algebra brings you to codes within codes, nested logic, the beginning of the need for spatial concepts, but you can learn more rules and manage.

"Then you get to geometry, and you can try to keep going that way, but it becomes completely meaningless because you don't have any conception of space. Two-dimensional. Three-dimensional. You haven't thought about numbers in that way at all," she says. And in fact, not just girls but a lot of boys opt out of math at this point. ("Math is so badly taught it's a wonder anybody catches on," she says, shaking her head.)

"So you have this little group of predominantly males who seem to have got it together and have that capacity for one reason or another. And we don't have a clue to why they develop that."

Her prescription for the classroom is to get kids started by preschool or kindergarten playing with the kinds of manipulative toys that allow them to make the connection between objects and numbers and teach them that math is rooted in spatial relationships. And if girls do start with a deficit in spatial abilities, there's evidence it can be remedied through the right kinds of sports, games, and hobbies. Maccoby and Jacklin found a decade ago that adults with the highest spatial ability are found in "cultures that allow independence to children." And: *"Where women are subjugated, their visual-spatial skills are poor, relative to those of men. Where both sexes are allowed independence early in life, both sexes have good visual-spatial skills."*

I'm going to come back to this subject in a later chapter because there's a lot that parents and the schools can do right now to make sure that the next generation of girls like Kelly, Adrian, and Nina starts out on the right foot. Lynn Fox pointed out to us that our schools already spend "a lot of time and energy helping little boys catch up" with girls' early advantage in reading and language skills. And McGuinness reminded us that parents and teachers are far more likely to let girls quit when they start having problems in math than they are to allow boys to give up learning to read.

Maybe in the future when all these factors of motivation, encouragement, and style are worked out, there will still be more men than women who choose careers in math, especially pure theoretical math. The students in Benbow and Stanley's study are not insignificant, after all. They're the top 5 percent of their classes. They're our most likely Ph.D.s. *But the sex differences in their scores alone can't explain the ratio of males to females in science and math careers.*

"I think there may be twice as many boys as girls who have these extremely high scores on the SAT at grade seven," Fox admits. "But out in the real world we're seeing at least ten times more men than women who are getting doctorates, or getting the high tech, high paying jobs. You still have the women with equal ability getting paid lower. *So I think there's a strong case to be made that there are some social factors affecting the ultimate achievement of men and women in science and technology. It isn't totally the result of there being slightly more men than women who have extraordinary aptitude.*"

o   o   o

I have to pause here and add the caveat that throughout the discussion of our survey results I've been talking about averages. Men as one group and women as another. None of those individuals in your world whom I asked you to strip of occupation and background and classify by sex are likely to fit the statistical average. No one would be able to launch a successful TV game show of making people predict on the basis of sex alone how fast someone would run in a 100-yard dash, what score they'd make on a math exam, or how they'd resolve a management dispute. (Although it's amazing how often people make assumptions like this in real life.) Psychologist Maccoby stresses that 90 percent or more of the differences between individuals—in personality, or preference, or performance—don't have anything to do with sex.

"That's why it's extremely unfair and wrong to try to make any judgments about how good a person is with respect to a certain thing just by knowing his or her gender," she told us. "Now of course, if you don't know anything else about them, you've improved yourself over pure chance by a tiny bit—4 percent or 8 percent or whatever—by knowing their gender. But all the sex differences are small." Only by dumping large numbers of males and females in the statistical blender do we get a sense of our unique talents and approach to the world.

So why do we bother? Well, I have a good reason. But first let me say that I don't think the women of tomorrow will need to go through this exercise. *I truly believe that in the not too distant future, it will be more important for a youngster to develop a strong sense of self-esteem and individuality than of masculinity or femininity.* That individuality will undoubtedly blend elements from both masculine and feminine ends of the spectrum, and all these elements will be equally valued.

We're not there yet, however. For millions of years, while we were still evolving and mere survival was a grim business, gender was one of the primary factors that defined an individual's course in life. That's a pattern we've only recently begun to break. The division of labor arose when reproduction and bare survival were the central focus of life. Women were bearing and nursing babies so it made sense that they tended the homefires and took care of the older children, too. Men were the ones who had to hunt for food and fight off intruders. The sensibilities and talents of men and women today have been subtly shaped by millions of years of filling these distinct roles in a successful effort to survive.

But somewhere along the line people got the causal sequence reversed. They began to believe that the roles were created to suit men's and women's natural temperaments instead of vice versa. The sexes were assumed to possess only the behavioral repertoires needed to fill those traditional slots. According to this thinking, men had originally been sent out to hunt and fight because they were exclusively aggressive, passionate, domineering, impulsive, and strong. Women, likewise, had been assigned childcare and basket weaving because they were immutably passive, unpassionate, submissive, nurturing, and frail. Neither sex had access to behaviors that were in the domain of the opposite sex, so no crossover of roles was possible.

It's now obvious, of course, that there are no strictly male or female behaviors. All human beings share the same spectrum of traits and abilities, differing only in degree. Every mature adult is a blend of values and strengths that once were considered exclusively masculine or feminine. But most cultures still penalize women for expressing traits that have been assigned to men (ambition, sexual desire), and ridicule men who display "feminine" traits (nurturance, empathy). The most exaggerated sex differences in behavior and attitude are, as you might expect, found today in societies with the most rigidly enforced sex roles.

It shouldn't surprise you that after a few million years of strict role-playing a lot of myths and misinformation about women as a group are still floating around. Only recently have we stopped taking them for granted and actually studied how girls and boys, men and women, act and think. And after countless thousands of hours observing and testing, *a new generation of psychologists hasn't found any evidence that the Victorian notion that women are shallow, suggestible, timid, passive, dependent, less analytic, lacking in ambition and self-esteem, or, as Freud postulated, ethically immature, is at all valid.* Yet, as our survey shows, some women still accept such notions.

(Unfortunately, there are misguided religious fanatics who also think it's important to keep up this charade "to save the family." But I agree with Maccoby and Jacklin's assessment: "Training a girl to be 'feminine' in the traditional nonassertive, 'helpless,' and self-deprecatory sense may actually make her a worse mother." Similarly: "A man who adopts the 'machismo' image may gain prestige with his peers, or enhance his short-term attractiveness to women, at the expense of his effectiveness as a husband and father.")

I think it's necessary for our generation of women to set the record straight about sex differences. Then perhaps we can avoid perpetuating myths about purported differences that don't exist, stop crying about the ones that do, and concentrate instead on putting our real advantages to work for us. With that in mind, let me tell you that all the research I've read on male/female differences has left me with two firm convictions:

Traditional male and female roles have never made full use of our inborn strengths, talents, and sensibilities or brought them the respect they deserve.

And, *men or women as individuals shouldn't be prevented from pursuing any career or lifestyle just because it seems to require skills or attitudes that don't fit traditional sex roles.*

The roles society has set aside for women have traditionally been based on quite a narrow view of what biology suited us for. One asset that biology provides, for instance, is fine dexterity in our hands and fingers. Culture has channeled that skill into sewing, typing, and tedious assembly-line work. Only in recent decades have we been allowed to develop our intellect along with our dexterity and to apply both to delicate jobs like brain surgery.

Hormones decree that women will never have the muscle bulk or upper body strength of men. Yet nothing in our biology demands that we hover at the sidelines cheerleading for male athletes instead of participating in sports that hone our own fitness, spatial skills, or sense of accomplishment. And not until the last few years has it been possible to gain an appreciative audience for newer sports like rhythmic gymnastics and synchronized swimming that showcase our own physical strengths.

What about our head start in verbal and language skills? It seems obvious to me that society's typecasting still causes more of this talent to be funneled into editing the boss's reports or answering telephones than into devising computer languages, writing books, or making stirring speeches. Our social savvy and communicative ability still get more exercise at cocktail parties or in settling family squabbles than in managing major corporations or negotiating international trade contracts. And even when a woman has succeeded in the realm of science and technology, history is apt to neglect her contribution. Take, for example, Lady Ada Lovelace, the girlfriend of Charles Babbage, the great British computer pioneer of the nineteenth century. Lady Lovelace, a mathematician, created the concept of the binary system, without which there could be no computer. History has neglected her discovery in favor of Babbage's crude attempt to build a computing machine.

Is it any wonder that more than half the women in our survey don't see any female edge in verbal and communicative skills? *Too often we surrender the head starts of childhood and adolescence. We let ourselves be slotted into roles that use only a fraction of our range of talents.* While our sensibilities and people-skills are shaping the character of the garden club or Junior League, men are out sharpening their often-less-adept skills in forums that bring economic rewards and prestige.

And that's another point. *Prestige.* Even professions that have developed to capitalize on stereotypically female talents and sensibilities are uniformly undervalued and low paying. Consider the "helping" professions—nursing, teaching, and social work (not to mention motherhood). And think of secretaries. In addition to their official duties, their organizational and people-skills provide what's been called the "social glue" that holds most large enterprises together. Yet their salaries remain lower than those of most truck drivers, whose education and range of talents can hardly compare.

What I want to emphasize is that there's nothing "natural" about any role we fill, except motherhood, and that one is burdened with an awful lot of social mythology, too. The stereotype of female nature has been narrow and limiting, locking us at one end of the spectrum of human possibility and calling it the low end because we were there. *It's time both men and women understood that feminine values and abilities have as much to contribute in the physics lab as in the grade school classroom.*

My second conviction is that individual diversity and adaptability make it ridiculous to bar women from any career, whether it's athletics or astrophysics. No one should be limited just because most other members of her sex wouldn't have the desire or ability to follow her.

Fifty-three percent of the women we surveyed felt there's no career that a woman with proper training is unsuited for. Among those who still think that everyone of our sex has certain limitations, 37 percent believe women are unsuited to be combat soldiers, 13 percent said fire fighters, 8 percent said military officers, and 4 percent said policewomen.

"Women don't have the strength, the stamina, and I don't think they have the instinct to kill," one of our executive assistants said, explaining her objections to women as combat soldiers. She's probably right about the majority of us, although I doubt that physical strength will count for that much in future high-tech warfare. And robots will make both conventional warfare and many heavy-duty jobs virtually obsolete. But I'm quite sure there are enough *special* women out there to fill any new opportunities that are opened to us.

Instead of declaring that no women or men will be allowed in certain jobs, it makes more sense to develop a list of *relevant* qualifications and let any individual who's interested try to meet them. Make sure any candidate for fire fighter is strong enough to drag a hose up a flight of stairs or climb a ladder in good time. Obviously, some women can meet the test because most big city fire departments now include small numbers of women. Seattle's fire chief has even said women have special qualities that are valuable to the force: "You can provide better service if you represent a cross-section of the community. Half the population is female." (In my personal view, robots, not men or women, should perform dirty and dangerous jobs like this anyway.)

Throughout society, a reevaluation and redefinition of femininity is underway. It's happening as more women break in and begin applying "female nature" to government, factory, courtroom, and boardroom. And it's getting a boost from psychology. Not only are researchers exploring the real differences between men and women, but psychologists who once defined human development by studying all-male examples are beginning to incorporate women's experiences into the fabric of human nature. *I believe these efforts are going to have two very positive results for our future: Not only will women's contributions to nontraditional fields come to be respected, but new value will be given to the professions built around caring instead of competing.*

Here's what I mean about psychology. Freud never could figure women out, so he presumed there must be something wrong with us. Without a penis, we were hardly subject to "castration anxiety" and so, under his developmental scheme, we could never achieve a fully mature superego or conscience. As a consequence, our moral sensibilities remained too tied in with our emotions, never maturing into the inflexible and impersonal sense of justice that men develop after coming to grips with their Oedipal conflicts. Throughout much of the twentieth century, theorists have followed Freud's pattern, drawing developmental timetables and goals from male experience, then trying to explain why women failed to follow them.

But since the late 1960s, a new generation of psychologists has begun to challenge this bias.

What Freud and all the others were laboring to explain is a rather obvious sex difference that seems to recur in every generation of men and women. We women tend to define ourselves in terms of our relationships, gauging our strength and morality by how well we nurture, care, and help. Men define themselves in terms of autonomy and competitive achievement. (Remember, we're generalizing again. Individuals can fall anywhere between these two extremes.)

No one knows exactly how this difference in sensibilities comes about. One theory finds its origins in the fact that both boys and girls are cared for primarily by their mothers. This means that in order to develop his masculine identity, a boy has to cut his psychological dependency with his mother despite his love for her. A girl, on the other hand, can develop her feminine self-identity without breaking the attachment. As we've seen, boys' and girls' childhood playgroups later reinforce these sex differences in how we define ourselves and what gives us pride and satisfaction. (Actually, I believe the origin of our tendency toward "connectedness" goes back even farther than parents and playgroups, perhaps to our genes. Remember that even as infants we're more attentive to people, male and female, than boys are, more interested in communicating and interacting with them.)

Whatever the origin of this feminine sense of caring and connectedness, psychology has always treated it as immature—for no valid reason —even though it may have been important in the development of civilization itself. As we've seen, society in general has also devalued the roles and professions that grew up around this sensibility, and disparaged any contribution it might make to "masculine" professions.

In her 1982 book, *In a Different Voice,* Harvard psychologist Carol Gilligan suggests it's time to redefine moral maturity for all human beings by incorporating feminine values into the ideal. Her most striking example of the female "voice" is the case of Amy and Jake, eleven-year-olds from the same sixth-grade class, who were asked in a study to resolve a moral dilemma. Both youngsters were "bright and articulate and, at least in their eleven-year-old aspirations, resisted easy categories of sex-role stereotyping, since Amy aspired to become a scientist, while Jake preferred English to math," Gilligan wrote. "Yet their moral judgments seem initially to confirm familiar notions about differences between the sexes . . ."

The dilemma presented to Amy and Jake was this: A man named Heinz is in a predicament. His wife is dying. He can't afford the drug that will save her. The druggist refuses to lower his price. Should Heinz steal the drug?

To Jake, the answer was clear from the start, Gilligan says. He saw the dilemma "as a conflict between the values of property and life," and since life is more valuable than money, Heinz should steal the drug. "Considering the moral dilemma to be 'sort of like a math problem with humans,' he sets it up as an equation and proceeds to work out the solution," she reports. "Since his solution is rationally derived, he assumes that anyone following reason would arrive at the same conclusion and thus that a judge would also consider stealing to be the right thing for Heinz to do."

But that's *not* the way Amy saw it. She immediately began to ponder alternative solutions so that Heinz wouldn't have to steal, and his wife wouldn't have to die. Maybe Heinz could borrow the money. Or sit down and work something out with the druggist. "Asked why he should not steal the drug, she considers neither property nor law but rather the effect that theft could have on the relationship between Heinz and his wife," Gilligan notes. After all, what's the wife going to do if Heinz steals the drug and she gets better temporarily, but then he's sent to jail and she gets worse? "Just as Jake is confident the judge would agree that stealing is the right thing for Heinz to do, so Amy is confident that, 'if Heinz and the druggist had talked it out long enough, they could reach something besides stealing,' " Gilligan says.

Amy's sensibilities "lead her to see the actors in the dilemma arrayed not as opponents in a contest of rights but as members of a network of relationships on whose continuation they all depend," Gilligan writes.

Whose solution is the most mature, Amy's or Jake's? According to the man who devised the dilemma, Amy's judgment is naive and immature compared to Jake's. Heinz's dilemma is one of a series used by another Harvard psychologist, Lawrence Kohlberg, in his twenty-year study of a group of boys. From the boys' responses over time, Kohlberg put together a six-stage sequence of moral development that's supposed to apply to all of us. Yet, Gilligan writes, women's judgments usually end up about where Amy's did on Kohlberg's scale, "the third stage of his six-stage sequence."

"At this stage morality is conceived in interpersonal terms and goodness is equated with helping and pleasing others," she notes. Kohlberg considers this "conception of goodness . . . to be functional in the lives of mature women insofar as their lives take place in the home," she said. He implies "that only if women enter the traditional arena of male activity will they recognize the inadequacy of this moral perspective and progress like men toward higher stages where relationships are subordinated to rules (stage four) and rules to universal principles of justice (stages five and six)."

Is this stage-three *"conception of goodness,"* this ethic of caring, really

immature and inappropriate for Amy to carry with her into the world of nuclear physics, genetic engineering, space travel, robotics, or high-tech medicine? I certainly think not. There are many women making their way into such fields who prefer to think of themselves as no different from their male colleagues, and perhaps they're right. Amy is not a prototype of all women, and Gilligan admits Amy's "voice" is not exclusively male or female. But it *is* an undervalued voice, one that's not encouraged in men and is seldom heard in arenas of power. *I think it's a priceless asset for the twenty-first century, and women are the ones most likely to articulate it.*

John Naisbitt, whose best-seller, *Megatrends,* described ten major forces reshaping human society, has belatedly noticed an eleventh megatrend— "a shift from sex roles to synergy . . . a greater harmony between qualities we used to consider either masculine or feminine."

"Although women are gaining access to power individually, the very nature of power will change as their numbers mount," Naisbitt told one interviewer. "A synergy of male and female leadership qualities will emerge, a new combination that is to everyone's advantage."

As our world becomes increasingly complex, we desperately need more voices like Amy's, male and female, bringing a fresh point of view, a humane sensibility to science and medicine as well as to politics, law, and business. Engineers are at work right now designing computers that can make human-like decisions, "Star Wars" weaponry that may be launched into space, and electronic networks that will bring the information of all the world's libraries into our homes. Biotechnologists are creating novel life forms that can provide us with new vaccines, revitalize agriculture on wastelands, and clean up toxic wastes. Harvard has launched a new medical school curriculum to put more emphasis on the "caring" aspects of medicine in an age when technology can give life to a tiny premature infant or prolong the dying of a person whose bodily functions have all been given over to machines.

The future can be a marvelous place if we develop these technologies wisely and apply them humanely. Now more than ever we need leaders in all fields who can make complex decisions on issues where there is no single right or wrong; who can cope with massive change without succumbing to stress and frustration; who can compromise their egos and passions in a world that can no longer afford to see differences settled through aggression. *Women are unquestionably well endowed for the task. The world can ill-afford to continue to operate using only half of its moral and intellectual resources.*

4 LIVING LONGER

Women are female mammals. As such not only they, but an unbroken chain of generations preceeding them, have been inescapably subject to the rules of evolution . . . The female gender is primary in *Homo sapiens* just as it is in all other species.

Does this make women naturally superior? Yes . . . Selection constantly favors increased longevity in women.

—Anthropologists Irven DeVore and C. Owen Lovejoy

We are always the same age inside.

—Gertrude Stein

Baby girls, like Adrian, Kelly, and Nina, born in the United States in the late 1980s can expect, on the average, to live to about 2065. That means they will live eight years longer than the boys of their generation. Some people would like you to believe that if these girls leave home, go out to work and grapple with the problems of the world, they'll wear out and die as quickly as their male peers. But the truth is just the opposite. Research is revealing dramatic evidence that staying home may be the worst choice a woman can make as far as her health and longevity are concerned. Here are the best strategies for women who want to beat the average life expectancy by a decade or more:

- Get a paid job.
- Better yet, get a job you like, and one that gives you some discretion and control over your work.

- Best of all, achieve success, recognition, and satisfaction in your endeavors. Earn a listing in *Who's Who*.
- Marry a supportive man and have children. Or marry and don't have children, which works almost as well.
- Learn to control your habits, eat the right foods, and exercise properly.

Obviously, increasing numbers of women are already adopting these strategies, most without even knowing that they're maximizing longevity along with their happiness and self-fulfillment. When I look at this trend, and the amazing strides scientists are making in understanding the aging process, *I can foresee the birth of another generation of girls sometime before the year 2000 who will live to see the twenty-second century dawn. And they'll face that dawn without the feebleness and deterioration that accompany advancing age today.*

Looking ahead, I'm going to tell you what researchers are learning about how and why we age and the prospects for slowing down the process. This is no idle curiosity. *Our survey revealed that a third of women would use life-extension drugs if they were available today.* Until such drugs come along, the best hope for longevity lies in those strategies I just listed, and I'll be talking about them in more detail. But *first I want to tell you about the best life-extension strategy of all: being born female.*

Remember that the creation of a male, from the arrival of the Y chromosome to the testosterone that floods the embryo, is a precarious business. The result, at best, is a creature with a single survival advantage over females: greater muscular strength. At every stage of life, men pay dearly to gain this advantage, falling victim to every threat from genetic defects to heart disease. *Women are biologically superior to men in every other physical category but muscles:*

- About three males are conceived for every two females, but more of the males are apparently miscarried or die in the womb.
- At birth, boy babies still outnumber girls, but only by about 5 percent. They're also more likely than girls to face birth injuries.
- Boys are more likely than girls to suffer birth defects and genetic diseases. So-called X-linked genetic diseases such as hemophilia and muscular dystrophy strike boys almost exclusively because they are carried on the X chromosome. Girls, with their two X's, usually have a good gene on the second chromosome to protect them. But the Y provides no such backup to a boy with a defective X.

- Infant boys suffer more illness and infection, and in the first month of life three of them die for every two baby girls. Throughout the rest of their lives, girls will outnumber boys.
- At every age, women have lower death rates from heart disease and heart attacks than do men. Even women who have high blood pressure and high blood cholesterol don't die as readily as men.
- Women are less likely to die of infectious diseases.
- Women in the United States now outlive men by about eight years. This gap has been widening throughout the twentieth century and shows no signs of narrowing even as overall life expectancy reaches new highs. Life expectancy for white women in the United States in 1982 was 78.7 years, compared to 71.4 years for white men. For black women, life expectancy was 73.8 years; for black men, 64.8 years.

"So women are an extraordinarily viable sex, right from the moment of conception," says endocrinologist Estelle Ramey, professor of physiology and biophysics at the Georgetown University School of Medicine. You can see the reality of these biological facts in any retirement community. The Sunbelt is full of widows. The streets are lined with beauty shops, not barber shops, and nice little places for lunch "with the girls." As of 1980, there were 131 women for every 100 men over age sixty-five. By 2000, there'll be 150 of us for every 100 older men.

As you can tell, *we women have a vital interest in encouraging scientists to figure out the female advantage and to unravel the secrets of the aging process, if for no other reason than to try to prolong men's lifespans. Otherwise a third of us will have to count on spending the last decade of our lives without male companionship,* or else come up with some new traditions for pairing up with younger men. (Robert Butler, the former head of the National Institute on Aging, confided at a medical meeting last year that his "number three daughter is marrying a younger man, which I thought was a pretty shrewd move on her part.")

Until some of these changes occur, however, it behooves women of our generation to plan for independence and self-sufficiency in our older years, including taking care of ourselves financially. And we should remember that decisions made now about retirement systems, age discrimination, nursing home and medical care for older Americans, and research funds on aging are truly women's concerns. (Only 5 percent of the elderly end up in nursing homes, but 75 percent of them are women.)

There are people, as I mentioned above, who would like to attribute our advantage to what I call the "hothouse orchid" effect: Women have been sheltered from the pressures and competition of the working world, so ever since medicine reduced the perils of childbirth and the threat of infectious diseases, we've had it easy. But all recent evidence contradicts this. First, human females are not unique in their longevity. The female survival advantage is found throughout the animal kingdom. Second, the advantage was noted at least as early as the eighteenth century. And third, the life expectancy gap is growing at just the time in feminine history when we're busier than ever, caught up in what one psychologist has labeled the "superwoman syndrome," juggling career, marriage, family, home, and social life. *(But, you'll soon see, being a so-called superwoman is hardly a health hazard.)*

At the beginning of this century, women outlived men by less than two years. (In some underdeveloped countries, the longevity gap is still only a few years, especially where no medical care is available at childbirth and female infants are less valued than males.) But in the United States today, with more than half of all women working, we have an eight-year advantage. And *women who do work not only are healthier than their male coworkers, they're actually healthier than housewives.*

The picture that's beginning to emerge from research is that *women are simply better prepared, mentally and physically, to meet the pace and challenges of life and work in a technologically advanced world.* There are lots of factors involved. But Ramey believes a major underlying cause is *hormones.*

(Ramey—respected, outspoken, and elegant as she nears seventy herself —thinks research in this field has definitely been inhibited by the myth that women are the "weaker sex." Not to mention the fact that medical researchers, just like the psychologists who probe moral development, haven't taken much interest in studying women. Not a single woman was included in the ten-year, $150-million federally funded study that determined the impact of cholesterol-controlling drugs and diets on heart disease. "We still don't know a thing about women and cholesterol," she says. "Nothing." And only after she and others raised a storm were women added to the Baltimore Longitudinal Study of Aging, which has been tracking the health of hundreds of men for a quarter of a century.)

The most obvious evidence linking hormones to longevity came from a 1969 study at Downstate Medical Center in New York City. It showed that castrated men, who no longer produce testosterone, outlive normal men. And the earlier the castration is performed, the greater the advantage. Every year of delay costs a quarter of a year of life expectancy. (Of course, none of us who appreciate men—nor men themselves, for that matter—would consider this an acceptable life-extension strategy.)

Throughout the life cycle, men die from accidents three times more often and from violence four times more often than women—partly a legacy of the lower thresholds for aggression that men seem to acquire in the womb, as well as their greater adult testosterone levels. It's also a legacy of those sex-segregated playgroups that boys and girls spend so much of their childhood in, and the different social roles boys and girls are encouraged to fit into.

"Girls in groups are encouraged to take psychological risks with other girls," Ramey notes. And they practice the kind of supportiveness and emotional intimacy that will make them so much better than men at surviving the psychological traumas of loss, disappointment, and bereavement when they get older. "Boys in groups are encouraged to take physical risks. That's why they have an accident rate that accounts for the great discrepancy in boys' and girls' death rates," she says.

"The other thing that's immediately imbued in little boys is the fear of failure, and I've always thought that this accounts for the incredible difference in the completed acts of suicide," Ramey says. "Starting from the age of twelve, three times as many boys as girls commit suicide, again by violent means. Women attempt suicide as they get older about five times as often as men, but three times as many men die of suicide. Men, it appears, are reluctant to fail at anything. They use techniques that make it impossible for them to contemplate failure—shooting, hanging, jumping off of buildings. Women are more inclined to use techniques that are essentially a cry for help because they can afford to fail at suicide as long as people pay attention to their agony—anorexia nervosa, bulimia, sleeping pills."

The accident rate for men also reflects the one area where women *are* actually "protected" from some of the work hazards men face. Thanks to the muscles testosterone builds, men still predominate in mining, construction, soldiering, and other high-risk jobs.

Another sex difference is found in the body's defense systems, and both genes and hormones seem to deserve credit. Women of all ages have more responsive immune systems than men, giving us greater protection from bacteria and viruses. Girls and women, for example, have higher levels of a protective blood protein called immunoglobulin M or IgM than males, and a gene on the X chromosome seems to be responsible. The X also carries other genes that influence various parts of the defense system. And after puberty, estrogens increase the efficiency of our immune responses.

Back in the era when much of the work men did was hard and dangerous and epidemics regularly scourged the country, it was probably fair to attribute women's brief survival advantage to our stronger immune systems and men's higher traumatic death rates. But technology—the increasing automation of work and the development of vaccines and sanitation practices during the last half of the nineteenth century—has eased those hazards. Overall life expectancy for men and women has almost doubled since the mid-nineteenth century.

Some of the biggest risks to life today—heart disease, alcoholism, lung cancer, suicide—arise from the way we handle pressure and stress. *It's becoming clear as the gap between men's and women's life expectancies grows ever wider that women have better ways of coping with stress, physically, mentally, and socially.*

From the physical side, think about how your body is designed to respond to stress. What, after all, did "stress" mean to the Cro–Magnon and the hominids who came before them? Millions of years ago, stress meant a physical threat to survival. The effective response was to prepare for "fight or flight." Your body doesn't realize times have changed.

"It doesn't matter whether the stress is that you've just lost your job or you're being attacked by a tiger," Ramey says. "The response is the same. It's stereotypic, push-button. The system just goes. The endocrine system fires from the adrenal cortex with cortisol. The brain fires, setting off the sympathetic nervous system, which releases adrenaline and noradrenaline. And the adrenal medulla releases additional adrenaline."

The effect of this cascade of hormones is to increase heart rate, heart force, blood pressure, and breathing rate. If the boss has just fired you, your cheeks flush and your heart pounds because your system is revving up your muscles to prepare to punch or run away. "The blood vessels to the muscles in the resting state are largely closed down," Ramey notes. "Just a small amount of blood is perfusing the muscles to keep them viable. When the muscles contract vigorously, as in exercise, the vascular bed just expands and blood pours in to provide the enormous amounts of oxygen and glucose working muscles need."

But you're not likely to run away or to hit the boss. You're just going to try to keep cool. "And that's like putting a clamp on an outflow system. Everything operates. The pressure goes up in the system. All the blood starts flowing toward the muscles. But the clamp is on. The muscles aren't working. You're just sitting there taking it. The pressure goes sky high. And every time the pressure goes up like that, you're damaging the endothelium, the lining of the blood vessels.

"When you're young, you repair the damage. After that, repair becomes more difficult. And every time you have a little breach in the lining, that's a place where lipids or fatty deposits slip in and little plaques form," Ramey explains. The result of plaque buildup is atherosclerosis, clogging or "hardening" of the arteries—the leading cause of death in the United States.

Although the same stress response takes place in both men and women, it's more extreme in men because they need a bigger head of steam to get their larger muscles fueled for action. Testosterone is the key, Ramey says. "It increases the intensity of the response to stress. Per unit stress, males secrete more adrenaline, which is a blood clotter. They get a more massive response of the heart in terms of rate and force. And they get a higher maximal elevation in blood pressure."

Women not only have a less intense response, but some researchers also think estrogen keeps our blood vessels more expandable so that our pressure doesn't shoot as high even when our hearts are pumping with the same rate and force as a man's. (Ramey recently saw another payoff to her years of pushing: The National Institute on Aging decided to pay for a study on the effects of estrogen on heart disease. So in the future we are going to learn even more about our natural protective systems, and how to enhance them.)

Besides preventing this mechanical damage to our blood vessels, estrogen also seems to help indirectly in fighting plaque formation. It influences the liver to produce high-density lipoprotein (HDL), which helps to disperse cholesterol. Testosterone, on the other hand, causes the liver to increase the ratio of low-density lipoprotein (LDL). LDL binds cholesterol and helps it to slip through gaps in the linings of the arteries and form plaques.

Every day, a man's arteries take more of a beating than a woman's, Ramey says. "These are small differences, but every single day of your life you're exposed to stress, whether it's sitting in a car as the traffic piles up around you, or jumping to avoid a taxi, or your kid coming home with bad grades. No one is sheltered from stress. But the female is getting a less vigorous response, and she does proportionately less damage per unit time."

The result is that women are about fifteen years behind men in accumulating significant heart damage. Men, on average, start to develop heart disease between the ages of thirty-five and forty, women between the ages of fifty and fifty-five. Men between thirty-five and fifty-five are twice as likely to die of heart disease as are women.

In evolutionary terms, it makes sense that women "stay viable about fifteen years longer than men," Ramey says. "That puts them right to the menopausal age, when they can no longer bear children." The human reproductive strategy is precarious and vulnerable enough without having fertile females contend with heart attacks, too. Women spend nine months in pregnancy, bear children one at a time, and have to protect them through the longest childhood of any animal species.

Longevity didn't matter so much in males as long as their testosterone-fueled muscles and temperament gave them early success in attracting females and protecting their turf. Anthropologists Irven DeVore, of Harvard, and C. Owen Lovejoy, of Kent State University, wrote: "A male who fathers a large number of children early in his life will have a high fitness, even if he fails to achieve longevity. On the other hand, the female's reproductive rate is linear with age, and she must survive in order to achieve her full reproductive potential."

(In fact, DeVore and Lovejoy say the only way males in nature can equal the "natural superiority" of women is by intensifying their parental involvement, thus making longevity important to their reproductive success. More on this later.)

So is there any way we can help men, without eliminating testosterone and losing the virile qualities most of us find so pleasant to have around? (I'm talking of course about the hormonal risks to their hearts. The lifestyle risks—aggression, high-fat diets, overindulgence of any kind, lack of exercise, lack of intimate and supportive friendships—are a problem men, and women, can already do something about.) The evidence so far looks promising, but it's still controversial. We are bound to hear more about it in the future.

Ramey and fellow endocrinologist Peter Ramwell have found direct evidence in dogs, rats, guinea pigs, and cats that testosterone makes the blood clot faster, increases the risk to the heart, and causes earlier death. However, this risk can be reduced considerably by giving men nothing more than plain aspirin or doses of an antigout drug such as indomethacin or Anturane, which slows blood clotting. Aspirin seems to give women some protection, too, although the effects are not as dramatic.

Some studies in human heart attack victims have found Anturane—and, to a lesser degree, aspirin—effective in preventing deaths from second heart attacks. But Ramey doesn't want to wait until after the first heart attack to offer protection. Her work with both male and female medical students has shown that one or even half a tablet of aspirin a day can reduce blood clotting in both sexes. She'd like to see the day when young men, and perhaps women, start taking daily doses of aspirin or some similar medicine as lifelong protection for their hearts.

Whether aspirin is ever used this way or not, other scientists are searching for even more dramatic ways to conquer the ravages of time. And perhaps even to defeat the aging process altogether.

o   o   o

In 1983, a man named Shigechiyo Izumi died in Asan, Japan, and became a champion of sorts. At 118 years, his became the oldest verified human lifetime on record. He displaced such hardy souls as Fanny Thomas of San Gabriel, California, who had died in 1980 after a life that spanned 113 years and 215 days. Izumi gave credit for his exceptional endurance to a life spent "not worrying," and Thomas attributed hers to three helpings of applesauce a day. But scientists are busy looking for more basic explanations. What they're finding may soon help us make those records commonplace.

Human life expectancy nearly doubled during Izumi's and Thomas's lifetimes, from less than forty to close to seventy-five years for men and women today. Much of the credit goes to Louis Pasteur, who put forward the germ theory of disease in 1865, the year Izumi was born. The medical revolution that followed brought us the miracles of vaccination, sanitation, and antibiotics. (The first doubling of life expectancy, from twenty years to forty, had probably required most of recorded history to accomplish.)

There's a logical question that might come to mind when you think about what modern medicine accomplished in so short a time: *If medicine continues to reduce the toll of heart disease, cancer, and other killers, can we double life expectancy again? The answer is, probably not. Of course, we need to do a lot more than eliminate disease. In order to double life expectancy again, we'll need a major breakthrough in the aging process itself, a discovery that extends the human life span.*

More than semantics is involved in these two terms. *Life expectancy* is the average number of years most of us actually survive. *Life span* is the maximum number of years that any individual of our species can possibly live. Izumi and Thomas greatly exceeded the life expectancy for people born in the 1860s, and even in 1985. But they didn't violate the maximum human life span, which is thought to be 110 to 120 years.

Only in recent times have scientists come to think of life span as a built-in limitation and of aging as an inherent process, separate from the diseases that complicate it. One of the pioneers of gerontology, Leonard Hayflick, of the University of Florida, estimates that if we could eliminate deaths from heart and kidney ailments, cancer, accidents, pneumonia and flu, diabetes, and all infectious and parasitic diseases, life expectancy might reach about 100 years. Others put it a decade or two higher. But then we reach a limit, a process we've only begun to explore: aging itself.

We can see and feel the outward signs of aging: our hair turns gray, our faces sag, and our lungs work harder to get us up the stairs. But there's a similar decline occurring at the cellular level, too. As we get older our aging cells no longer process nutrients, clean up wastes, defend us, or perform the other vital chores of life with the same vigor. As function declines, we're left vulnerable to disease or accident. If these risks were eliminated, presumably the system would, in time, simply fail to maintain life and we would truly die of "old age."

Until ten years ago, very little money was available to probe the mechanisms that govern this process, and money is tight even today. Still, the field has lured some dedicated researchers, and their work is beginning to pay off.

Theories about how and why we age tend to fall into two categories. First is the premise that aging is a preprogrammed event, governed by one or more "death clocks" ticking away in our cells. At some preset moment, perhaps, a clock switches on a dormant gene, and a killer hormone begins to gum up our smoothly running system. Or perhaps the clock itself is set to run down, leaving our carefully orchestrated systems free-running and without direction until the parts begin to fail and the whole mechanism grinds to a halt.

The second category holds that aging is the result of either damage that accumulates in our DNA over the years as our repair mechanisms slip up or damage to other cell mechanisms caused by the wear and tear of daily activities. There's a lot of room for overlap in these theories. Some researchers believe aging is not a single process at all but a series of events controlled by different signals in each of our tissues and organ systems.

Proponents of the "clock" theories of aging point to a now-famous finding in Hayflick's lab in 1961. He showed that embryonic human cells nurtured in a lab dish would grow and divide for only about fifty generations. Then they died. Some innate timer in the nuclei of the cells seemed to count and bring an end to their divisions. Only cancerous cell lines seem to be able to throw off this limit and become "immortal." (At least one researcher, however, Vincent J. Cristafalo of Philadelphia's Wistar Institute, has been able to extend the lifespan of cultured human cells 30 to 40 percent by spiking their nutrient medium with the adrenal hormone hydrocortisone.)

But Hayflick doesn't think this provides a simple explanation of aging and death. We don't age simply because some crucial cell populations in our bodies stop dividing. "Most gerontologists believe that the most important age changes are not produced in rapidly dividing cells but in the more highly specialized cells that divide slowly or not at all," he notes. "These might be neurons, endocrine cells, muscle cells, sensory cells, or cells that give rise to the immune system." It's likely that we age and die before these cells ever reach the limits of their capacity to divide, he believes. But the same "clock" mechanism that limits cell division probably causes other cell functions to run down, too. In cells growing in a lab dish, he notes, all sorts of activities begin to slip up before the last division is reached.

Hayflick suggests that these changes in activity that come with aging may simply be part of a series of genetically programmed events that guide our development from conception to maturity to death. Aging, in other words, may not be an accident but a planned and orderly sequence of events. "There may even be *'aging genes'* that instruct systems to slow down or shut off," he notes. And the cells of different organs and systems might be programmed to shut down at different rates.

A handful of biochemists around the country are busy with a tedious search through the hundreds of enzymes and other proteins produced by young and old cells, looking for consistent changes in older proteins that might reveal "aging genes" at work. Morton Rothstein, at the State University of New York at Buffalo, for instance, has found an enzyme in rat livers that differs in young and old animals. The sequence of amino acids, the building blocks of the enzyme, are strung together differently, indicating that "a very similar but clearly different gene" is at work in the older animals, he says.

But the prize for the most stunning evidence of the clock theory must go to W. Donner Denckla and his "death hormone." Denckla, an endocrinologist, thinks the key to aging is a clock that's programmed to begin shutting down at the end of adolescence. This shutdown process is controlled by a death hormone secreted by the pituitary gland, he believes. He calls the hormone DECO, for "decreasing consumption of oxygen," which is the impact it has on cells.

When Denckla removed the pituitary from aging rats and then gave them supplements of other critical hormones that the gland controls—thyroid, cortisone, and growth hormones—signs of rejuvenation appeared. Their hearts, lungs, and immune systems regained the strength of youth. Twenty percent of them lived to an age that would translate to ninety-five in humans. *This was the first time any researcher had reported actually reversing the aging process.* Denckla also gave crude extracts of this pituitary substance to young rats, and signs of aging appeared.

The work was beginning to look very exciting to those of us who want to see people live longer, healthier lives. In 1981, Denckla was confident that he was just about to isolate this hormone. Then antibodies could be found to block it, or the signals that cause the pituitary to release it could be identified and countered. But in the wake of the recession of the early 1980s, his funding was slashed. Tragically, Denckla left his post at the National Institute of Alcoholism and Alcohol Abuse and gave up the research altogether.

Moving away from the clock idea, a theory of aging that's less popular today contends that our DNA becomes so riddled with mutations and errors during a lifetime of abuse—from smog, sun, and toxins to radiation —that eventually our repair processes are overwhelmed. From faulty DNA our cells make faulty blueprints, produce defective proteins, and assemble shoddy products. The products don't work efficiently, or don't work at all, and systems begin to fail. A variation on this theory says that it's not the buildup of little mutations that fouls up the works but a few catastrophic errors in key genes. Perhaps the genes that oversee DNA repair or regulate the immune system.

Of course, built-in inefficiencies in the cell's repair systems would make aging just as inevitable as death hormones would. But the late George A. Sacher, of Argonne National Laboratory in Illinois, argued that this view is more promising for those who hope to be able to intervene in the process.

The clock ideas, Sacher said, are really based on the premise that the natural state of man is immortality. Sometime during evolution, however, aging genes or death clocks got inserted into our systems. According to one explanation, nature needed a way to get rid of old, infertile humans so they wouldn't compete with younger ones for food and scarce resources. Another possibility is that aging clocks arose to get rid of individuals who were still able to reproduce but who'd accumulated too many mutations in their sperm and egg cells, thus threatening the next generation with an intolerable load of defects. A third rationale is that aging genes are simply useless corruptions that accumulated in our systems. Evolution hasn't weeded them out because they supposedly don't harm us until our reproductive years are over, and thus they don't impair the survival of our lineage.

Sacher preferred to view aging from a different perspective: *Living things are mortal, and evolution works by enhancing systems that assure our survival, not by setting up booby traps to destroy us.*

If our life spans weren't under *positive* genetic control, he contended, then we'd never have been able to develop into big-brained, intelligent creatures. Increasing the size of an animal's brain does two things: It reduces the number of young a mother can bear with each pregnancy. And it increases the length of time it takes for the young to reach maturity. So both the reproductive years and the overall life span of the species have to be lengthened just to keep the population size up.

Within a period of about a million years before the emergence of modern humans, early man doubled his life span and tripled his brain weight, Sacher noted. A creature timed to self-destruct couldn't have made this amazing change. A species can only increase its life span substantially if it can find a better way to carry out "the normal vital function of stabilizing and protecting the essential information molecules (DNA) in the organism." Sacher believed the length of our lives is controlled by a handful of genes that regulate our DNA repair systems.

Indeed, Sacher and Ronald W. Hart found proof for this theory when they studied the DNA repair processes in two species of mice, one of which had a life span of three and a half years, compared to eight and a third years for the other. The cells of the longer-lived mouse patched up their genetic damage two and a half times faster than did those of the shorter-lived mouse. Hart and another researcher, Richard Setlow, looked at the cells of half a dozen other species, from shrew to elephant to man, and also found that long-lived species had greater repair capacity than short-lived ones.

Repair systems, of course, aren't perfect in any species. Eventually damage accumulates to the critical point in all systems, and that brings on the changes that we associate with aging. *If this theory proves correct, Sacher felt, it offers the very real possibility that we'll be able to increase further our own life spans through genetic engineering.* After all, the rapid growth of our brains and the lengthening of our life spans during the Pleistocene Period could have taken place only if the number of key genes that had to be altered was small.

Whatever theory of aging they prefer, several groups of scientists now agree that changes in a small number of genes could make a critical difference in both our health and our life spans. Prime targets are the genes of the major histocompatibility complex or MHC. This knot of genes clustered together on a single chromosome has so many functions it's been dubbed a "supergene." The MHC governs the antigens or chemical markers that tag each of our cells and allows our internal security forces to tell "self" apart from foreign tissues and invading germs. These are the antigens that cause the body to spot and reject transplanted kidneys and hearts. But the supergene does much more.

Roy Walford, of the University of California, Los Angeles, a slightly offbeat but enormously well-respected guru of aging research, thinks the immune system is the master "pacemaker" of aging, and the MHC is its regulator. The MHC influences not only our immune responses, but also our systems for repairing DNA and other machinery inside the cells and for removing potentially dangerous molecules called "free radicals." Walford has shown that nearly identical strains of mice that differ only in the genes of the MHC will have different maximum life spans.

By manipulating the function of the fifty to one hundred genes of the MHC, he believes, we may one day be able to take control of the aging process.

Walford isn't waiting for genetic engineering, however, to try to extend his own life. For more than five years, this sixty-year-old scientist has been living by a strict regimen that's come to be known as "undernutrition." In the 1940s, it was found that the life span of young lab rats could be extended by a third if their calorie intake was cut back by about the same proportion. The diet still contained all the required nutrients, so the rats were not malnourished. Just undernourished. *It's still the only method that's ever been found that can successfully extend the actual life span of a mammal.*

Walford has repeated and expanded these studies at UCLA, finding that the regimen also delays the onset of normal age-related changes in the immune system and decreases the incidence of heart and kidney disease, cancer, and arthritis. He and Edward J. Masoro, of the University of Texas Health Sciences Center in San Antonio, have also found that underfeeding can increase the life span of mice even when it's not started until middle age.

Walford and his colleagues aren't sure how food restriction causes changes in the aging process. But *they are confident we'll eventually develop scientifically calculated diets to combat cancer, heart and kidney ailments, and arthritis and other autoimmune diseases,* which are caused when the body fails to tell friend from foe and begins to attack its own tissues.

The life-extension diets that you've heard about most, such as *Life Extension* by Durk Pearson and Sandy Shaw, in books and on TV talk shows, are much less rigorous than Walford's, and based on a different theory of aging—*free radicals.* Denham Harman, at the University of Nebraska, proposed, in the 1940s, that the primary agents in aging are free radicals. These unstable, highly reactive molecules are byproducts of normal cell activity, formed when oxygen is used to process food and generate energy, particularly in the mitochondria or "powerplants" of our cells. Free radicals bombard the genetic material and other sensitive structures, eventually wrecking the mitochondria. Fewer mitochondria means less energy for moving muscles, manufacturing hormones, and running other life functions.

Harman and others have shown that the life expectancy of mice—although not their life spans—can be prolonged dramatically when they're given free-radical inhibitors. The supplements also retard the development of age-related diseases. The inhibitor substances—called *antioxidants*—include vitamins A, E, and C, the trace element selenium, and food additives like BHA and BHT.

Hundreds of clinics around the country are now offering a more controversial anti-aging treatment that its advocates claim can prevent tissue damage from free radicals—*chelation therapy*. It involves infusing EDTA —ethylenediamine tetraacetate—into a patient's blood. EDTA is a "chelating" agent, which binds itself to iron, copper, and other metals required for the formation of certain free radicals and removes them from the body. (Its only approved use in orthodox medicine is in the treatment of lead poisoning.)

For more than three decades, chelation has been used as an alternative therapy for one of the major afflictions of aging, heart disease. Advocates claim the treatment removes accumulations of metals that might otherwise speed up the formation of plaque along arterial walls. As plaque softens and ceases to grow, supporters of the therapy say, blood flow improves, reducing the risks of stroke and senility and allowing more oxygen and nutrients to reach all body tissues. (Older women often suffer from iron, calcium, and other mineral deficiencies, that can lead to anemia and osteoporosis, so chelation isn't a therapy to rush into without a thorough assessment of your total health needs.)

Several hormones have also been found that seem to inhibit the diseases of aging and perhaps even slow the aging process itself. One of these is thymosin, discovered twenty years ago. It's produced by the thymus, a gland right behind the breastbone that has important roles in keeping our immune system strong. The thymus reaches its peak and starts to shrivel away by the time we reach puberty, and many researchers believe this gradual failure of our defenses is one of the most damaging effects (if not the cause) of aging. Allen L. Goldstein, of George Washington University, one of the discoverers of thymosin, and others are now seeing what the hormone can do for aging mice.

One of the most exciting and underfunded areas of research concerns a hormone that seems to give some of the same benefits as undernutrition. It has an unpronounceable chemical name, dehydroepiandrosterone, or DHEA for short, and it's produced by the adrenal glands. Production peaks in one's mid-twenties, then declines steadily after that. DHEA was discovered more than thirty years ago, but was virtually ignored because no one knows to this day why your body makes it.

Biochemist Arthur G. Schwartz, of Temple University, in Philadelphia, got curious and started using the hormone on mice. DHEA prevented the development of breast cancer in a strain of mice genetically susceptible to breast tumors. It also inhibited development of lung and colon cancers and delayed the onset of an inherited blood disorder. And it helped genetically obese mice to lose weight without curbing their appetites. (More about this benefit later.) The combination of effects sounds almost too good to be true, doesn't it? Even the normally cautious and low-key scientists working with DHEA have a hard time trying to restrain their enthusiasm.

Unless federal funding policies change, I can't really tell you that you'll be able to benefit from this hormone anytime soon. The money for long-term studies on humans is scarce. And unfortunately, DHEA is a natural substance that's been available for so long it's no longer patentable, so drug companies aren't interested in spending millions of dollars to test it. Some companies *are* at work trying to make derivatives that could be patented, however.

This problem of funding priorities goes much beyond DHEA. *Our government spends billions of dollars supporting people in nursing and convalescent homes and trying to patch up the ravages and misery caused by the diseases of aging. I don't begrudge the sick and elderly all the help we can give them, but our approach is too short-sighted.* I agree with what science writer Albert Rosenfeld said in an *Omni* column in 1983:

> What if the March of Dimes had elected during the decades of the 1940s and 1950s to devote most of its resources to putting polio victims into iron lungs instead of concentrating on basic viral research and vaccine development? We now know that to have spent *less* money on infantile paralysis research would have been a massive extravagance. Think what we would have been spending all these years on polio care versus the negligible costs of vaccination and prevention, let alone the untold amount of human anguish that has been prevented.
>
> . . . The message should soon get through to the politicians in our federal government that we can no longer afford the *iron-lung approach to aging.* Money put into aging research is money put into our national savings—at high rates of interest in the form of health and vigor, dignity and self-respect, and, of course, dollars and cents.

Our survey showed American women definitely have a strong interest in improving health, enhancing their mental and physical capacities, and even prolonging life.

Of all the possible technological breakthroughs ahead—in health, energy, education, domestic environment, work environment, birth control and reproduction, transportation, even control of the weather—we asked women which would have the greatest positive effect on their lives. *Sixty-seven percent say a breakthrough in the field of health would benefit them most.* This was highest, as you might imagine, among the oldest age group we surveyed—74 percent among women thirty-five to forty-four, compared to 58 percent of women twenty-five to thirty-four. (It surprised me that the women we talked to in Japan and South Africa ranked health second behind transportation and education, respectively. The English women put health ahead by 43 percent, but they're the only ones to give weather control a big vote—17 percent.)

As I mentioned before, *33 percent of the American women we surveyed say they would use life-extension drugs if these were available.* (So would a fourth of the English we talked to. But only 12 percent of the Japanese women and 7 percent of the South Africans we contacted would use these medicines.)

Even more than life extension, the women we surveyed are interested in enhancing their energy, memory, and intelligence. *Half the women we surveyed say they'd use energy-boosting medicine if it were made available; 44 percent would use memory-enhancing medicine; and 41 percent would use intelligence-boosting portions.*

We *can and will* have all these things. Only the timing is in question, and that's largely a matter of priorities and money. These are things that you and other women, as voters, politicians, government officials, and scientists, can influence greatly.

o   o   o

This takes us back to those strategies I began with, the things women today can do to insure longer and healthier lives.

I want to start with the last strategy I listed, because it's an area where I'm afraid too many women are heading in the wrong direction. I mentioned in the last chapter how we women have tended to let slip the head starts nature endowed us with—our social, verbal, and communicative skills; our native ambition and self-confidence. *We could easily surrender some of the survival advantages nature handed us, too, if we pick up the bad habits of the men we work with,* and if we don't take the time and trouble to learn about the benefits of nutrition and exercise.

Let's turn now to the life-extending strategies that have to do with jobs. They may surprise you but they're no real surprise to social scientists. *When Lois M. Verbrugge, of the University of Michigan's Institute of Gerontology, looked at the health of American women, she found well-documented and very consistent evidence, not only from recent surveys but from ones conducted before World War II, that "having a paid job is associated with good physical health."*

"Women who are currently employed (with a paid job) are notably healthier than unemployed women and women outside the labor force," she finds. They have fewer chronic complaints, spend fewer days in bed, spend less time in the hospital, and use less medical care. The difference is most dramatic among middle-aged and older women, from forty-five to sixty-four. A national health survey in 1977–78 found working women in this age group suffered fifteen days of restricted activity a year, compared to thirty-eight for nonworking women; five days disabled in bed, compared to thirteen for nonworking women; and 12 percent of them suffered limitations due to chronic conditions, compared to 32 percent of nonworkers.

The women with the "poorest health profile" are housewives and others who aren't even looking for paid jobs. The health of unemployed women—those who are looking for a job but haven't succeeded—is closer to that of housewives than that of working women. ("All of these statements are true for men as well," Verbrugge notes.)

Researchers looking for direct signs of health risks in women report similar conclusions. When epidemiologist Helen Hazuda, of the University of Texas, San Antonio, looked at blood levels of HDL, (which helps disperse cholesterol, you'll recall), she found working women had significantly higher levels than housewives and thus were more protected against heart attacks. She conjectured that the work environment may be "healthier for women's psyches."

Of course, not all work environments are equally healthy for our psyches or our bodies. Nevertheless, all the evidence says you're better off at work than at home, but it also knocks down some old clichés about what kind of work is most stressful. If you still think the person at greatest risk of a heart attack is the high-powered executive, the woman with the weight of a multinational corporation on her shoulders, you've got it wrong. The person most in jeopardy is more likely to be the harried file clerk in the back office.

The key to health and happiness on the job is control, the ability to influence what work you do and how. Some of the highest risks of heart disease among women have been found in those working in dead-end sales, clerical, and other low-status jobs. These are often women who dislike their jobs, feel oppressed by their superiors, but keep their mouths shut for fear of being fired. Many of them work not by choice but from economic necessity. Their health risks are in sharp contrast to those of women who are working by choice, especially at careers they feel committed to.

Don't be afraid of ambition and competitiveness. The very best thing you can do for your own health and longevity is to achieve success and prominence, and preferably a listing in Who's Who in America. I'm not just speculating on this. In 1979, the Metropolitan Life Insurance Co., which has a vital interest in how long people can be expected to live, published a study confirming this. Prominent women listed in the 1964–65 edition of *Who's Who* were followed up for twelve years. Their death rate turned out to be 30 percent *below* that of their contemporaries in the rest of the population.

The "exceptional longevity" rate of these distinguished women would have been even more favorable if 12 percent of the group hadn't been made up of performers and entertainers. Women in this category actually had a death rate 43 percent above average. (Figures like this make me glad I gave up acting and dancing for publishing.) On the other hand, women correspondents and journalists died at a rate 3 percent above that of their contemporaries.

But look at all the other occupations: Famous women scientists had a death rate 30 percent below that of their contemporaries; business executives had a 26 percent advantage; educators, including college professors and presidents, 36 percent; government officials, 55 percent; archivists, librarians, museum directors, and curators, 54 percent; artists, illustrators, and sculptors, 45 percent; political leaders, 48 percent; community service leaders, 52 percent; physicians and surgeons, 14 percent; judges and lawyers, 22 percent; and architects and designers, 19 percent.

A decade earlier, Metropolitan Life had done a similar study of prominent men in the United States. The results were startlingly alike. The men in *Who's Who* also had an overall death rate "30 percent below that of their counterparts in the general population." (To make the male study feasible, the researchers had to use only 5,800 of the names listed—about one-sixth of the men in that edition. But to get enough women to study they had to use every one in the book—2,352. I certainly hope opportunities for women in the past twenty years have changed those numbers.) This confirmed many earlier studies showing that "the most favorable longevity is enjoyed by men of high educational attainment and professional accomplishments" and "men in the more favored socioeconomic segments of the population."

That means educated, successful, respected, and well-heeled. *So, if you're looking for a long, healthy life, don't be afraid to work hard and to be ambitious.* People who not only enjoy what they're doing, but who have learned to cope with the normal stresses and uncertainties of professional life are better off. And if they do it well and it brings status and wealth, that's even better. *The people at most risk are those who feel helpless and overwhelmed by life.*

Verbrugge's statistics confirm that "life satisfaction is a strong predictor of later good health status and of longer life . . . Employed women who like their jobs or who are working by choice rather than solely economic need have better health and less medical care, restricted activity, and medical drug use than less satisfied workers." (This all bodes well for our health and well-being in the future. As you'll see later, *three-quarters of the women we surveyed expect to work most of their adult lives, and only one-quarter of these listed financial necessity as one of the reasons.*)

Now, I don't want to leave you with the impression that every housewife, now or in the future, is destined for a short, sickly, and unfulfilled life. We're talking about averages. And as Verbrugge says, none of the statistics prove that "the homemaker role is intrinsically unsatisfying. There are many happy, content homemakers; and there are many discontented working women. *The critical finding is that happiness matters in one's work activity, whether that is at home or at a paid job."* Still, housewives overall *are* the least happy and least healthy women in this country. They're much more likely to attempt suicide than are women in any other occupation, except prostitutes.

The greatest jeopardy to happiness and health comes when a person perceives that the role she's filling is not valued, and unfortunately our society tells women in many subtle and not-so-subtle ways that it no longer puts much stock in lifelong homemaking. That's not a conspiracy on the feminists' part, and it didn't happen overnight. It's simply a reflection of changing economic times, and ironically, our own longevity. In an agricultural age, when children were valued as economic assets on the farm, infant mortality was high, and women themselves expected to die in their forties, childrearing was truly a vital and lifelong profession. But today we live to be nearly eighty and average one and a half children apiece. That's hardly a lifetime job. I find it tragic that many girls like Kelly are still being raised to think that childrearing is their major contribution to society. (More of this in a later chapter.)

This brings me to the fourth item on my longevity strategy list. If you were still under the impression that high-powered jobs lead to early graves, you may also believe that women who combine career and family responsibilities are asking for heart attacks. Wrong again. *It's time to stop wringing our hands about that "superwoman" nonsense.*

Women with "multiple roles"—that is, employed married women, with children or without, and employed single women who have kids at home—"have much better health than other groups," Verbrugge says. "The best health is found among employed married mothers, though employed married women without children are very close to them. . . . For men, too, those with the triple roles of job, husband, and parent have the best health profile. . . . *The evidence suggests that people can accumulate roles with no health debit so long as they are satisfied with their choices."*

(Working is also the healthiest way to spend a pregnancy. A recent University of Washington study found that women who work during their pregnancies have fewer emotional and physical problems than those who don't, probably because they keep busy and get more social support. They suffer less backache, sleeplessness, vomiting, loss of appetite, worry, and depression. And the women with the most prestigious jobs have the fewest problems.)

The impact of children isn't really as small as it looks in Verbrugge's statement because she's presenting an overall average. *Parenthood can actually be quite good or bad for your health at any given time, depending on the number of children you have, how old they are, and whether you're raising them alone.* The scientific evidence isn't consistent on this, but it seems to indicate that "having preschoolers or numerous (three or more) children can pose problems and stresses for working women and ultimately jeopardize their health," Verbrugge says. And the highest health toll, as you might imagine, seems to be levied on single working mothers with *numerous* youngsters at home and no partner to share the load.

This brings us back to the question of whether or not women are satisfied with their choices, and also whether they're backed in those choices by a supportive partner. When University of Illinois researchers Catherine Ross and John Mirowsky looked at depression among husbands and wives, they found it to be most severe for both spouses when the wife works but neither she nor her husband wants her to. Their moods improve—although his much more than hers—when she wants to work and he supports her decision, but he doesn't share the burden of home and child care.

Her mood is brightest, and his doesn't seem to be dampened any, when the burdens of job and home are shared equitably. This is what the researchers call *"parallel marriage"* and it's the sort of mutually supportive style of relationship that promises to improve both the physical and mental health of men and women in the future. (I'll get back to this in a later chapter, too, because that's the sort of partnership with a man that the overwhelming majority of you told us you want.)

As more and more women take charge of their own lives, train for careers that excite and challenge them, and team up with men who are willing to pull their weight at home, I foresee even greater prospects ahead for the health and longevity of both sexes.

5 FIT AND FEMALE

Crash programs fail because they are based on the theory that, with nine women pregnant, you can get a baby in a month.

—Anonymous

A woman can never be rich enough or thin enough!
—attributed to the Duchess of Windsor, Barbara Paley, and others

Which one of the following biotypes describes you best?

- You can eat whatever you want, maintain a great figure, and never fool with diets or jogging.
- You seem to gain weight just by looking at food, and all your faithful dieting doesn't help.
- You gorge like a Roman noble, never exercise, and still can't seem to flesh out your bony frame.

I know most of you picked the second category because *our survey showed 79 percent of American women actively diet anywhere from a few days to every single day of the year.* Only 19 percent of women say they *never* diet. Another 38 percent say they diet up to a month a year. And 41 percent say their dieting runs from two months a year to "always —every single day." (In contrast, 75 percent of the Japanese, half of the

English, and a third of the South African women we talked to say they never diet, perhaps, in the case of the Japanese, because their diet is low in fat to start with.)

In the past few years, science has verified what most dieters *know* but don't want to admit: *Dieting is self-defeating. The more you do it, the less likely you are to lose weight or ever be able to return to normal eating habits without rebounding to an even heftier size than before.* In the process of figuring out why this is so, researchers have also confirmed some of the common wisdom of dieters: *Various people's bodies respond differently to the same calorie intake.* We're in the process now of completely revising our thinking about how people gain and lose weight.

This is an area where science is going to affect you very personally in the immediate future. Women have been the targets of most of the fad diets of the past thirty years, and these diets have done little but make us feel like failures. Research is now providing us with the information we need to begin to understand our own bodies and to pattern our lifestyles, exercise, and eating habits around our individual nutritional and metabolic needs. And for those of us who still need help, it'll soon make available weight-control drugs that really work.

I predict that women of Kelly and Adrian's generation will look at the thousands of diet books on our shelves today the way we look at Victorian corsets—as amusing antiques from a period of self-imposed torture and ignorance of our own bodies. This is another area where I think a knowledge of our personal biology will lead to better self-understanding and self-respect and provide us with greater and more precise control of our own lives. *In the future we're going to work with our bodies, not fight them. The women of tomorrow will be leaner, healthier, stronger, and full of the energy they need to enjoy their busy lives.*

Now the old dogma of weight control is simple: 3,500 calories equals a pound of body fat. A moderately active woman between the ages of twenty-three and fifty, who stands five feet four inches tall and weighs 120 pounds needs to take in an average of 2,000 calories a day just to keep from losing weight. If this were really true for everyone, however, most American women would be Twiggy-slender, because federal statistics also show we consume about 1,500 calories a day. This dogma contradicts something painfully obvious to all of us: some people stuff themselves and never gain weight. Others eat sparingly and never lose it. You may stay slim effortlessly on 2,000 calories a day while a friend of the same age and build stays pudgy on 1,200 calories.

It wasn't until the past decade that truly sophisticated research techniques actually confirmed this phenomenon. The work is so new that most medical doctors are actually unaware of it. They roll their eyes at fat patients who swear they exist on cottage cheese. But the truth is, most overweight people don't eat any more than do thin people.

Now scientists are beginning to explore *how* some bodies can handle calories so differently than others. (Saying it's "metabolism" doesn't help much because that term includes all the physical and chemical processes that go on inside your body.)

Some of the most exciting work in this field will start in 1986, in Beltsville, Maryland, at the U.S. Department of Agriculture's Human Nutrition Research Center. There, in a computerized chamber the size of a large bank vault, human volunteers will sleep and exercise and eat precisely calculated meals, and while away days or weeks as sensors monitor the oxygen they take in and the heat and carbon dioxide they give off. The chamber is called a calorimeter, and it will be the first one in this country large enough for humans to live in.

Using the chamber, USDA scientists will be able to recalculate, for the first time in almost a century, the calorie values of the foods we eat and the total amount of energy the average American needs, depending on his or her activity levels. (Our lifestyles have obviously changed a great deal since the 1890s, and it's a sure bet those early calorie counts don't tell us what we're getting when we eat a chemically processed frozen dinner or a pizza with artificial cheese.)

Even more interesting to me are the experiments that will analyze how different bodies use the energy they take in. (None of us, after all, is an "average American." We need a way to calculate our *individual* energy needs.) Research has already provided plenty of ideas to follow up. I know you've probably heard some of the more fashionable catchwords because each new concept has been exploited by the diet industry as soon as it emerged from the lab: set points, brown fat, thrifty genes, sodium pumps.

One of the basic concepts that's surfaced so far contradicts what all the diet books tell you: ***It's actually the chemical plant in your own body and not the presumptions of your willpower that determines your weight.*** Your body has a *set point* that, like a thermostat, adjusts your metabolic rate, or knocks out your appetite, or sets you to dreaming of donuts in an effort to keep you at the weight it "wants" you to be. The thermostat is probably headquartered in the hypothalamus, the section of your brain that controls your hormonal flows and regulates your appetite, body temperature, blood pressure, and responses to stress. The set point for fatness is probably just one of many pacemakers your body uses, without the help of your conscious mind, to keep its systems in balance.

Unless you're a pathological eater, you probably know right off what weight your body seems to consider natural. It's the weight you drift back to after an illness has caused you to lose five pounds or a holiday binge has added five. It's the point you tend to hover at when you're ignoring your weight. (Some of you may be scoffing: "Hah, if I didn't diet every minute I'd be a 300-pound blimp in a month." But it's precisely *because* you're dieting that your body can't pace itself naturally. More on this shortly.)

How does your body adjust its metabolic rate to compensate for too many or too few calories? This is where *brown fat* or BAT—brown adipose tissue —apparently plays a role. This is a tissue that might provide the key to some people's fast metabolism, their ability to eat just about anything without gaining weight. Brown fat seems to excel at *futile cycling,* burning calories simply to generate heat. It's the tissue that keeps hibernating animals warm through the winter.

Brown fat really is *brown* because each cell is crowded with little structures called mitochondria, the powerhouses that convert calories to heat and energy. Researchers at the University of Ottawa have found that brown fat provides a way for animals to adapt their body temperatures to colder climates. When they put slim rats in a cold chamber, the rats shiver for awhile—a way of generating heat through muscle activity. Then the shivering stops as mitochondria in the animals' brown fat switch on and begin to generate enough heat to maintain their body temperatures. Leave the rats in a cold environment and their brown fat layers will actually increase while each cell develops proportionately more and more mitochondria.

Now there's another way to increase the amount of brown fat besides chilling the rats. You can tempt them to overeat by offering them an unlimited diet of novel foods (from fruitcake to spaghetti) on top of their ordinary chow, as researchers at London's St. George's Hospital medical school did. The rats ate an average of 80 percent more calories than normal but increased their weight only 27 percent. Again, it was brown fat that was responsible for trying to burn off as many of these excess calories as possible, more efficiently, of course, in some rats than in others. The overfed rats actually increased their stores of brown fat just as the cold rats did.

Just how much of a role brown fat plays in human weight control is still being debated, although some scientists think brown fat may burn off as much as 10 percent of the unneeded calories we eat in a day. We don't even know how much brown fat adults carry, although most of it seems to be sandwiched between the white fat layers along our spines, upper backs, and the back of our necks.

Our brains apparently gauge how much we've eaten by monitoring our insulin levels, which shoot up as our blood sugar rises during a meal. The hypothalamus then causes the release of the stress chemical noradrenaline, which spurs brown fat cells to speed up their burn rate. Your metabolic rate, or calorie-burning rate, normally rises after any meal, but it increases dramatically after a real splurge, just as it did in the overfed rats.

Your body works quite hard, as you can see, to keep your weight stable. And there are plenty of things you can do to help. I'm going to talk about how you can safely adjust your set point to a lower fat level and turn up your metabolic rate right now. We already have the keys to throwing away our calorie charts. Exercise is the easiest key. The timing and content of your meals are another. And drugs that raise the burn rate in brown fat are a third. I'll come back to all these later in this chapter, *but first I want to show you how crash dieting can defeat your body's weight control efforts and lock you in a vicious cycle that will actually make you fatter.* Personally, I have never punished myself with crash diets. Instead, I get on the scale each morning to make sure I haven't gained an extra pound or two. The moment I do, I cut back immediately on the *amount* I eat.

Almost any diet looks promising at first because you actually *do* lose pounds. Of course, what you're losing isn't fat. It's salt, minerals, and water, the kind of weight that goes back on in a matter of hours as soon as you start eating normally. If you continue a strict diet you may actually start losing muscle, and even some fat. But then your weight levels off. I know most of you've experienced that frustrating point, after the first easy five or ten pounds, when you just can't seem to lose any more. So you give up the diet, and the weight you lost creeps back on. Plus a new pound or two. Then you start a new diet. The doctors call it "yo-yo dieting."

Here's what happens: Your body of course, can't tell a severe self-imposed diet from plain old famine. And your body has evolved all sorts of mechanisms to keep from dying of starvation. If you cut your calorie intake drastically, your body tries to "save" itself by cutting its energy requirements. It simply turns down the burn rate and slows your metabolism to keep from dipping too far into energy reserves. Of course, what your body regards as energy reserves is what you call flab.

In pathological forms of dieting like anorexia nervosa, a body's energy requirement to preserve life may fall as low as 500 calories. Imagine what happens then if that person tries to go back to a more normal diet, even a low 1,500 calories. Her body will store most of that extra 1,000 calories a day and continue to put on pounds even after she's regained her starting weight. Most of that weight, too, is fat, not muscle. For all her body knows, she could be a Stone Age woman enduring seasonal cycles of feast and famine. And after a period of near-starvation her body intends to stock up all the reserves it can during the cycle of plenty. It raises her set point and becomes thrifty with every calorie.

The same phenomenon has been observed in prisoners of war and other victims of malnutrition, who balloon up to obesity when food is given to them. And years of yo-yo dieting can trigger the same thriftiness in most of us, defeating our best efforts to starve to a size smaller and stay there.

(Thriftiness, of course, may be even easier to trigger in those of us who are already genetically susceptible to it. This is where the *thrifty genes* concept comes in. Some of us may have simply inherited the kind of metabolism that's better suited to survival in the Ethiopian desert than in a land crowded with McDonalds. Whole ethnic groups, in fact, including American Samoans and the Pima Indians of Arizona, whose ancestors endured harsh cycles of drought and plenty, seem to have inherited the thrifty trait. The tragic result is that they now suffer from some of the highest diabetes and obesity rates in the world.)

It's almost a cliché among doctors treating fat people that even those who starve down to their ideal weights seldom stay there. And it's not because they start stuffing themselves either. Rudolph Leibel, at Rockefeller University, notes, "formerly obese patients often complain of persistent feelings of fatigue, mental depression, intolerance of cold environments, irregular menstrual periods, and inability to ingest a normal number of calories per unit of body weight without beginning to regain some of their lost weight." (These are the same symptoms that anorexia patients report.) So he set out to see if losing large amounts of weight was associated with a change in metabolism.

He found twenty-six very fat patients and calculated, through the use of a liquid diet, exactly how many calories it took to keep each one's weight stable. Their energy requirements, as it turned out, were very close to those of a group of normal weight people who'd never been obese. Then Leibel put his fat patients on an extremely low-calorie diet until they'd lost an average of one hundred pounds each (an ordeal that's dreadful even to contemplate), and measured their energy requirements again. *In their slimmed-down state, these patients had to eat 28 percent less than other people the same size who'd never been fat just to keep from gaining weight.*

In other words, Leibel points out, their metabolic rates "were more 'normal' in the obese state than after weight loss. In fact, weight loss seemed to be associated with a substantial increase in the efficiency of the body's metabolic processes." This, of course, is the last thing these people needed to hear after coming off months of a miserable near-starvation diet and just wanting to eat like normal people again.

Other researchers have found that drastic weight loss alters more than metabolic rates. Rats that have been put through repeated cycles of food restriction—a laboratory version of yo-yo dieting—die sooner than rats on steady diets. In humans, too, obese people whose weight goes up and down drastically die at a much higher rate than do people who are just as fat but don't diet. (I'm certainly not arguing for obesity or against trying to lose weight. But there are much better ways of doing it, as you'll see.)

All this comes down to a simple fact: a fat body operates differently from a slim body. Some of the differences may be *consequences* of being fat and of your body's attempt to keep you that way. Other differences may have helped *cause* you to get fat in the first place. Scientists are pursuing these differences at the level of cells, hormones, and enzymes—the kind of information that will help us find new ways to break out of the self-defeating cycle of dieting. Here are some of their findings:

- *Fat cells:* One thing that yo-yoing causes is a permanent increase in the number of fat cells in your body. Semi-starvation dieting shrinks your fat cells but it never gets rid of any. And as soon as you start eating normally again, these cells not only refill but multiply. One study shows that the fat cells of obese people scoop up sugar from the blood and turn it to fat more enthusiastically than do the fat cells of slim people. Even those hunger pangs and food fantasies that cause you misery during a diet may be your brain's way of responding to the "requests" of shrunken fat cells to be filled.

   Very simply, your body craves stability. But you teach it through constant dieting to expect massive changes in its fuel supply. So it becomes even more determined to prepare for the worst, to resist the next famine—or the next diet—*by actually storing more fat.*

   Another finding: The most dangerous fat to accumulate, as far as health is concerned, is in potbellies and flabby necks, arms, and shoulders. Those saddlebags on your thighs and rear don't look very good, but they're not associated with as many health risks. One possible explanation for this has been proposed by Leibel. He finds that abdominal fat cells are covered with a higher proportion of receptors that stimulate the breakdown of fat (beta receptors) than are the fat cells in hips and thighs. This means these fat cells release more fatty acids into the blood, and high blood fat levels are a risk factor in heart disease. It also means, however, that potbellies are usually easier to get rid of than saddlebags.

· *Insulin:* One factor that spurs the creation of these new fat cells is insulin. Overweight people produce higher levels of insulin than do people of normal weight. Insulin speeds up the conversion of sugar from the food we eat into fat and sends it to fat cells for storage. High insulin levels also increase your hunger pangs and your taste for sweets.

One reason so many overweight people develop diabetes is that this overabundance of insulin seems to cause the body to develop a resistance to it. (This is different from the type of diabetes that arises in children who produce little or no insulin.) By losing weight, most people can lower their insulin levels and bring diabetes under control.

· *Brown fat:* Genetically fat rats seem to carry just as much brown fat as do slim rats, but thcy can't get it to burn calories and generate heat as efficiently. They never adapt as well to cold. And they store the excess calories as weight. Some fat people may have underactive brown fat, too.

· *High blood pressure:* The obese suffer from hypertension at twice the rate of slim people. Doctors have usually considered fatness itself the cause, as the heart strains to pump blood to all those extra pounds of bloated tissue. But Paul Ernsberger, of Cornell University, has found that, in rats at least, cycles of drastic weight gain and loss can cause a distinct form of hypertension, a kind that in humans can bring on congestive heart failure.

· *Muscle mass:* The thing you lose most of in dieting is lean body weight, not fat. And if your diet is too drastic, especially if it's low in protein, part of the muscle you waste away can be heart muscle.

· *Sodium pump:* As much as 30 percent to 40 percent of the energy your body uses is spent maintaining the balance between sodium and potassium in your cells. An enzyme called sodium-potassium-ATPase serves as the "sodium pump" that lets potassium in and keeps sodium out. The process not only uses up vast quantities of calories but produces much of the heat that keeps our bodies at 98.6 degrees.

In a result that is still controversial, Jeffrey Flier, of Beth Israel Hospital in Boston, has found that the blood of fat people contains about 20 percent less of the sodium pump enzyme than normal. And that may leave them with more unburned calories to store as fat.

- *Growth hormone:* Growth hormone plays a critical role in the body's ability to break down fat. The pituitary glands of very fat people produce only a tenth as much growth hormone as do normal people's, according to research at the University of Cincinnati College of Medicine. If a fat person loses weight, however, hormone production returns to near normal, indicating that this slowdown is a consequence, not a cause, of obesity.
- *Adrenaline:* Studies at the Medical College of Wisconsin–Milwaukee could explain why very fat people have so little energy and have such a hard time sticking with an exercise program. Researchers have found that when obese and slim women perform the same exercises, the slim ones respond by producing twice as much adrenaline and thus experiencing a greater energy "rush." And it looks as though the adrenaline response, like the growth hormone response, may return to normal if the overweight person manages to reduce.
- *Satiety signals:* Dieting teaches a person to ignore her own body's signals of hunger and satiation. Instead of eating a nutritious and reasonable meal or snack when she's hungry, the dieter waits until an appointed hour and eats what's on the list. She eats grapefruit even if her body craves something sweet. This sets her up for capitulation and a guilty binge when the cravings get too strong. Who needs the chronic stress and anxiety that come from ignoring your own body?

Besides, the brain may actually set up a specific craving because the body *needs* a certain nutrient. If nerve cells in the brain, for instance, are low on supplies of the amino acid tryptophan, which they use to manufacture the messenger chemical serotonin, the brain may create a demand for carbohydrates. (Actually the tryptophan, like other amino acids, is supplied by protein. But tryptophan has a hard time competing with its fellow amino acids to get into the brain. Carbohydrates in the diet give it a boost.) A person who understands the signals can eat an apple or a cookie and go on about her business instead of waiting until she's driven to gobble down a dozen donuts.

So after I've told you all this, what can you do about that extra twenty pounds or more you're carrying? You've already fasted and splurged so many times that your insulin and fat cells are up, your sodium pump and growth hormones are down, you're afraid of your own appetites, and you hardly have enough energy to climb the stairs at the end of the day, much less jog.

There are no quick miracles, but you *can* take charge again. And it's important that you do. Earlier this year, a federal health panel labeled obesity a potential killer and warned that 34 million Americans are at least 20 percent overweight and at significantly higher risk of hypertension, heart disease, diabetes, gout, gall stones, arthritis, and certain cancers.

Getting active is the best prescription I can give you. And before you groan and recoil, let me explain why. *The truth is, your set point and your weight are much more closely related to how active you are than to how much you eat. For most of us, behavior modification needs to be directed toward our activity levels, not our eating habits.*

That's certainly not because you're likely to walk, jog, or swim away all the excess calories you eat. You can, of course: If you spend your lunch hour jogging at a six-minute-mile pace you could run off 900 calories. But most of you are more likely to do something less strenuous, especially if you're already overweight and out of shape. You may take a brisk walk, say three to four miles on your lunch hour, or a quarter-mile swim. That burns 300 calories, only 200 more than you'd burn if you just sat at your desk for that hour.

Now I don't belittle those 200 calories. They would burn off a dish of ice cream. And in fact, if you did that amount of exercise every day for a year without changing your eating habits much, you'd lose those extra twenty pounds. (If that's too slow for you, just think how many months or years you've wasted trying to get rid of twenty pounds by dieting.) But brisk aerobic activity—the kind that speeds up your heart rate and keeps you breathing a little harder for a half hour or more—has much greater benefits than only burning the calories while you're doing it:

- Exercise raises your metabolic rate for at least an hour after you finish, and perhaps all day (this point is hard to gauge until we can get people into that big calorimeter and monitor them after a good hard ride on the exercise bike). This means you're burning away more calories even as you sit at your desk after your lunch time walk, swim, or run.
- Exercise actually seems to lower your body's setpoint, resetting the thermostat to hold you at a lower weight and body fat level.
- Exercise builds muscle and burns fat. Severe dieting, as you saw, destroys muscle, and weight gained on the rebound replaces it with

fat (not the good brown kind—just plain old white fat). As you exercise, your scale may not show any dramatic weight loss for quite awhile as you trade fat for muscle, because muscle tissue is heavier. But you can actually improve your figure and drop a dress size or two even before your total weight changes. The same 130 pounds can look dumpy or sleek, depending on how much of it you carry as flab.

Remember, too, muscles *use* energy. Fat stores it. The leaner you are, the more calories you'll burn and the easier time you'll have overcoming occasional indulgences. Healthy women usually carry anywhere from 15 percent to 25 percent of their weight as fat, the rest as muscle, organs, and bone. Too many American women now are more than 30 percent fat, much of it thanks to dieting.

· Exercise raises your levels of HDL, the "good" cholesterol; improves your glucose tolerance and flattens out the up-and-down swings in blood insulin; strengthens your bones; makes your heart stronger and more efficient; reduces stress; and can even relieve some depressions.

· Finding an activity you like and pursuing it has *got* to be much more pleasant and not nearly as stressful as denying yourself food all the time. (Especially knowing that you're doomed to ultimate failure.) Active people, free of all those repressed cravings, can afford to listen to their bodies and indulge in special treats now and again without falling prey to guilt and self-loathing.

As a dancer, I took my body seriously long before fitness became fashionable, and I still try to get to ballet class at least three or four times per week, to walk instead of riding, to use stairs instead of elevators. Exercise lifts my spirits tremendously, clears my mind, refreshes me after a stressful day, and gives me the energy I need to go back to a hectic schedule. If you think exercise is boring or takes too much discipline, then you just haven't looked hard enough for an activity that suits your lifestyle. (And how could anything be more boring than dieting?) *I was glad to find that 63 percent of the women on my New York staff say they never diet, and 57 percent are on a regular exercise program.*

We live in a highly automated world, and it's going to get more so in the future. Fewer and fewer of us will get physical exercise on the job, and frankly, the labor-intensive jobs that remain aren't anything I'd want to go after anyway. The nice thing about the future is that as the work week inevitably gets shorter we're going to have much more leisure time. And

I think we're going to respect ourselves enough to devote some of that time not only to hobbies and entertainment but to self-improvement, mentally and physically. I have high hopes for girls like Adrian and Nina, who'll grow up not just exercising but involving themselves in sports and developing a confident sense of control over their own bodies. (More on women and sports shortly.)

First let me tell you about a few other things researchers have found that will increase your body's ability to burn calories and keep your appetite under control.

- The act of eating speeds up your metabolism by 30 percent, so it's best to eat a number of small meals throughout the day rather than two or three big ones. That keeps you burning calories at a higher rate longer. It also prevents those big swings in insulin levels that can fire up your appetite.
- If you do have a few large meals, eat them early in the day, when you're likely to be most active. Exercise boosts the burn rate you get after a meal.
- Overeating can also boost your calorie burn rate. So if you splurge and overeat one day, here's what to do the next morning to burn off as many of those excess calories as possible: Eat your normal breakfast, wait about forty-five minutes, then exercise lightly. According to the experiments of Cornell researcher David Levitsky, the act of eating raises a lean person's metabolic rate from one calorie a minute to 1.3. A light workout like a brisk walk raises that rate to 6.3 calories a minute. And if a person really overdid it the day before, this routine will have her using energy at 6.5 calories a minute.

  Your body, you see, really can sense that it's out of balance and fire up systems to get things back under control. But, as other researchers have found, those systems fire up higher in a person who's aerobically fit. And your body can't work miracles, of course, so don't make overeating a daily habit.
- If you aren't fit enough to trust your body to cope with too many extra calories, try to stick to foods that won't cause an insulin surge. High insulin levels will just increase your appetite and make it easier for you to overeat. But here's another area where old nutrition dogmas are crumbling: To control your blood sugar levels and thus your insulin swings, you can't just go by the old rule of avoiding simple carbohydrates like sugar and sticking to complex carbohy-

drates like starches. The truth is, no one had ever tested what various carbohydrates actually do to your blood sugar until a few years ago. And when Phyllis Crapo, now at the University of California, San Diego, did the tests, she got astonishing results.

Ice cream, for instance, does almost nothing to your blood sugar. On the other hand, a slice of bread, white or wheat, will send it soaring even higher than will a Mars bar. So will a white potato. But a sweet potato brings the same flat response as ice cream. Carrots and parsnips produce a blood sugar swing higher than that of honey, almost at the level caused by pure glucose. (So those carrot sticks dieters munch on, though low in calories, may be setting them up for worse hunger pangs.) And carbohydrates in combinations like cheese and bread or bread and beans produce unexpected effects that can't be predicted without testing each combination (bread with cheese shoots blood sugar up, but with beans gives a slow rise). David Jenkins, of the University of Toronto, has prepared a startling list from this research, and I'm sure we're in for more surprises as our old assumptions about food finally get put to the test.

This "glycemic index" uses a value of 100 for the blood sugar rise caused by white bread. Any numbers above that indicate a faster blood sugar rise, and below that a slower rise.

Fruit

Apple 53
Banana 79
Plum 34
Orange 66
Cherries 32
Grapes 62
Grapefruit 36
Peach 40
Pear 47
Raisins 93

Legumes

Kidney beans 54
Soy beans 22
Dried green peas 56
Red lentils 43
Chick peas 49
Butter beans 52

Sugars

Fructose 30
Honey 126
Maltose 152
Sucrose 86

Pasta and Rice

Brown rice 96
White rice 83
Spaghetti (white) 66
Spaghetti (whole wheat) 61

Dairy Products

Ice cream 52
Skim milk 46
Whole milk 49
Yogurt 52

Breads

White   100
Whole wheat   99
Whole grain rye   58

Cereals

All Bran   73
Corn Flakes   119
Shredded Wheat   97

Potatoes

Sweet potato   70
Boiled new potato   81
Baked potato   135

Please don't take a look at this table and decide to live on ice cream, because there are other considerations besides blood sugar to think about. Like calories. And nutrients. And high fat content. One recent study at the University of Illinois at Chicago found that rats on a high-fat diet gained a third more weight than rats who ate the same number of calories on a low-fat diet. This contradicts previous findings that a calorie is a calorie, whatever its source, and I'm sure we're going to hear more about it in the future.

For those of you who have been dieting so long that you just can't seem to get your bodies back on balance without help, or those with the misfortune to have inherited a thrifty metabolism, scientists are already testing promising new weight-loss pills. The pills fall into two categories. One would turn off your appetite. The other would safely speed up your metabolic rate.

The most effective drugs known for suppressing appetite are amphetamines, but of course their dangers far outweigh their benefits. In 1982, researchers at the National Institutes of Health located "appetite receptors" in the hypothalamus, the actual sites where amphetamines apparently go to stifle the appetite. Pharmaceutical companies are now at work on drugs that can perform this task without the side effects of amphetamines.

There are other satiety drugs already being tested. (Your body undoubtedly has a very complex network of reporting stations that help the brain decide how well your energy needs are being met. So there are all sorts of possible ways to intervene, some of course more effective than others.) For instance, a hormone called cholecystokinin, secreted by your gut in response to food, can help you feel full and tell you you've eaten enough. Gerard Smith, of Cornell University, has shown that obese patients *do* eat less after an infusion of it. Whether that will help them lose weight permanently is still being tested. (As you probably know, not all of us stop eating just because we're not hungry. We eat because we're lonely or depressed or restless or bored.) Until a pill form is developed, however, cholecystokinin has to be given intravenously, so it's not something one could easily use oneself yet.

One thing that no one knows yet is whether using pills to suppress your appetite and cause a drastic weight loss will be any more effective than strapping you in a hospital bed and enforcing a near-starvation diet. Either way, the body may simply adapt its energy requirements and defeat you just as it did Leibel's patients. *The best strategy may be a slow and steady weight loss with the help of a combination of appetite suppressants and drugs that raise the metabolic rate, and a more active life so that the weight you lose will be fat not muscle and you won't have to keep on the pills forever.*

This brings us back to DHEA. Remember, this is the hormone that shows lots of promise, at least in mice, as an anti-aging drug. It also causes fat mice to lose weight rapidly without changing their eating habits. Researchers at Jackson Laboratory in Bar Harbor, Maine, and a New York City firm called Progenics, Inc., have developed a synthetic derivative of DHEA that, they say, increases the body's fat-burning capacity. Human tests in diabetics and obese patients are already under way, and if all goes well, the drug could be available to everyone in two to three years. (A word of caution: You can already buy something labeled DHEA in health food stores, but it contains little of the real thing. Also, the hormone itself hasn't been tested in humans, and it could have unintended effects, like altering your sex hormone levels. DHEA was used at one time in the manufacture of birth control pills.)

Now many other companies—including Beechum, Hoffman-LaRoche, and Lilly—are already doing animal tests with other drugs that offer the hope of safely raising our metabolic rates to burn off excess calories. (Lots of agents, including cigarettes, raise metabolic rate. They aren't hard to find, but most also speed up heart rate and have other destructive side effects, too.)

It shouldn't be long before those who need help losing weight can get it. With these aids, and a new understanding of how our bodies operate, any woman who takes responsibility for herself ought to be able to maintain a healthy and attractive weight. Don't get me wrong. That doesn't mean all of you will look like high-fashion models. Nothing can change the basic body structure you were born with. But you should be able to keep the body you were given lean, fit, healthy, and energetic.

I can't imagine a future in which women won't care what they look like, but I do hope we won't be so obsessive about worshipping one particular body type in the future. Society has always tended to glorify a single "ideal" female body that typifies the role it wants us to fill. The ideal has ranged from the fleshy, big-hipped madonnas of classical paintings to today's lithe fashion models and movie stars. *But women of the future will have more numerous avenues for success and respect than being mothers or decorative items. As our role models, the people we admire and seek to emulate, become more diverse, so will our notions of attractiveness.* Women gymnasts, astronauts, judges, and politicians won't all be rated against Victoria Principal, just as no one would think less of male football players, stockbrokers, doctors, or physicists for failing to look like Robert Redford. I think we women will be less self-conscious and insecure about our looks when that's no longer the only "accomplishment" the world judges us by.

I also predict that part of any definition of beauty and health in the future will include fitness. In fact, it's already begun. Today, fitness doesn't mean bulging muscles, but strong, healthy hearts and lungs. You may dismiss sweat as a fad when you look at photos of celebrities who weight-train like Shari Belafonte-Harper and Ally Sheedy in *Vogue*, or watch the women of the movie *Flashdance* pumping iron. But our whole definition of health has been undergoing a change, and I think fitness is the wave of the future.

Health used to mean simply the absence of disease. Taking care of your health meant brushing your teeth every day and maybe seeing a doctor for a health check once a year. Then came an emphasis on prevention of disease, and we began to assume more personal responsibility for keeping ourselves healthy. Now we're starting to add a new perspective. We want to work actively not just to prevent disease but to *maximize* our physical and mental capabilities, as well as our life spans.

We'll do this in our individual ways, seeking varying amounts of help from technology and medicine. There will be many more miracles of invention, such as implants that restore feeling and movement to people with damaged spines. I would say that genetic engineering and bionics represent two very promising areas of frontier medicine. Genetic engineers, for instance, are eliminating the need to vaccinate people with dead or weakened viruses to protect us against diseases like flu, hepatitis, rabies, or polio. Instead, they're identifying the specific viral particles or antigens that trigger our bodies' defensive responses, then using cloning techniques to mass-produce synthetic versions of the antigens. An injection of these will forewarn and forearm our immune systems without risk of side effects. In the not too distant future, other gene-spliced drugs will be used to dissolve blood clots, boost the immune system generally, suppress appetite, or even enhance one's memory capacity. Monoclonal antibodies—substances derived from a single cell and genetically manufactured in quantity—are already being used to treat certain forms of cancer, and, along with the substance interferon, are two encouraging areas of cancer research. I am personally most encouraged by the beginning of genetic engineering research that may bring help to the unborn. Mothers carrying babies with a wide assortment of possible genetic defects or diseases will, in certain cases, see their unborn cured through sophisticated gene-splicing techniques.

We are all familiar, of course, with the story of Dr. Barney Clark and his successors, but the implanted heart is a small part of the bionic story. Scientists are working on everything from an artificial pancreas that will bring permanent relief to many diabetics to bionic ears that will translate sounds into hundreds of electric impulses to be relayed to a wire in the cochlea, the nerve center of the ear. Over the next fifteen years, advances also seem likely in a wide range of areas, with bionic lungs, livers, skin, even eyes.

As our knowledge of cerebral biochemistry increases too, we're going to have much better drugs to cure depression, relieve panic and anxiety disorders, and even alleviate schizophrenia. And new scanning techniques, such as magnetic resonance imaging, are giving us "windows" far more sophisticated than the old-fashioned X ray through which to observe functions and to diagnose malfunctions of our internal systems.

But I predict that lifestyle changes will improve our health as much in the future as medical breakthroughs like these. Once again, it is science that provides us with the understanding to make those changes.

In the near future, genetic screening will give each of us the information we need to minimize the risk of cancer, heart disease, mental illness, arthritis, and other ailments. We already know that a certain percentage of people with inborn vulnerabilities will get lung cancer if they smoke, develop dangerous anemias if they're exposed to specific drugs and chemicals, suffer heart disease if they don't severely cut their blood cholesterol, face skin cancer if they spend time in the sun, or even become obese if they don't remain active. But which person on the beach or in the office or factory is the one at risk? Scientists are already beginning to pinpoint the genetic quirks that make us vulnerable to such hazards and are developing simple lab tests to detect them.

Women of tomorrow will undoubtedly start life with a list of their inherent strengths and weaknesses to help them plan their lives and careers.

Perhaps some of you today don't want that much responsibility, but Nina's children and their contemporaries will come to expect and welcome this degree of control over their own fates.

The field of nutrition is rich with new findings right now, and they reach far beyond weight control. A very fundamental debate is raging over whether we're the best-fed people on earth or are slowly deteriorating because of our highly processed diets; whether there's an optimum way to eat or if the sensible "varied diet" your mother urged on you will cover most of the bases; whether vitamins and other nutritional supplements are a necessity or a waste. *I know these are questions that concern most of you because the majority of women we surveyed* do *read the nutrition labels on the foods they buy,* do *worry about additives and preservatives, and are aware of the nutritional value of their daily diets.*

Sixty-two percent of the American women surveyed read food labels for nutritional content either generally or all the time. Another 35 percent read labels only on items they're specifically concerned about. And only 3 percent never read labels. (Eighty percent of the South Africans, 65 percent of the English, generally or always read labels. Only 42 percent of the Japanese women do, but they usually buy fresh food.) *Seventy-eight percent are either quite concerned or very concerned about additives and preservatives in food,* while 22 percent aren't concerned. *And a whopping 95 percent of women are quite aware or very aware of the nutritional value of their daily diets.* Only 5 percent say they're not at all aware.

I certainly share this concern and awareness. And I firmly believe the new information coming out of nutrition research will allow us to fine-tune our individual diets for *optimal* eating. That means diets that strengthen our immunity, cut the risk of disease, lengthen our lives, and improve our memories, endurance, and energy levels. Those low-fat and low-salt, high-fiber, fruit, vegetable, and carbohydrate diets now being recommended to prevent cancer and heart disease are a step in the right direction. But even those who've drawn them up recognize that not all of us are vulnerable to salt, cholesterol, and so forth. In the near future, as researchers pin down the molecular chain of events involved in cancer and other diseases and in aging, we should be able to tailor personal diets based on knowledge of our own biochemistry.

And whatever help we're not able to get from the foods we eat I believe we'll find in individually calculated nutritional supplements. For several years now I've been taking a daily packet of vitamins, minerals, and nutrients formulated for me by Michael Colgan, of the Colgan Institute of Nutritional Science, in San Diego. For me, the results have been excellent, including the fact that I've never suffered from hay fever again. (You can chart a program for yourself from his book *Your Personal Vitamin Profile.*) Unfortunately, most of the supplements people use now are ineffective, Colgan says, because they're taken in haphazard combinations that ignore how nutrients interact in our bodies. His own work is still experimental and thought of as somewhat controversial by the traditional medical community who know little about nutritional medicine anyway. But I definitely think this is the way of the future as we come to understand more and more about how our bodies operate at the molecular level.

o   o   o

Increasing numbers of women, emboldened by their new sense of physical competence and control over their bodies, are testing their mettle in competitive sports. I've watched with delight as the old concept of female frailty has crumbled. Anyone watching the 1984 Summer Olympics—gymnast Mary Lou Retton's flying, twisting vaults; Joan Benoit's vibrant face as she circled the coliseum in her marathon victory; Flo Hyman's crushing spikes in volleyball—had to realize that ***strength, speed, discipline, and mental toughness are part of our female repertoire.*** Women have what it takes to become champions on courts, tracks, and ski slopes as well as in the office, Senate, science lab, or Space Shuttle.

We've come a long way in a very short time, and now it seems almost ludicrous that fifteen to twenty years ago, researchers were still seriously debating whether women could safely participate in sports at all. We've learned since then that bouncing or blows to the breasts don't cause cancer, and our reproductive equipment is at least as well protected as men's against the jarring of physical activity. Heavy training can sometimes stop menstrual cycles in very lean women, but their periods resume without problems when training slacks off. Athletic women actually have an easier time in childbirth than inactive women. ***The question today is not whether we can do it at all, but how far we can go.***

The turning point for women athletes came in 1972, when Congress passed Title IX, which bans sex discrimination in school athletics. Within ten years, a third of all high school athletes were girls, compared to only 7 percent before Title IX. The number of women in intercollegiate sports increased tenfold. Scholarships and prize money expanded. In fact, many of the female athletes we cheered for in last year's Olympics got their start this way.

Also in 1972, the Amateur Athletic Union (AAU) finally allowed women to enter the venerable Boston Marathon for the first time. Twelve years later, after an intense lobbying effort by women runners, a women's marathon was added to the Olympics. (Of course, there are still some middle-distance races, like the 5,000-meter and the 10,000-meter, unavailable to women, and women still remain barred from a third of the Olympic sports categories altogether. So the lobbying goes on for 1988.)

However, we are gaining acceptance for newer events that showcase feminine strengths, such as synchronized swimming and rhythmic gymnastics, which are already Olympic events. Team aerobic dance has been accepted by the AAU as a competitive sport and may reach the Olympics in the 1990s. (And that will be much more exciting to watch than Greco-Roman wrestling or hammer throwing!)

Today's women are the first to break into competitive athletics with the same intensity as men, and their performance is improving dramatically. *In competitive track and swimming events, the last two decades have seen women come to within 10 percent or less of the best men's times.* As male runners strive to improve their times by seconds every year, women are shaving minutes off their records. Nina Kuscsik led the women who finished that first Boston marathon in 1972 with a time of three hours and ten minutes. Joan Benoit's world-record-setting pace at Boston in 1983 was two hours and twenty-two minutes. In skating, skiing, rowing, basketball, diving, gymnastics, and cycling, women are setting new standards, pushing back the old limits.

How far do the experts think our bodies will take us? There are some basic biological differences between the sexes that can't be ignored, although they're not nearly as great as we were told twenty years ago:

- *Upper body strength:* Men have broader shoulders, and testosterone gives them more muscle bulk. (A man is about 40 percent muscle, a woman, 23 percent.) As a result, their arms and shoulders have twice the strength and three times the power of a woman's. Women, of course, can greatly increase their upper body strength with training, but they remain less powerful than men the same size. On the other hand, with proper training we can develop at least two-thirds the leg strength, power, and work capacity a man has.
- *Flexibility:* Women's joints are more flexible, their bodies more agile.
- *Aerobic capacity:* Our ability to take in oxygen and get it to our muscles is about 15 percent less than men's. It is partly because our hearts and lungs are smaller and partly because our blood has about 10 percent less hemoglobin, the oxygen-carrying pigment in our red

blood cells. Of course, through training we can increase our aerobic capacity, just as men can. But exercise-physiologists believe there'll always be some gap.

- *Energy reserves:* Because the average woman has a higher percentage of body fat than a man, she has a greater reserve energy supply to call on after the glycogen in her muscles is depleted in long-endurance activities. That fat layer also makes us more resistant to cold, a boon to English Channel swimmers, the best of whom have always been women.
- *Heat tolerance:* Women sweat less and therefore lose less water and salt during exercise. But they also dissipate less heat and so are more vulnerable in hot weather than men their size.

Of course, as I've pointed out throughout this book, these are averages, and individual men and women can fall anywhere along the spectrum. *Instead of classifying people by sex, physiologists and biomechanics experts have been busy in recent years figuring out which body types are best suited to which sports and professions, regardless of gender.*

Research by the Seattle Fire Department, for instance, has shown that a person needs a lean body weight (muscle, bones, and organs) of at least 120 pounds to develop the strength needed to pass its training program and handle heavy equipment. (For a rather lean woman, with about 20 percent fat, this would mean a total weight of 150 pounds.) And using this selection standard the department has had good success in recruiting and training able women to become fire fighters.

Since 1976, when the first female cadets arrived at West Point, researchers there have been measuring the differences between men and women and tailoring a training program that will let women reach their top physical capacity. They've modified some tests, such as the indoor obstacle course, that require a level of upper body strength most teenage girls can't muster, even with intense training. But they've found other exercises, where the females may soon outstrip the males.

Robert Stauffer, West Point's director of research and evaluation, said that if society continues to encourage women in their pursuit of excellence, "I think the difference between men and women in such popular sports as running will probably narrow itself to 3 percent in terms of performance times."

Other exercise physiologists predict that *women may eventually pull alongside men in the marathon, and even outperform them in the grueling sport of ultramarathoning—races of fifty and one hundred miles.* In sports that depend on absolute strength, speed, or power, however, the best men will probably always be better than the best women. (Remember, of course, that the best women athletes may still beat the majority of male competitors in their events. And at the level of club, school, and intraoffice competition, many women will beat most of the men they play.)

But tennis great Billie Jean King thinks we'll never really know what the exceptional and motivated woman can do as long as girls grow up thinking from an early age that no matter how good they are, professions like baseball are closed to them. King has raised what in the future is going to be the most controversial issue for women in sports: *Will the barriers between men's and women's sports ever be dropped completely, allowing any person who can qualify to compete, just as anyone who qualifies can now become a fire fighter or an astronaut?*

Sports competition is just about the only area left where women don't compete with men to reach the top, King says. She compares being at the top of the women's tennis circuit to being the champion in yesterday's black baseball leagues. " 'Separate but equal' means women will always be second-class citizens in sports," she believes.

"Not all women are cut out physically for all sports or to compete with all men, but for those who can, the possibility should be there—and the rewards may be great," writes King. "I believe that in every aspect of sports, women would achieve much higher levels of performance if they entered the crucible of competition with men on an open basis, from the beginning and throughout the educational process."

Others worry, however, that because of the biological differences between the sexes, most girls wouldn't get to play sports at all if they had to compete with boys for places on the team or league. And most scholarships and prize money would fall back into men's hands, where it was thirteen years ago.

This is an area where I think it's futile and unrealistic to try to ignore biology, although I was surprised to see how many women don't recognize the inherent difference between the sexes on this point. (Remember, 44 percent of the women we surveyed think the sexes are *equal* in sports ability and other physical skills.) I sympathize with those few young girls, wherever they are, who dream of pitching for the Mets or fighting fires. It's not my cup of tea, but nonetheless they should have the chance to try. That's no reason, however, to abandon the separate athletic programs that allow girls and women to develop their own physical capacities.

After all, beating men isn't what athletics is all about for most of us. Girls like Nina who grow up playing basketball, soccer, tennis, or other games will learn that it's not unfeminine to be aggressive, to want to win, to go after what they believe in. Increasingly, they'll experience the boldness, mental discipline, self-confidence, and grace under pressure that sports can teach. And this can't help but serve them well later as they pursue excellence in the office, factory, or lab.

6
SEXUAL STRATEGIES

Wherever we are, whatever our romantic ups and downs, the important thing to remember is that we are developing our own personal sense of values. We certainly have the right to experiment sexually, to try various relationships and get to know different lovers—as long as we are doing what we want and not being pressured into sex. We are not "bad girls" for doing this. We are women stretching our wings.

—Shere Hite

rop into any group of singles and listen to the conversation. You'll reach the same inescapable conclusion I did: Despite all the how-to books on sex and the advice columns in women's magazines, women today aren't sure what men expect of them, or if they think they know, they don't like it. And vice versa. If you *do* go to bed with him on the first date, he'll drop you. If you *don't* go to bed with him by the third date, he'll drop you. You think you want a sensitive man, then you get swept away by a strong, silent stud.

Despite today's confusion, no one is willing to give up. Women *and* men still dream of marrying and living happily ever after. And that means we all have some learning to do about sex.

Within the next few decades I believe women are finally going to explore and learn to enjoy our own sexuality. And I predict an end to much of the anger and confusion between the sexes as we also come to appreciate the quite different quality of male sexuality.

It's no wonder, of course, that both sides are confused today. Only twenty years ago our social mythology still portrayed "nice women" as sexless. Then along came Alfred Kinsey, who publicly acknowledged our passions. The so-called Sexual Revolution of the 1960s and 1970s was supposed to bring fulfillment to all. But it only added to the confusion by assuming that our newly rediscovered sexual needs must be the same as men's—that we could all be happy just by "moving the fig leaf to the face" and jumping into any bed.

Our survey results indicate that confusion still reigns. *Fifty-nine percent of the women we surveyed believe most men tend to feel more casual about their sexual relationships than do women, and I certainly agree.* Another 19 percent said men aren't any more casual than women, and 21 percent aren't sure. (In contrast, 25 percent of the women we talked to in Japan, 37 percent in South Africa, and 40 percent in England think women can feel just as casual about sex as men.)

But only 32 percent of those who think men are more casual believe it will always be this way. Some 44 percent think things will become equal in the near future, and 24 percent aren't sure what will happen.

I'm not sure whether the women who expect a change are counting on men to get more serious or women more carefree. But I think they're in for some disenchantment either way. The comments from women in our New York office revealed a deep ambivalence in their feelings. Sixty-one percent of them claim women can be just as casual about their sex lives as men, but they say it with an almost defiant we-can-if-we-want-to-but-we-don't-want-to attitude: "I think women can feel casual. I just don't know if they want to as much as men." "I think they can, but most don't." "Do men feel casual about sex? If men feel casual about sex, then, yes, we can, too." "Women can when they choose to."

One of my executives thinks some women, in their attempt to find sexual liberation, have become even more casual about sex than men: "Women have come full circle and have become the worst of what we think of men—callous, using men for sex. There are many women in my circle of friends, professional women, who talk about using men just for sex."

Even some of the women who think we *can't* be as casual as men expressed the hope this would change: "Their psyche is still emotional and they can't feel as casual. They may think they are but *we're not capable yet.* I think we try." "It's bred in us. Maybe in three more generations . . ."

I don't think three or even thirty generations will do it. *It's time to recognize that men and women have some innate differences that aren't likely to change in the next few hundred or even thousand years.* Saying we *could* act like men if we wanted to is beside the point. For the most part, we're designed to *want* and be happiest getting something different. *This is another point where self-understanding can help us to make more realistic choices for the future. And we do have choices to make, because, as you'll see, some of the taboos that restricted our sexuality in the past no longer have any relevance in an age of birth control and overpopulation.*

It's useless to politicize the differences between men and women, or punish one another for them. After all, we've always found a way to enjoy each other's company in the past. And that little thread of sexual tension that runs through all our encounters adds a spice that few of us would want to live without. *I think we're going to find even better ways of getting together in the future, in a wide variety of relationships that fulfill women's needs as well as men's.*

o   o   o

Even before they learned to talk or stand on two legs, our male and female ancestors had developed two distinct sexual strategies. *Their legacy has left us, today's men and women, with very different sexual styles and turn-ons.* The ultimate goal, of course, was the same for all life and for either sex: to survive long enough to produce babies to carry as many of one's genes as possible into the next generation. I realize that's hardly the goal most of us set for our lives today. But we're the descendants of individuals who played that evolutionary game very successfully, and the traits that helped them succeed still run like an undercurrent through us.

Even our sexiness has ancient roots. *We humans, male and female, are among the most sex-driven of all creatures,* probably because we're so inefficient at reproducing. Our babies are born usually one at a time, after long pregnancies, and require years of care before they can fend for themselves. So humans couldn't afford to waste time with seasonal breeding cycles or periods of rut and heat. We're constantly sexy. (Don't get the mistaken notion that we developed a sex drive because we *want* babies. Primitive humans took quite awhile to figure out that sex and pregnancy were even connected. It just turned out that those amorous folks who did it the most also left the largest number of descendants. That's how we inherited their strong sex drive.)

Now back to our separate strategies. A woman who wants her genes to survive has a big stake in every child because she can bear and raise relatively few in a lifetime. Men, with only an investment of sperm, can father dozens of offspring. Since the female investment is so costly, an obvious question to ask is why females ever let males have a share in the process at all, allowing them to contribute half of each child's genes. Many fish, lizards, and other creatures get along quite well without sex or males. Every one of their offspring is a complete replica of its mother, a sort of immortality for her.

The traditional answer evolutionary biologists give is that males provide genetic variety, a stirring of the species' gene pool with every mating. Variety raises the odds that, in periods of turmoil and change, at least a few individuals will have the traits needed to survive. So mammals gave up their exclusive lineages and "invented" the male to give their offspring a better chance at survival and keep their genes well represented in the species' pool. (I'm speaking now as though evolutionary strategies were conscious decisions, and of course they weren't. Individuals made choices, and only from the perspective of millions of years can we judge which way of doing things was most successful.)

Sex left women with a new task: weeding out the losers and making sure offspring carried genes from only the most suitable men. *So from the start, we decided which type of men would succeed. We truly made them what they are.* As Harvard anthropologist Irven DeVore puts it, *"Males are a vast breeding experiment run by females."*

Men court, and we choose. It's an ancient ritual. "Among all peoples it is primarily men who court, woo, proposition, seduce, employ love charms and love magic, give gifts in exchange for sex, and use the services of prostitutes," University of California, Santa Barbara, anthropologist Donald Symons wrote in *The Evolution of Human Sexuality.* ". . . Everywhere sex is understood to be something females have that males want . . . even where women are believed to derive as much pleasure as men do from sexual intercourse."

Because we hold the power and make the choices and stand to lose the most from a bad decision, our sexuality is not as impulsive as men's. Our turn-ons have a mental and emotional side. With only a little sperm to lose in a mismatch, men can afford to be less discriminating in their arousal. In fact, Martin Daly and Margo Wilson, of McMaster University in Ontario, Canada, note that males of many species have a harder time than females just recognizing their own species: "Male butterflies court falling leaves and male frogs mount galoshes." (Among humans, it is men almost exclusively who develop erotic fetishes for feet, shoes, stockings, diapers, feces, whips, or even streetcars—hardly the stuff of reproductive success.)

A word of caution: *Don't get the idea that because women are more careful and deliberate about sex that we must also be passive or even monogamous.* Primatologist Sarah Blaffer Hrdy, in *The Woman That Never Evolved,* took a long look at the behavior of apes and monkeys for clues as to what our prehuman sisters might have been like and the foundations they set for our sexuality. She found no reason to think women are innately demure or noncompetitive about sex. Instead, primate females are discriminating, manipulative, and smart about sex. And they don't consent only to conceive. For instance, female monkeys and apes sleep around with many powerful males, apparently just to keep them guessing about who's the father and thus gain more protection for themselves and their young. (At a fairly recent point in human evolution, as you'll see later, we apparently modified our strategy and traded some of this sexual freedom for economic security and the chance to raise bigger families.)

The fact of our choosiness brings up another question: Why, if we had the power and made men what they are, did we at one time favor the philandering gadabouts? Surely among all those Homo erectus there were a few suitably big and tough ones who were less promiscuous. And after all, we had no reason to help men succeed with *their* strategy of fathering as many offspring as possible. Or did we? DeVore says the answer lies in our sons. They carry half our genes, and the fate of our lineage lies in their reproductive success. We chose the fathers to get the traits we needed in our sons. (Again, at a certain point in evolution our infants began to need greater investments from their fathers, and we began to modify our choice of men. More shortly.)

o   o   o

Perhaps you resent all this talk of early humans and apes, the very idea that our low-brow past intrudes on the relationships between intelligent men and women today. But it does. The choosiness is still there. We still deliberate before saying yes. *Even in this liberated age, the majority of women admit they're not as interested in casual sex or sex just for the sake of orgasm as men are. Please don't interpret this to mean that women don't like sex. Every survey shows we do. But most of us also rank the many pleasures it can provide in a different order of priority than men. And not all relationships provide the sexual rewards most women rank highest.* The result of our survey is borne out by many other findings:

- My friend Shere Hite found in her nationwide study of female sexuality that women want intimacy, attention, and affection from intercourse more than they want orgasms. "The overwhelming majority of women answered that sex meant a great deal to them, and the reason almost always given was because it was a wonderful form of intimacy and closeness with another human being," she wrote in *The Hite Report*. Even most of the women who never achieved orgasm during intercourse said they liked the act. And in fact, "even women who did orgasm during intercourse most frequently gave affection and closeness as their basic reason for liking intercourse, rarely mentioning orgasm."

- When *Parade* magazine conducted a representative survey of American sexual attitudes last year, it identified eight equally prevalent sexual styles ranging from "The Pansexual"—high in life satisfaction, sensuality, and eroticism—to "The Nonsexual"—low in all three categories. There were *no* categories that were exclusively male or female, but clear sex differences did show up: 86 percent of women, compared to only 59 percent of men, said it's "hard to have sex without love"; only 66 percent of women, compared to 77 percent of men, said sex is important; and only 60 percent of women, compared to 81 percent of men, said having an orgasm is important.

- More than thirty years ago Kinsey found that women, even those who've been very active sexually, "may go for weeks or months or even years with very little outlet, or none at all. But then after such a period of inactivity the high rates of outlet may develop again. Discontinuities in total outlet are practically unknown in the histories of males." That last statement may reflect some wishful thinking on the part of the men Kinsey interviewed, although Kinsey included all sources of orgasm from petting and nocturnal emissions to intercourse with animals as part of "total outlet." But the pattern for women is typical even today. If a woman isn't in love, or can't at least fantasize that the man she's with has potential, she'd often just rather skip it.

One of the single women in my office summed up the feeling: "Women don't go out with just anyone. Women don't have sex just to have sex. If you *do* just have a one-night fling, you do it because you want to be close to someone. What I mean is that women even in a casual relationship cannot feel casual about it like a man can. A woman puts more than the physical into a night of sex. She has to feel good about the person she's with before she'll have a one-night fling."

More and more researchers are beginning to look to the behavior of homosexuals for clues to male and female sexuality in their most undiluted forms—female attitudes, needs, and values untempered by those of males, and vice versa. The sexual activities of gay males tend to be quick and genital and involve a variety of partners. Lesbians tend to engage in loving, tender, and nongenital activities with relatively permanent partners. *The vast majority of us still prefer to try to blend those two styles, and always will.* It's a lot of fun, for all the tension it creates, and I think life—and certainly sex—would be terribly dull without it.

"Sex with love is the greatest thing in life," Mae West was fond of saying. "But sex without love—that's not so bad, either." There's no doubt that most women, even the sexiest among us, still prefer the "with love" variety, and I don't think we should be embarrassed about it or think we have to adopt the stereotyped, male style at some point in the future. But remember, there's a lot of stereotyping and fantasy involved on both sides of our romantic rituals.

"Males have the reputation for being hit-and-run experts," says former Kinsey associate C. A. Tripp. "Females have the reputation of wanting things to last forever. In practice, it's not that way at all for either side. In practice, women are very fussy and not ready to net everybody in sight. And the males are so dumb, they just fall right in and always go after the high risk ones. The reason they want to get away is they want to play Romeo and Juliet and climb the wall all the time."

o   o   o

Just as the average man and woman today differ in their priorities about sex, they differ in what it takes to arouse their passions. Women respond most to touch, physical contact, and certain mental cues. Normal men, on the other hand, are easily turned on by looking.

Kinsey sampled the erotic responses of men and women to dozens of cues and found that men were much more likely to be turned on by looking at women, nude or clothed, than women were by looking at men. Men were also much more turned on by fantasizing about sex, listening to off-color stories and jokes, and looking at women's genitals, their own genitals, photos and paintings of nudes, burlesque shows, other people or animals such as dogs or cattle engaging in sex, and photos and films showing sex acts.

Now, women may giggle at pictures of male nudes or enjoy the naughtiness of looking at them, but most don't feel sexually aroused by them. Some women are in fact so turned off by male nudes they get enraged to moralistic frenzy. My experience in publishing *Viva* magazine and pioneering the first male centerfolds taught me that painful lesson. We put out the first issue in October 1973, and it raised an incredible storm. Despite *Viva's* literary quality, and the fact that we dropped male nudity after the first year, some magazine sellers actually continued to keep it under the counter until we stopped publication in 1978.

If visual erotica has little effect on the average woman, it's not because women's bodies are different or our sex drives are lower. It's just that our minds have the final say about what turns us on. Researchers at both the Mount Sinai School of Medicine and at Brown University did some experiments that show just how strong the mental side of female sexuality is. These are the sorts of tests that require wiring people's genitals with probes while they watch erotic films. The erotica actually brought just as strong a physical response from the women's bodies as it did from the men's. But the men *felt* turned on and the women didn't.

So plain old nudity or sexually suggestive material just doesn't throw that mental switch for most women. But add *romance,* and more than half of us will respond. In Kinsey's study, women were sexually aroused as often as men by reading romantic literature (60 percent of women, even in 1953), and aroused more often than men by romantic movies (48 percent of women).

In real life also, we usually wait for our minds to size up the situation before our bodies get swept away with passion. While a man looks at a prospective date's face and figure and makes a quick decision about whether he's willing to sleep with her, she watches and listens for clues to his character, reliability, social status, and earning power. She may have no interest in marrying the man or in having children, and no need for support or security, but the checking process goes on anyway, unconsciously, perhaps even cooling her initial attraction to him if the cues are wrong.

This bias in the mental programming may lead a woman to marry an older man, even though a younger one would match her better in terms of life expectancy and sexual peaks (his at twenty, hers in her thirties). And it's almost a cliché that men, even those who don't have any interest in children, are universally attracted to young, reproductively fit women.

Few women seem interested in overriding this mental check and surrendering themselves to passionate abandon. ***Only 12 percent of the women we surveyed say they'd use proven aphrodisiacs if these were available.*** This included highs of 15 percent to 17 percent among younger women, working mothers, professional and managerial women, and those with higher incomes. (My staff is somewhat unrepresentative of American women on this point, too, because 44 percent of them would use such love potions if they could. So would 28 percent of the English women. In contrast, almost *none* of the women we talked to in Japan or South Africa had any interest.)

Remember here that as I've talked about men and women, I've been talking about averages. It's not hard to find individuals who don't fit them. *Women in particular show a wider range of variation and depart from the averages more than men do, Kinsey found. For instance, a third of women may be as affected by erotica and fantasy and the other "psychologic stimuli" he tested as the average male.*

"At the extreme of individual variation, there were . . . 2 percent to 3 percent of the females who were psychologically stimulated by a greater variety of factors, and more intensely stimulated than any of the males in the sample," Kinsey wrote. ". . . A few of the females were regularly being stimulated by psychologic factors to the point of orgasm, and this almost never happens among any of the males." His studies turned up women, for example, who "have daytime fantasies which may so arouse them that they reach orgasm without any physical stimulation of any part of their bodies. It is only one male in a thousand or two who can fantasy to orgasm."

In the *Parade* magazine survey, 44 percent of women scored high on "eroticism" (which included being aroused by oral sex, pornography, and erotic fantasy) and 57 percent rated their sex drive as "strong." (A higher proportion of men—73 percent—said their sex drives are strong, but remember that leaves more than a fourth of men who *don't* have strong libidos.)

Sex drive is a misused concept anyway. For instance, Kinsey concluded that because males are conditioned to be aroused by so many things they see or hear or think, they feel a greater *desire* for frequent sex. Some people interpret this to mean that men have a stronger *need* for sex than women, as though men's desires are powerful primal urges that can't be denied or controlled. But women are no less "driven" than men when aroused. The old cry of "don't leave me like this" goes for women as well as men. Shere Hite certainly heard from numerous women who were angry to the point of tears and even mayhem when their lovers finished their own orgasms and rolled over to sleep, leaving them frustrated.

The science of sexology in the past three decades has begun to dispel a lot of mythology about sex drive, the physiology of sexual arousal and response, and the female orgasm. (Even after Kinsey broke the ice, this wasn't an easy field to work in. When William Masters went to the Washington University library in 1954 to get started, he found that only full professors were allowed to check out the *Atlas of Human Sexual Anatomy*. He was an associate professor at the time. And when he and

Virginia Johnson tried to publish their first scientific papers in 1960, the gynecological and psychiatric journals rejected their work as pornographic.)

It's now clear that women are born with all the brain chemistry, sex hormones (including testosterone, the same hormone that fires up men's "drives"), and the erectile tissues necessary to become aroused and achieve orgasm as quickly as a man *if the stimulation is right.* Masters and Johnson, for instance, have found very little difference in the way men's and women's bodies respond to arousal, except that some women have the capacity to achieve a whole series of orgasms in quick succession. Those researchers also debunked the old myth that vaginal orgasms are somehow different from or better than those caused by clitoral stimulation. In reality, the body's response is the same in either case.

So if orgasm were all that counted, masturbation would achieve the same effect as intercourse. Eighty-two percent of the women in Hite's study said they masturbate, and 95 percent reach orgasm easily this way (so much for the myth of "frigidity"). But only 30 percent of the women could achieve regular orgasms from intercourse alone, without extra clitoral stimulation. This is almost the same result Kinsey and other researchers have reported. Of course, the overwhelming majority of women still *like* intercourse, if only for the intimacy and closeness it provides. And Hite also found that, as you might expect, women who understand their own bodies and have the self-confidence to guide their partners' movements have an easier time reaching orgasm during intercourse.

In the future, I hope we'll stop condemning and ridiculing one another, labeling men pornographic and perverse or women frigid and uptight just because we don't respond to the same things. A woman isn't threatening her partner's masculinity when she initiates (or refuses) sex or suggests something new to improve their lovemaking, and a man is *not* degrading his wife, lover, or any other woman when he enjoys looking at erotica.

It's pretty obvious just from reading Dear Abby columns that this message hasn't sunk in. Earlier this year she printed another one of those letters from a twenty-seven-year-old wife and mother who found "pornographic girlie magazines" her husband had hidden and was hurt, disgusted, and angry "to discover he was reading such filth." Fortunately, Abby had the sense to advise the woman to get some counseling and quit harassing a grown man over reading habits she obviously didn't understand. Researcher John Money worries about the impact of today's antipornography craze on the next generation of boys: "What's going to happen to the young boy whose feminist mother goes crazy when he reaches puberty and peeks at [men's magazines]. Will he be told he's horrible and degrading to women? When he later gets excited at seeing his wife or girlfriend naked, he's likely to be so ashamed he'll become impotent."

It's time to reject the blind politics that tries to shame men or women for their perfectly normal sexual feelings or fantasy lives. Many gentle and moral men (and women) are pleasantly aroused by erotica, and many non-frigid women (and men) don't like one-night stands. *Despite all the turmoil and backlash confusing us today, I think people of Adrian's and Nina's generation are going to reintegrate sexuality, in all its rich variety, into normal human relationships.*

"I once asked Dr. Kinsey what sex would be like 500 years from now," Tripp recalls. "He said, 'Of course, I don't know, but I'm sure of one thing: it will become part of the general knowledge of people that individuals vary enormously, so it won't be so surprising that people have idiosyncratic requirements. People will have a more fluent readiness for surprise and for variation and not get into thinking that some role that works fine in sex, such as bondage, is necessarily something that you use outside the bed-room.' " I hope this understanding *won't* take us another 500 years.

o   o   o

Researchers still don't agree on why women learned to enjoy sex and how female orgasm ever evolved. (Male ejaculation and orgasm, of course, are no mystery. They have an obvious reproductive function.) It could have been to encourage us to sleep around more. Or it could have been just the opposite—one of the rewards of giving up the sexual freedom of our monkey and ape cousins and inventing monogamy. *Let's look back at our prehuman ancestors again briefly, then at all the trouble human societies have gone to just to keep female sexuality in line. And finally, why our society no longer really cares whom we sleep with.*

Some anthropologists think the success of humanity—and the invention of recreational sex—is actually rooted in the development of monogamy. According to this view, when certain species of ape-like creatures (homi-nids) made a commitment to stay together and share work and play, they set the stage for learning to walk upright, forming complex social groups, growing bigger brains, using tools, and developing civilization. Owen Love-joy, an expert on the biomechanics of locomotion, began to think about monogamy as he tried to figure out why our ancestors started walking on two legs. The commonly accepted theory was that they stood up to free their hands for using tools. But Lovejoy's work with Lucy, a 3.5 million-year-old prehuman skeleton from Ethiopia, showed that our forebears started walking long before they learned to use tools or developed large brains.

Lovejoy proposes that we're the descendants of "socially and sexually innovative apes." What they developed was a whole package of innovations that helped them overcome the serious disadvantages of our reproductive strategy—nurturing one baby at a time through a long, vulnerable childhood. The central problem the females had to solve was to find a way to care for several little ones at a time. This they did by standing up, freeing their hands to carry and care for the kids, Lovejoy proposes. Then the females got the males to stand up and use their hands to bring home the bacon.

To induce the males to share food and stick around to help feed the kids, Lovejoy says, females extended the estrus cycle until they became constantly sexy. They also hid all signs of ovulation so that males who were interested in getting them pregnant had to hang around and keep trying just to make sure. And perhaps as a bonus, to help them endure this constant amour that their strategy required, females developed the capacity for orgasm so that sex became fun for everyone. (Our cousins the gibbons, however, are much more faithfully monogamous than we and have sex only every few years.)

But females also had to keep males in the area from fighting over sex all the time and preventing social harmony, Lovejoy believes, so they developed pair-bonding, special feelings of attachment between couples, even love. That way, a fellow could go off to find food and still be reasonably sure some of the kids he was supporting were his. (Cuckoldry, after all, is a reproductive disaster for a male, in evolutionary terms. *The more help we wanted from men over the millennia, the more sexual exclusivity we had to give them,* as you'll see.) Perhaps females even began to require more elaborate courtship, cutting down their chances of pairing up with a passing Lothario who didn't intend to stick around or already had mouths to feed.

Female apes and chimps never got around to trading their sexual freedom for monogamy or dividing up the labor of childrearing. Their reproductive rate remains precariously low. Females are able to bear a new infant only every five years or so. And as a result, without human protection, both species will soon be extinct.

Lovejoy's theory has plenty of dissenters who say monogamy didn't come along until property was invented. And in fact, prehuman females could have stood up and wangled more help from the males without having everyone divide up into couples. Hrdy thinks females gave up estrus, became constantly sexy, and learned to experience orgasm to motivate them to mate with several powerful males and keep lots of guys hanging around. Unsure of their paternity, these males at least wouldn't harm the infants and might give them and the mother extra protection and food.

One thing is certain: By the time human cultures began to record their histories, people had become consciously aware of the connection between sex and babies and had hemmed sex in with all sorts of religious, legal, social, political, and economic restrictions. With the advent of property and patriarchy and the passing of wealth from one generation to the next through first-born sons, genetic lineage and family name took on a new significance. Cuckoldry mattered. Eighteenth-century scholar Samuel Johnson reflected this thinking when he pointed out the great difference between a man's infidelity and that of his wife: "The difference is boundless. The man imposes no bastards on his wife."

Men feared women's sexuality, and they reined it in powerfully. Intercourse became a property right, and the law made women and children men's chattel. (Not necessarily one woman at a time, either. George P. Murdock's *Ethnographic Atlas* catalogs 849 of the world's societies, of which societies 708 allow a man more than one wife—polygyny. In only four societies may a woman take multiple husbands—polyandry.) Women in such a situation could be one of only two things, madonna or whore, wife or mistress, good girl or bad, sexless or depraved. Both extremes equally distorted our natural sexuality.

The Roman Catholic Church, which held the power in Europe for more than a thousand years, taught that *all* sex was corrupt. It was the means by which "original sin" was passed to new generations, and until recently even husbands and wives were to engage in it dispassionately and for procreation only. Romantic, courtly love, invented as an aristocratic diversion in the twelfth century, separated pure, chaste, heavenly love from sex. Tragedy awaited lovers like Tristan and Isolde, who debased their feelings by actually copulating. By the thirteenth century, the Catholic Inquisitors declared lascivious dreams and erotic fantasies as signs of demon possession and burned at the stake thousands of women who confessed under torture to such thoughts.

Women were finally saved, John Money says, by being declared sexless:

According to the doctrine of the Inquisition, women were so sinfully incapable of resisting concupiscence (lust), including the imagination of copulating with Satan or his demons, that the redemption of their immortal souls required the sacrifice of their mortal bodies by burning them alive.

The price that women had to pay to be rescued from the fires of the Inquisition was the renunciation of all claim to concupiscent sexuality and eroticism, and the assimilation of an antithetical new doctrine of women's preternatural moral purity, erotic apathy, and sexual inertia.

This new doctrine reached its zenith by the mid-nineteenth century. It declared that women copulated not out of lust, but in order to be relieved of their husbands' attentions, and to fulfill the obligations of maternity.

Next it was men's turn to be punished for their sexuality. "Degeneracy caused by masturbation . . . replaced demon possession as the explanation for virtually all of the afflictions, social and personal, of humankind," Money says. "Maybe you could even say it was the price men paid for the wickedness of being the Inquisitors, because we suddenly had this new belief that all sexual evil was in men."

By the early 1700s, with witch-burning in decline, "Onania, Or the Heinous Sin of Self-Pollution" was being blamed for cholera, consumption, lethargy, untrustworthiness, love of solitude, bashfulness, unnatural boldness, disgust for simple food, confusion of ideas, acne, round shoulders, and hundreds of other diseases, habits, and traits.

The "secret vice" was even blamed for the urbanization of society that was taking place toward the end of the nineteenth century. John Harvey Kellogg, the inventor of Corn Flakes, a health food intended to aid the cause of abstinence and chastity, warned in his 1888 edition of *Plain Facts for Old and Young* about "The Race Ruined by Boys." The human race was "growing weaker year by year," and the chief cause was "secret sin." "Even the country boys of today cannot endure the hard work which their fathers did at the same age; and we doubt not that this growing physical weakness is one of the reasons why so large a share of the boys whose fathers are farmers, and who have been reared on farms, are unwilling to follow the occupation of their fathers for a livelihood. They are too weakly to do the work required by an agricultural life, even by the aid of the numerous labor-saving inventions of the age," Kellogg wrote.

Money believes we haven't come all that far in our sexual attitudes in the past hundred years, and I agree. We're still blaming society's ills on sexual freedom. Just sequester sex within marriage, return women to the kitchen, take away men's erotic magazines, and life will revert to a Norman Rockwell painting, the Moral Majority implies.

The truth is, restrictions on sex are crumbling because the world has changed and the primal bargain is broken. Men are no longer willing to provide economic support in return for guaranteed paternity and exclusive rights to a woman's sexual favors. The legal, social, and religious taboos that once enforced the bargain are now meaningless.

Changes taking place in western society since the beginning of the twentieth century made it inevitable that something like the sexual revolution would take place. The country shifted from a rural to an urban economy (and certainly not because of the "secret sin"). Large families became economic liabilities rather than assets. The world developed a legitimate concern about overpopulation. Motherhood lost its status as a valued lifetime career. Men no longer considered carrying on the family name and passing wealth along to genetic descendants a prime goal. New birth technologies like embryo transfers and artificial insemination promise to blur further the meaning of family lineage. Finally, the Pill completed the trend by cutting the remaining links between sex and reproduction.

There's no turning back. We women can do what we want with our sexuality now. But we haven't yet decided how to handle our new sexual freedom. And men haven't quite figured out what we want from them now that their economic support and thus their power over us has diminished.

o   o   o

It's too late to go back to the days when sex was cloistered in marriage, guarded as a sacrament. The majority of Americans, including the overwhelming majority of young people, have already come to accept that. When Daniel Yankelovich surveyed American values to see how they had changed between 1940 and 1980, he found that the majority of us no longer oppose sex before marriage or living together without tying the legal knot. The number of people who embrace the new socio-sexual reality will grow with every generation. *Glamour* magazine's annual poll of women's attitudes showed in January 1984 that two-thirds of young women, between the ages of eighteen and twenty-four, think premarital sex is acceptable.

The majority of us accept sex without marriage, and we surely realize by now that young people will continue to experiment with sex for many years before they or we think it's the right time for them to marry or get pregnant. *Only one in five of the women we surveyed said she'd want to have children before she reached age twenty-five.* But so far we've left sex education to the TV soap operas. I hope that in the future the voice of sanity will win out over the morals of a bygone era, and we'll start providing adolescents with the educational guidance and contraceptive protection they'll need for their first attempts at sex and love. It's tough enough for youngsters just to risk their emotions and egos in those first encounters without risking shame and trauma and the fear of unwanted pregnancy.

It amazes me that in a nation as forward-thinking and supposedly as progressive as the United States that we have a teenage pregnancy rate that is one of the highest in the western world. Let me quote a recent article that appeared in *The New York Times:* "American teen-agers become pregnant and give birth and have abortions at significantly higher rates than do adolescents in other industrialized nations, according to a study released . . . by the Alan Guttmacher Institute. Moreover, *the United States is the only developed country where teen-age pregnancy has been increasing in recent years* (emphasis added)," the study reported.

"The pregnancy rate for Americans 15 to 19 years old stands at 96 per 1,000, compared with 14 per 1,000 in the Netherlands, 35 in Sweden, 43 in France, 44 in Canada and 45 in England and Wales . . ."

What interested me most about the Guttmacher Institute study was that those countries that had the most enlightened and liberal attitudes toward sex—*countries in which sex education and contraceptives are easily available—were the ones that had the smallest incidence of teenage pregnancy.* What is worth noting is that teens in these European countries engaged in sex no less frequently than did their American counterparts, but had been better educated about the importance of using birth control. I wish that our schools and our educators would take this message seriously. The abortion issue in this country would become far less explosive if we were able to educate young women and men more effectively about the ABCs of reproductive biology and so prevent millions of abortions from ever taking place. Fewer girls in the future will end up in Kelly's position —married, divorced, and left with two children to raise while her friends are just finishing college—if we enlighten the young about the value of contraception.

I predict that most of the women of Adrian's and Nina's generation will experience a whole series of love relationships, some of them lasting for years, before they choose someone to marry and perhaps start a family with. They'll still play the dating game. They'll allow themselves to be wooed and won. But they'll also be more self-reliant economically, socially, and emotionally. They won't romanticize and idealize every man who comes along or fall into depression when they're not in love. They'll explore their own bodies, learn what gives them pleasure, and have the self-assurance to guide their lovers in pleasing them. They'll experience intense passion, and even heartache and jealousy, as well as playful fun.

None of my forecast, of course, fits with the "utopian" prophesies you've heard from so many sociologists since the mid-1970s. Their visions all strike a common theme: an end to games-playing and the rituals of courtship and chase; low intensity, nonpossessive "cool sex"; a universal touchy, feely, sensual communion where jealousy would be unlearned, relationships "open," and passions mellowed. I don't for a minute believe it, and neither do the experts who understand human biology. ("The biggest game of all, of course, is playing like there isn't any such thing as a game you're playing," Tripp says. "The hippies were very strong on this.") I also can't believe many of us would want such a future.

We *will* stop thinking of sex as a demonic or sinful force, but it would be wrong to deify it as a mystical source of peace, healing, happiness, or enlightenment either. Sex is a natural function, and it's also a powerful source of tension between men and women. I don't think that will change in the foreseeable future. The built-in desires, the cautions, the programming are still with us even though they set us up for a world that no longer exists. Any changes in them will be gradual, evolutionary, not revolutionary.

Courtship and a certain amount of social games-playing will always be with us, and so will romantic, high-intensity love, despite the 1960s predictions of men like Marshall McLuhan. You may profess to hate the dating game, all the maneuvering that singles have to go through today just to meet prospective partners. Well, technologies like computerized video dating services may help more of you find prospects in the future, but the actual sorting and matching up will always be something you'll have to do in person. That wasn't true, of course, when sex and marriage were too important to society to leave the pairing-up process to the whims of love. At that time, families took care of the arrangements. But we certainly aren't likely to go back to arranged marriages.

"In the future, as now, most couples will marry for 'modern' reasons— for companionship, regularity of sexual contact, and emotional support— and (for most) with the expectation of rearing children," according to Yale University sex researcher Lorna J. Sarrel. She made her predictions in a 1984 report of the Sex Information and Education Council of the United States (SIECUS). "These personal bonds, as opposed to bonds for survival and economic necessity, are and will continue to be fragile."

Sarrel also made a prediction Kinsey would have seconded: "The single most significant trend affecting adult sexual relationships in the foreseeable future is the trend toward diversity in the form of relationships. Adults will cohabit, marry, divorce, remarry, establish informal and complex kinship groups, have nonmonogamous relationships of varying kinds, and have both same-sex and other-sex relationships. In fact, many individuals will experience *all* of this in a single lifetime. We had better begin preparing ourselves and others for flexibility."

I'm sure our increased tolerance and flexibility are going to help us understand men and be more generous in dealing with their needs, too. I think all of us realize that sex isn't "all men want," at least not once they get past the teen years, just as hugging isn't all most women want. Men, too, want emotionally satisfying relationships. They want love and long-term commitment and, often, families.

We're in a transition time now, and psychologists report record numbers of men are seeking counseling and psychotherapy. They're feeling angry and impotent, emasculated by demands they don't understand and fear they can't fulfill. And we women often have expectations that show a basic misunderstanding of male nature and upbringing. We expect the men we love to share with us the same kind of soul-searching, highly intimate conversations we have with our women friends. That's seldom going to happen, even if we don't pair up with the "strong, silent" types. This difference in style and approach certainly doesn't mean men don't have feelings. But the more irritated and resentful women get, the less likely men are to share their feelings with us in any form.

Ironically, we women seem to be turning that old madonna-or-whore dichotomy against men right now. Feminist magazines question whether a man who likes erotic photos can be a good father or treat his wife as an equal, as though a little healthy lust and adventuresome sexuality couldn't be part of a good mommy or daddy's makeup. And we're also sending out schizophrenic signals about which of the two "types" we prefer. The British press actually worried itself for weeks about whether Prince Charles was becoming a "wimp" because he now prefers fatherly pasttimes over the blood sports of his bachelor days.

I think the sparring and game-playing between men and women will be less confusing and threatening in the future, when both sexes understand our new roles better. Men who grew up after the "sexual revolution" often seem annoyed that women who are obviously attracted to them still need to be wooed and convinced. But most women have mental checks to run through before their arousal is complete, and that's not likely to change.

A self-confident woman shouldn't feel pressured or put-upon by male interest in sex. There's no reason at all that male desires should make us resentful or anxious. Yet many women still feel a twinge of anxiety, even the most independent and competent of us, because we were raised to believe our success and our survival depend on pleasing men, attaching ourselves to them, and being taken care of.

Women of tomorrow will be able to relax and feel more comfortable about their sexuality. They will please themselves first. And they won't consider themselves bound by any social rules about when to say yes or no. A woman will do what she wants on the first date, or on the third. I realize that there's still a double standard at work today. Some men try hard to get a woman into bed, calling her uptight if she says no but scorning her if she gives in too easily. *I have no doubt that a woman like Adrian will laugh at any man who tries to make innocence, or the lack of it, a measure of her worth.*

Even the most successful women today have almost teenage fantasies about finding the perfect love. Few women really feel emotionally complete without a relationship with a man. I think we're always going to *want* such relationships, but as we become absorbed in our careers and in achieving larger goals we won't have the same desperate need for men in our lives in order to feel successful and fulfilled. The age at which we marry will continue to rise, and this should allow us to relax a little more in our dating. We can learn to put more of our loving feelings into satisfying but temporary relationships and take longer, more realistic looks at the men we're considering marrying.

Too many intelligent women today get carried away with romanticizing every halfway acceptable man who comes along. Romance is wonderful, but blind romance hasn't proven to be a good guide to picking marriage partners, as our 50 percent divorce rate shows. When *Psychology Today* polled its readers in 1983, 96 percent of the respondents said romance is important to them. But the readers also had very diverse opinions about what was romantic. One-fifth described an unusual sexual adventure. One-half said romance involved pain or suffering. Their own experiences also offered "little evidence that romance flourishes, that love survives, or that marriage works."

I think that's because too many of us approach love and romance unrealistically. No two people who think they're in love can even be sure they're feeling the same thing for the same reason. The state of being in love is controlled by an area of the brain I've already talked about a great deal, the hypothalamus, and the pituitary gland, which it controls. (There are people with certain pituitary diseases or hypothalamic tumors who don't fall in love at all.) The initial attraction between two people—love or lust at first sight—seems to rely on a rush of natural amphetaminelike chemicals in the brain. But this giddy high, as we all know, doesn't last. Long-term bonding seems to rely on natural opiates in the brain, an internal addiction if you will.

Euphoric love, John Money says, sustains itself at its highest degree of "agitation" for a maximum of about two years, then "tranquilizes into a more quiescent fondness and continuing erotosexual attachment." Love can go on indefinitely, but not at the "same high peak of insane intensity."

And what sets off this response in our brains? Money likens the process of falling in love to what animal behaviorists call "imprinting." According to Money, we all carry "lovemaps" in our minds, images of the ideal partner coded into our psyches during childhood. We search the world for people who, like Rorschach inkblots, seem to fit the images in our minds. We project onto others what Money calls "loveblots," our own impressions of their needs, feelings, personalities. "The loveblot exists not as an individual, self-understood and self-defined, but as one whom one endows, Pygmalion-like, with one's own precepts and meanings," he says.

In other words, if you see your "prince" in every nerd in the bar, it's because you're projecting your own loveblot onto him. And each of these men, of course, is looking at you through his own loveblots. If the image you're projecting onto someone is wildly out of touch with reality, that euphoric agitation isn't likely to last long. The chances for a long and happy match are best, Money notes, when "there is a very close fit between the actuality of each partner and the loveblot image projected on to him or her by the other partner, and this is a two-way fit . . . It is irrelevant whether the two partners are replicas or polar opposites of one another in temperament, interests, achievements, or whatever. What counts is that they fulfill each other's ideal in imagery and expectancy, even though neither may be able to spell out this expectancy in words." In other words, you can't always explain what you want, but you know it when you see it—or think you see it.

Sadly, that's about all the help science can give us so far in making better matches. And unless love is declared a disease, there's not likely to be much money to study it in the future, either. (Several researchers who've used federal money to study love have already been humiliated with infamous Golden Fleece awards from the famous Senator William Proxmire, acts which certainly will deter others from beginning new studies.)

So if we do get ourselves into a relationship with an appropriate loveblot, and we marry, do we eventually have to settle for "quiescent fondness" in our sex lives, too? Not necessarily. It's familiarity and predictability that most often knock the sparks out of sex, as Kinsey found. An aging male may lose interest in his partner, he reported, "as her every wish, interest, and expression become too well known in advance of sexual activity." These are the Mom and Pop marriages, where sexual tension has long since vanished and two identities may have merged into one.

Some people, both men and women, will seek to restore sexual excitement by having affairs. Sociologists Philip Blumstein and Pepper Schwartz, of the University of Washington, in a nationwide study published in 1983 in *American Couples,* found that after ten years of marriage, 30 percent of men and 22 percent of women have had at least one extramarital affair. Those figures aren't likely to decline much in the future, and secret affairs will probably continue to greatly outnumber "open" relationships, where husband and wife accept or even encourage each other's philanderings. Despite all the books and unlearning workshops, scientists say the state of being in love will always carry with it a certain unpredictable load of jealousy and possessiveness.

(By the way, the impulse to cheat will always be there, too; it is inherent in our nature. But it's silly to use biology to justify affairs. It's true that a little cheating on the sly was once an evolutionary advantage to a male, but since sex and reproduction are no longer linked and success isn't measured in numbers of children, affairs are biologically pointless. Temptation will always be with us, but decisions about whether to *act* on our impulses are always under our conscious control.)

In the future, however, I think more and more couples will find ways to keep the sexual zest alive without turning to new partners. Tripp believes the secret lies in keeping up a little "resistance," or, as he likes to say, "making Romeo climb the wall forever." What's required is something to add a touch of disparity, of foreignness, of unpredictability to the relationship—not enough to shatter the bond, but enough to put some tension back into it. (We all know great sex often happens after a spat, as long as the spat was not too nasty or brutal.)

"Resistance can be symbolic," he says. "Put it in humor and the subconscious will pick it up—things like 'next time I marry I'm going to pick someone who serves me breakfast in bed.' The unconscious has no sense of humor. Friendly distance is important. This will work even among longtime partners who know consciously what the other is doing." Tripp points out that those words women think they want to hear most—"I love you, darling, more than life itself"; "I don't know what I'd do without you" —can be "absolute poison" for sexual excitement.

Studies of commuter marriages, where husbands and wives work in separate cities and get together only on weekends, show that great sex can flourish during their brief time together. A few years ago an article in *New York* magazine interviewed couples who were emulating the lifestyle of Simone de Beauvoir and Jean-Paul Sartre, committed lovers who maintained separate homes for fifty years. These "apartners," as the magazine dubbed them, compared their sex lives to a constant courtship or honeymoon. In the case of both commuter couples and apartners, of course, the men and women each must bear the routine chores and strains of daily life alone. Not everyone would want this existence. But they also manage to keep from taking each other for granted, and that definitely helps their sex lives.

As women become more independent and self-reliant, developing vital and interesting lives outside their marriages, I think couples who live together will stop taking each other for granted, too. Both partners will grow and change over the years, developing their separate identities. "Theoretically, the more you equalize the sexes, the more you reduce predictability, and that's equivalent to keeping the resistance up," Tripp says. A man and woman can be close friends and still be a little coy, a little unpredictable, even after twenty years together. And that's definitely a plus in the bedrooms, today *and* tomorrow.

HOMEFRONT 2000

7

FUTURE FAMILIES

What we now think of as a traditional marital pattern, in which the husband is employed and the wife stays home and cares for the household and children, is actually a consequence of the Industrial Revolution. . . . A pattern that appeared with industrial society may disappear in a postindustrial period. No one pattern can be stable and function well for all time.

—Catherine E. Ross, John Mirowsky, and Joan Huber

Those interested in perpetuating present conditions are always in tears about the marvelous past that is about to disappear, without having so much as a smile for the young future.

—Simone de Beauvoir

The majority of girls born in the United States this year will grow up expecting to create nuclear families—mother, father, and children living together in their own home. But the America of the 1980s will barely recognize the unfolding twenty-first-century family.

Most of the girls of Kelly and Nina's generation won't marry until the second decade of the twenty-first century, when they're in their late twenties or thirties. I truly believe they'll make better choices, too, by waiting until they're older. And in all probability they will live with a man first before deciding to marry him, as many already do.

Almost all of these girls will grow up expecting to pursue careers. If they leave their jobs at all when their children are born, it'll be for a few years at most. Their husbands will share the responsibility of raising the children and running the home, and they'll expect their wives to share the financial load. The difference in wages for men and women will have narrowed.

Couples like Paul and Nina will be partners in every sense.

Grandparents and other relatives, as well as friends and neighbors, will also play vital roles in future family life, easing the pressure-cooker emotions that often build up inside isolated nuclear families today. Children will develop greater independence and have a wide network of adults to turn to for love and support. Although both parents will work, the twenty-five-hour work week, plus the option of working from home via computer terminal, will provide more time than ever before for families to join together in sports, hobbies, travel, and community activities.

In some ways, I believe home life in 2020 America will be more like that in 1885 than in 1985, because a new spirit of community will flourish among us. All of us will share the sense of security provided by living in an extended family, of having a personal identity much larger than our job descriptions, and of having some control over the world in which we live and its future.

Unlike anytime in our past, however, we'll also be very tolerant of diversity, and we'll certainly see plenty of it in our sexual and marriage and family patterns. *The American family isn't dying, it's diversifying.* If families are in turmoil today, it's largely because so many people, men and women, still cling to the notion that the family style of the past one hundred years is somehow "natural" and necessary for our continued survival. As you'll see shortly, neither assumption is true. But first, take a look with me at what women today believe families of the future will be like.

Nearly two-thirds of the American and English women we surveyed believe the typical family of the future will be a mother and father with children, what we call a nuclear family. But there's a sharp difference in expectations between working women and housewives on this point. Seventy-five percent of women who don't work believe the nuclear family will predominate. Only 58 percent of women who work agree. And only 50 percent of the women without children choose this family style. (Only 39 percent of the women on my staff, 55 percent of the Japanese women we surveyed, and 30 percent of the South Africans think the nuclear family will be typical.)

Actually, the nuclear family has been in a steep decline over the past fifteen years. Married couples represented 70 percent of American households in 1970. By 1984 they made up only 58 percent of our households. When you look at the figures for families with children at home, the proportion headed by married couples dropped from 89 percent in 1970 to 78 percent thirteen years later.

I imagine nostalgia prompted many of the women we surveyed to predict the resurgence of nuclear families. "We've reached saturation with divorces, and people are going back to nuclear families," one of my account executives, a new mother herself, believes. "Everything goes in cycles," one twenty-four-year-old staffer says. "The baby boomers are having a baby boom right now and probably people will go back to having children at a younger age." She and her husband, however, don't plan to start a family until she's thirty. (And as you'll see later, *three-quarters of the women we surveyed think the ages between twenty-five and thirty-five are ideal for having children.*)

The late anthropologist Margaret Mead suggested almost twenty years ago that marriage in the future will develop into a two-stage experience. The first stage would be an "individual" marriage, a legalized version of today's less formal living-together arrangement. (By 1984, 4 percent of American couples were living together unmarried, more than triple the number in 1970. A third of these people had been divorced, and more than a quarter of these family units included children.)

Under Mead's proposal, people in step-one marriages would not have children and they could dissolve the union rather easily. Step two would be a "parental" marriage. Getting out of it would be harder, and both parents would be obligated to share in the rearing of the children even if the union were dissolved.

I think probably more and more couples in the future will go through the two-stage commitment like the one I imagined for Paul and Nina. And we may eventually want to give formal legal status to that first stage of the union, as many couples are already doing by drawing up contracts specifying each partner's rights and responsibilities. More importantly, I think we'll give greater legal protection to children to assure them some stability as a series of birth and stepparents move through their lives. A Duke University law professor has even suggested a new concept of "non-exclusive parenthood" that would give legal protection to important emotional relationships between children and their grandparents, stepparents, and other special adults. More on this later.

Some 17 percent of women believe we'll return to an extended family pattern—a mother, father, and children with grandparents or other close relatives nearby. The biggest support for this family style comes from working mothers (21 percent) and younger women age twenty-five to thirty-four (20 percent). In contrast, only 13 percent of women thirty-five to forty-four believe extended families will be typical. (One in five women in England and South Africa and only 14 percent of the Japanese women we talked to think the extended family will be typical.)

This is the lifestyle my family still cherishes, even though we're living on two continents now, and I fervently believe more people will go back to it. My parents spend half the year in New York with me; I try to spend a month in South Africa every winter; and nieces, nephews, and other family members shuttle back and forth for frequent visits. I can't imagine life without these close family ties.

I especially agree with the thinking of one of my sales people that grandparents are going to become an important part of the American family again in the future: "I think more and more we're headed for the extended family because older people are getting healthier and more functional with the leaps being taken in the medical field and research. So older people will be around to help with the family and won't be a burden. I don't mean that young couples will dump the kids on them, but I feel that older people will want to get involved." I know my parents certainly feel that way. My mother, proud as she is of my career, would almost certainly prefer that I had given her grandchildren rather than having been successful in business, and she dotes on my brother's children.

The majority of the world, of course, has never moved away from the extended family in the first place. One of our secretaries, a native of Brooklyn, says she's never left her multigeneration family and doesn't plan to: "This is what I have now. It's what I grew up with. My children will also have that. I think as the world gets more and more complicated, we need family systems to help us raise our kids. I see the extended family as staying around because we need it."

For people who don't have family, or can't be near them, there are other ways to be surrounded by loving and supportive people of all ages.

Women without children voice the biggest support for communal groups of couples who share childrearing and other tasks. Twelve percent of the childless women select this family style, compared to 6 percent of the women who have children, and only 3 percent of housewives. Overall, only 7 percent of American women think communal groups will predominate. (In contrast, 26 percent of my staff and 20 percent of the women we surveyed in South Africa see this as the typical family of the future. Only 11 percent of the Japanese and 9 percent of the English think so.)

Several of my staffers recognized that this sort of arrangement is already a lifesaver for many divorced women trying to raise their children alone: "It's happening now, and it's becoming very common, especially with the divorce rate so high and so many single women with children. They're finding it hard to raise the children on their own financially, and I think the communal group will come together because of economics more than anything else."

"Everything's changing so much, I don't think it's easy to stay near your relatives anymore," says another woman on our staff, who shares an apartment with a single mother and her young daughter. "Economic considerations preclude staying wherever your family is because your job takes you somewhere else. So I do think it'll be like an extended family, except it will be made up of friends sharing interests, finances, etc. That could include relatives, too. It's what women and children are doing now. What they have to do."

For many people who can't live near their own parents, grandparents, and other family members, I think friends and neighbors will increasingly serve the role of extended family. I don't mean communes of the 1960s sort, where people live in a single housing unit and pool all money and chores. I predict more people will live instead in the sort of housing communities I imagined Kelly, Adrian, and Nina enjoying.

In our large cities, young couples are already moving from isolated suburbs into denser, more energy-efficient housing clusters where they can live only a short commute from their jobs. Like most urban dwellers, they have fewer children than do couples in rural areas, and they depend on neighbors and support services, such as day care centers, to help with family responsibilities. (We're certainly not going to return to an isolated pastoral lifestyle in the future, and American women recognize that. *Some 61 percent expect to live most of their lives in suburbs within commuting distance of a city. Another 22 percent expect to live in urban neighborhoods,* 15 percent in small towns or villages, and only 2 percent in rural areas.)

One of the most startling cultural phenomena of the last ten years has been the resurgence of major American cities. Downtown city centers like Baltimore, New York, or Boston were presumed lost to urban decay as recently as the mid-1970s. The trend toward suburbia that began immediately after World War II, and saw its heyday in the 1950s and 1960s, resulted in the abandonment of many urban neighborhoods. Yet, so many of the children who were raised in the suburbs during this period have traded in green lawns and open-pit barbecues for brownstones and one-bedroom apartments. The city has triumphed in the 1980s, and young professionals in their twenties and thirties are often deciding to raise families in small and expensive city quarters rather than head for the suburbs.

I'm not certain that this urban gentrification movement will go on forever. Cycles are quite common in social history, and I predict that many of the children of today's so-called Yuppies will abandon the city—in the same way their grandparents did in the era following 1945. The suburb, with its quality schools and large housing plots, will provide an allure for the young couples of 2001 that their parents never understood. I'm reminded of Marjorie Morningstar, the heroine of Herman Wouk's novel of the same name, who forsakes a life and upbringing in the city to raise her brood amid a spacious suburban setting.

Few housing developments today include day care services and convenience stores on site, or even large, secure playgrounds. Builders, however, are already designing innovative projects for retirees, young singles, married couples buying for the first time, and even "mingles"—the industry term for two young single professionals who pool their money to buy a first home. But they're not yet thinking ahead to provide the sorts of services that couples who work and raise children so desperately need. *In the future, I believe housing developers are going to begin building these features into new family-oriented condominium, townhouse, and apartment complexes the way they now include clubhouses, swimming pools, and tennis courts.*

It's not just young couples who'll benefit from creation of a communal version of the extended family. Listen to geriatrics expert Alex Comfort (who wrote *The Joy of Sex*): "The decline of the kinship family has borne excessively hard on the old—dependency is rejected, and they become increasingly isolated in a forced 'independence,' which is worsened by the shortage of kin. Perhaps more than anyone they would benefit from a 'spreading' of the couple-preoccupied family into something more like a tribe of friends."

There are some other family styles that'll be with us in the future, too, although I think they'll always be in the minority.

Only 6 percent of American women believe single women with children will form the typical families of the future. However, that figure includes a low of 2 percent of the younger women we surveyed and a high of 8 percent of the women thirty-five to forty-four. This is the age group that's feeling the pressure of the biological clock. Their answers may reflect the fact that, like the woman in *The Big Chill* sorting through her male pals for a sperm donor, many singles in this group are seriously considering whether to raise a child on their own. And the most recent advances in birth technologies are assisting such women in achieving their goals (see chapter 8).

Thirty-nine percent of women say that, if they were unmarried, they'd be very concerned about growing old without having children. Another 27 percent would be moderately concerned, 21 percent slightly concerned, and only 11 percent wouldn't be concerned at all. *Forty percent of American women say they'd at least consider getting pregnant and raising a child on their own if they were single and wanted children.* (That includes 16 percent who'd definitely consider it, and 24 percent who say they might.) Another 58 percent say they probably or definitely wouldn't consider it. (In contrast, about three-quarters of the women we surveyed in Japan and South Africa and two-thirds of the English wouldn't consider single motherhood.)

"I would pick single women with children as the typical family of the future because the divorce rate is so high, and also, I've thought to myself that I would like to have a child but not a husband," a twenty-five-year-old secretary told us. "I don't see marriage on my horizon. I've seen a lot of my friends get caught either in a bad marriage or a divorce. Just because two people are married doesn't mean that makes a family . . . I'd rather be single than be stuck with someone I don't want to be with . . . Too many unhappy marriages these days."

"It's not necessary to be married to have kids, and if I didn't have a mate I'd find other ways, other male figures like my Dad to help," a thirty-six-year-old single woman says. A new mother in the office says: "I had considered this before I was married because I wanted a child. Now after having a child, I would have second thoughts about going it alone. But, because I would want a baby, I would still consider it, knowing it to be a selfish decision."

Others feel it's too difficult financially, and unfair to the child: "It's hard enough to raise a child, prepare a child to cope with normal life with two parents, much less one." I think deliberate single parenting will always be an option, but I can't believe it will ever predominate as our favorite family style.

Of course, most of the families in this category today didn't start out to be single-parent families intentionally. Eleven percent of U.S. households in 1984 were headed by women without husbands, and 60 percent of these households included children. Only 2 percent of households were headed by men without wives. *Together these single-parent families represent nearly a quarter of all American families with children.* Today's figure is twice what it was in 1970. Nearly half of all children today will spend at least part of their childhood with a single parent. Many of the women who head these families are widowed or divorced. Others have never been married, and most of these women became mothers unintentionally. *Al-*

most 20 percent of all babies in the United States are born to single women.

I certainly believe in the future; as we develop more enlightened attitudes toward sex education and contraception, the only single women who'll be having babies will be those who make a deliberate choice to do so. And as a result, I think we're actually going to see fewer single-parent families.

Only 3 percent of the American and English women we surveyed think childless couples will predominate in the future, and 2 percent voted for single adults without children. (Of the women we talked to in Japan and South Africa, however, a surprising 12 and 13 percent, respectively, expect childless couples to be the typical family of the future.)

Today, about a quarter of Americans live in single-person households, signifying a trend that the 1980 census clearly revealed. In vital inner cities, this is especially so. In New York, for example, there are fewer than two people per house or apartment. While this may represent the extreme, we'll continue to have a large single population at any given time, since young people will leave their parents' homes and set up housekeeping long before they're ready to pair up or marry. Divorce will also bring many back to singledom. And being single will never again carry the stigma it did until quite recently, when family ties and marital status defined a person's (especially a woman's) role in society. But I think for the great majority of both sexes, being single will always be a stage on the road to a relationship.

Census figures show that the number of confirmed singles—people who've never married—has actually been *declining* since 1920, when 12 percent of the men and nearly 10 percent of the women in the forty-five-to-fifty-four age group had never been married. (That's the age group at which demographers give up on them, right or wrong.) By 1982, only 5 percent of men and 4 percent of women in that age group had yet to marry. So 95 percent of Americans will at least give marriage a try.

Children aren't going out of style either, but whether people choose to have them alone or as couples, they're going to have fewer of them than in the past.

Two-thirds of the American women say the ideal number of children in a family is two. Another 20 percent say three children is ideal. The rest are split at each end of the range, with 5 percent favoring one child, and another 5 percent choosing more than three. Of the women who are childless now, 14 percent say one child is ideal. (More than 80 percent of the women we surveyed in Japan and South Africa and 70 percent in

England choose either two or three children, with two getting the edge in each country.)

A third of all the women we surveyed, including more than half of those who have no children, believe the American government should use tax incentives and welfare payments to encourage smaller families (as the Chinese do already). Overall, 55 percent of women *don't* think the government should use such measures to hold down the birth rate, and 10 percent aren't sure. The greatest vote against comes from housewives, by 66 percent. Women in professional and managerial positions are almost equally divided, with 43 percent saying yes, 45 percent no, and 12 percent undecided. (English women also opposed government intervention, with 40 percent against and 33 percent for. Views in the other countries were much stronger, with two-thirds of the Japanese women voting against government sanctions and two-thirds of South Africans voting for them.)

Those who say no believe such action "smacks of Big Brotherism" and that "birth control education is the way to do it." Even those who say yes apparently do so reluctantly: "I don't like government interference, but in my heart I feel we should have a smaller population." And, "I would automatically say no, but we're going to have to do something similar to the Chinese, and very soon. We're running out of space, and the government seems lackadaisical in its approach to the space program, which might be an alternative to our population problem."

Again, if we'll just stop clinging blindly to old notions about sex and prepare young people for the future instead of the past, I don't think we'll ever need to have the government step into our personal lives this way.

o o o

Two hundred years ago, economic life centered around the home and farm and intertwined with family life. Husbands and wives did much of their work side by side. Then our agricultural society gave way to the industrial age, and more recently to an economy based on the exchange of services and information. Work moved from the homestead to the factory and now the office (although the computer could now move much of it back to the home, as you'll see later). *Men left home to work; their wives remained behind; and the style of marriage we call "traditional" got its start. In the past fifty years, however, our marriage styles have been shifting again as wives go out to join their husbands in the work force. But the change is not yet complete. A major point of discord remains: Most men haven't yet reclaimed their share of the load at home.*

Those early manufacturing industries also created thousands of jobs for women, but they didn't really change the lives or expectations of *married* women. Brown University historian Joan Wallach Scott points out that employers hired mostly unmarried women between sixteen and twenty-five to run the machines of the textile mills and button factories. These were the daughters of farmers and artisans, girls who otherwise would have worked in cottage industries or domestic service until they married. Most went into the mills expecting eventually to marry, and to leave work when they did, Scott says. There was no job advancement for them if they stayed on, and few women did.

Both for women and for men, the industrialized American city with its squalid quarters and harsh conditions was often a miserable place at the turn of the century. If you've ever read muckraking authors like Upton Sinclair, John Spargo, or Ida Tarbell, you know that poverty took an exacting toll on many female workers. And novels of the period, from Dreiser's to Dos Passos's, are filled with stories of exploited mill girls who took up prostitution or of wronged garment workers who became labor leaders.

A Japanese writer, Hisako Matsubara, provides an interesting perspective when she tries to explain what lay at the root of this urban disaffection. "In the United States," Matsubara writes, "an agrarian structure prevailed until the beginning of the industrial age. Cities of a million people came into being only in the wake of this revolution. The explosive, even chaotic, growth of American cities caused a stratification of class that undermined America's agrarian society. Life became a harsh dream for those millions who were forced to subsist in major cities, and an abiding aversion to technology resulted. This aversion continues to this very day.

"The Japanese, however, had no such unpleasant experiences. Their transition to a new age represented no social or ideological break with the past. Their major cities continued to swell during this period, but such growth occurred within an ordered historical framework. Instead of reacting with disdain, they embraced change with wonder. It amazes countless visitors that, within the Japanese consciousness, traditional and modern values can coexist even today in such harmony."

At the beginning of this century in America, with urbanization and the expansion of commerce came the growth of clerical and service jobs and an increased demand for female labor. Many women could now choose to go to an office rather than a factory. At first, as before, the jobs went to the young, single, and childless women. Most married women worked only if their husbands couldn't provide for them. But the economy continued to grow, and employers began to turn to the "next-most-acceptable category of women: Starting in the 1940s women over the age of thirty-five, whose children were in school or grown, reentered the labor force in large numbers," according to University of Illinois sociologist Catherine E. Ross and her fellow researchers. *By 1947, 20 percent of married women worked.* "In the 1950s growth in female employment reached the sanctum sanctorum—married women with young children." And once a married woman goes to work, for whatever reason, the researchers note, she's likely to continue.

As more and more married women began to work, increasing numbers of people came to approve of it. In 1938, only one person in five approved of married women working if they didn't have to. By 1978, three-quarters of Americans approved. *Today, some 62 percent of married women work, and because they do, the very nature of marriage is changing.*

Ross and researchers John Mirowsky and Joan Huber say that *America is now in transition from "complementary" marriages to "parallel" marriages. And the men and women most depressed about their lives are those who are still in the intermediate stages of the change.*

Look at the four types of marriages they've identified and see which one fits your situation best:

- *First* is the traditional, or complementary, marriage in which the husband works, the wife stays home and cares for the children and the house, and both approve of the arrangement. Although some people still think of this as the bedrock American family, only 17 percent of our families still fit this picture. This marriage style is second only to the modern parallel marriage in promoting a couple's mental health and happiness. But the wife suffers more depression than her husband "since he has the power and prestige associated with economic resources, whereas the wife is assigned the lower prestige, invisible, and less rewarding household chores." (These are the types of relationships that for decades have produced data showing marriage improves men's mental health but not women's.)
- In marriages of the *second* type, the wife works, but neither she nor her husband wants her to. This is the situation that causes the greatest depression for both spouses, the researchers found, and it's the only marriage style in which husbands are *more* depressed than their wives. (Again, some earlier studies have concluded that when women go to work, their husbands' mental health suffers. The Illinois researchers believe that's true only for men in this transi-

tional, second type of marriage whose pride and self-esteem are wounded when their wives have to go to work.)

- In the *third* type of marriage, the wife works, both she and her husband prefer it that way, but she still maintains most of the responsibility for the home. (I can tell from our survey that most of you are going to find yourself in this category.) The mood of both partners is much better than in the second type of marriage, but the wife obviously doesn't benefit as much as her husband. After all, his standard of living is improved by her paycheck without any extra effort on his part, but she ends up holding down two jobs. It was in these marriages that the Illinois researchers found the greatest *gap* between the wife's depression and that of her husband.

- *Fourth* is the parallel marriage, in which work inside and outside the home is shared equitably. When her burden is eased, the wife's mood improves tremendously, and, in contrast to what you might expect, *"the husband's depression is not increased by doing more housework."* The researchers suggest from this that wives in the third type of marriage are depressed *not* "because housework per se is a depressing activity but rather because it consists of menial work performed by a person of lower status for a person of higher status. When the husband shares the housework, then neither spouse is doing service work for the other, and the invidious status message is replaced by a sense of equity."

In case men have any doubts about what's expected of them around the home, our survey makes it clear: More than three-quarters of women, with children or without, working or not, expect men to share equally in virtually all household responsibilities. Here are the percentages of women who think each of these tasks should be equally shared: raising the children, 98 percent; deciding on investments, 96 percent; deciding on household budgets, 95 percent; planning social activities, 95 percent; housecleaning, 93 percent; tutoring and transporting the children, 92 percent; washing dishes, 87 percent; yard work, 83 percent; grocery shopping, 81 percent; cooking, 80 percent; paying bills, 79 percent; doing laundry, 77 percent; planning meals, 73 percent; doing home repairs, 72 percent.

Some women say each job doesn't necessarily have to be split fifty-fifty. If one partner hates doing laundry and the other hates grocery shopping, these can be traded off. But all expect the chores to be divided equitably. (The attitudes of the women we talked to in Japan and South Africa contrasted sharply with those from our American survey. Only 17 percent of the Japanese, for instance, thought men should share in housecleaning, and only a quarter of them even expected men to help raise the children. Englishwomen's views were much closer to those of Americans, with two-thirds expecting men to share the housecleaning.)

Reality, however, doesn't meet most women's expectations right now. Among the women in our survey who are married or living with someone, here's the proportion who believe they and their partners are actually splitting these responsibilities equitably: raising the children, 85 percent; deciding on investments, 82 percent; deciding on household budgets, 84 percent; planning social activities, 81 percent; housecleaning, 41 percent; tutoring the children, 64 percent; transporting the children, 59 percent; washing dishes, 44 percent; yard work, 61 percent; grocery shopping, 40 percent; cooking, 38 percent; paying bills, 43 percent; doing laundry, 32 percent; planning meals, 28 percent; doing home repairs, 46 percent.

The figures were about 10 percent higher for professional and managerial women in the categories of housecleaning, meal planning, shopping, cooking, washing dishes, and doing laundry. *But at best, only half of these women think their partners do an equitable share of these chores.* The experiences of these professional women could reflect another finding by the Illinois researchers, that the husband's share of the housework increases the more his wife earns and the less he earns. Still, a Gallup poll of female executives conducted in 1984 for the *Wall Street Journal* found, as we did, that despite "their demanding work schedules, many of the women carry more of the burden of family and domestic responsibilities than their husbands do." Some 54 percent do all or most of the bill paying; 52 percent see that the laundry is done, and 47 percent do most or all of the meal planning and grocery shopping.

Many women indicated to me that their partners are willing to *help* to one degree or another when they are asked to, but the women are still responsible for keeping up with what needs to be done and for overseeing the work. One of our managers says her partner does "whatever I can cajole out of him. Actually, he grew up on a kibbutz in Israel and is into equal work loads. But men can be men, and whatever he can get out of he'll try." But in my home—and I have household help now—it would drive me crazy not to be in charge!

The results of our survey are confirmed by many other findings. *Parallel marriages are preferred by most Americans today, especially younger ones.* For instance, a Connecticut Mutual Life Insurance Co. survey revealed that 63 percent of men and women prefer "an equal marriage of shared responsibility in which the husband and wife cooperate on working, homemaking, and child-raising." In a poll conducted by *The New York Times* and CBS News, only 2 percent of the eighteen-to-twenty-nine-year-olds said they preferred traditional marriages in which one person is the homemaker and the other the breadwinner.

But other studies also confirm that responsibilities in the home *aren't* parallel yet. *Glamour* magazine, in its 1984 survey of American women, for instance, found that 72 percent still do most of the housecleaning, 75 percent cook most of the meals, and only 40 percent say their partners share equally in caring for the children. Last year, too, *USA Today* asked both men and women who does the most household chores and found that 86 percent of men and 93 percent of women agree that women do. In *American Couples,* sociologists Pepper Schwartz and Philip Blumstein report that husbands of women who work "help out more" than the husbands of housewives, "but their contribution is not impressive." Many husbands they interviewed were actually vehemently opposed to sharing the housework, and even those who gave lip service to equality didn't actually put in the hours that their wives did.

Sometimes, of course, we women defeat ourselves by setting up impossible standards for shiny floors, ironed pillowcases, and meals from scratch that only a home economics teacher would consider valid. Then we run ourselves ragged pursuing an absurd level of perfectionism, and resent the men in our lives for not helping us achieve it.

"We trade off in chores," one of my account executives wrote. "What I wouldn't want to do, he'll do and there are other chores such as housecleaning I wouldn't let him do. I'm a perfectionist and no one can do it as good as I can, so there's no sense in my even trying to let him houseclean . . . Laundry, he doesn't do." Another sales person says she doesn't let her husband touch the laundry because "he might screw it up." (This reminds me of a recent cartoon by Jerry Van Amerongen, which shows a man banging an unopened tin can against the kitchen counter, ignoring the can opener lying nearby: "Cohabitation Axiom No. 6: The less it appears you know how to do, the less you'll have to do.")

The Illinois researchers found that *when a man begins to move from the third to the fourth stage of marriage and agrees to take on more of the household chores, his solution "will typically consist of a maximum possible reduction of the total housework load and a more equitable division of the remaining chores."* In other words, he's not going to take your list of chores and divvy it up. He's going to take it and say "let's forget ironing the pillowcases, wax the floors twice a year, eat Lean Cuisine three nights a week, and I'll split the rest of the work with you." And why not?

As you'll see later, the "science" of home economics came along early in this century when homemakers were just about out of a fulltime job and raised the level of busywork to a point that would have astounded our great-grandmothers.

I can also predict that as men accept more responsibility around the home, the pressure for mechanization of household chores will greatly increase, and so will the number of household robots! Men have automated or hired out most of the repair work and manual labor they used to do around the home, and the same thing will happen to "women's work" once it's shared.

We can expect better understanding among both husbands and wives in the future as the transition from traditional to parallel marriages is completed. The big problem for men during these transitional times, they say, "may be one of self-esteem—of getting over any embarrassment, guilt, or apprehension associated with their wives' employment." I don't think this will be difficult for the next generation of men and women, because they're going to see both of their parents going off to work and will grow up with new expectations about masculine and feminine roles. Men won't base their manhood and self-worth on being providers, and women won't fall into the Cinderella role of expecting to be taken care of. Few men will be able to afford the traditional stay-at-home wife anyway, and few women will want to fill the role of self-sacrificing martyr, putting husbands and families ahead of their personal goals.

Physiologist Estelle Ramey, who's still actively pursuing her research at seventy, says the mark of a good marriage is a husband who realizes that "it would be a burden if his wife expects to get all her sustenance and kicks out of life just through him and encourages her to get off his back. My husband forty years ago recognized that. I was a physical chemist teaching at Queens College when I married him. He was just graduating from law school. And he was a very ambitious young man. He wasn't going to have a lot of time to listen to my whining about how I could've been great. So from his point of view: get the hell out of the house! Whenever I faltered in my determination because I was tired, he'd say 'Ah, no you don't. You'll make life a misery for me.' And now in self-defense he was smart, because he was right. I'd have made life a misery for him."

If men's problem in the transition is their egos, *for "the wives the central problem is getting their husbands to share the housework. Since the wife's and husband's earnings affect the amount of housework the husband does, any trend toward equality in the division of household labor depends on the outcome of the struggle for economic equality in the workplace,"* the Illinois researchers concluded. I firmly believe that by the time women of Nina's generation are ready to marry, equality will be taken for granted in both these realms.

o o o

Only 29 percent of today's women pick motherhood as the career choice with greatest appeal. This figure rises to 33 percent among the women in our survey who already have children. But among those who are childless, only 16 percent say motherhood is the most appealing career. Even among the housewives, only 40 percent list motherhood as their top career choice.

If unemployed women are excluded from the sample altogether, then business executive ranks several points higher than mother on the career list. And among all the younger women, aged twenty-five to thirty-four, business executive comes in only one point behind mother. *Overall, more than two-thirds of women find some other career more appealing than being a mother.* (Only 23 percent of the women we surveyed in Japan, 13 percent in South Africa, and 12 percent in England chose motherhood as the most appealing career, so women's ambitions are an international phenomenon.)

This doesn't mean, of course, that only a third of women are going to want to have children. After all, we just saw that two-thirds of women would be anywhere from moderately to very concerned about growing old without having any. And nine out of ten women in the *Glamour* survey rated marriage and children as important to them. What our survey result *does* mean is that the majority of women in the future aren't going to make motherhood their sole life work. And some may decide to forgo it altogether if it conflicts with other life goals.

Thirty-one percent of the childless women in our survey say they would consider remaining childless to concentrate on a career or other personal goals, and another 20 percent have already decided not to have children.

I discussed this a lot with the women on my staff, and one thing they all stressed was that the conflict between career and family depends heavily on how much money a woman makes and whether she has a supportive partner: "If you can't afford day care or babysitters, this can definitely get in the way"; "It depends on if the husband helps and what kind of career she has"; "If a woman wants a career, a husband, and children, she can't constantly focus on all three at the same time"; "It depends on backup and the question of money"; "It depends on the needs of that particular child and on the motivation of the mother."

As you'll see, more women are spending less time at home after bearing children, and more fathers are starting to share the parenting responsibilities. In the not-too-distant future, as childcare services improve, the work week is shortened, and employers adopt more supportive policies about working parents, this conflict between bearing children and building a career should be lessened. For some women it already has. Columbia University's Graduate School of Business tracked down women a decade after they had received their MBA degrees and found that those who had married and borne children had achieved the same standing in their professions as those who had remained single.

Women tend to have more anxiety these days about whether their careers are causing them to cheat their children than vice versa. For years now we've been subjected to nostalgia for mothers in aprons sending their children off to school with bellies full of hot oatmeal and greeting them after school with homemade cookies. You might think from reading psychologist Lee Salk and others like him that working mothers are spawning a generation of unloved and insecure emotional cripples who'll never be able to cope with life. In fact, research shows that the children of working mothers are often better off than the children of full-time homemakers.

This is good news because even today 60 percent of mothers with children under eighteen work, including 52 percent of all mothers of preschool children. And this percentage is certainly going to increase. *Whatever twinges of guilt and anxiety they may feel, our survey makes it clear that American women intend to spend less time at home in the future, and most don't believe their children will suffer.*

Three-quarters of the women we surveyed say they would prefer to stay home while their child was young, if they had the financial choice. Another 13 percent say maybe, and 10 percent say no. Only 60 percent of working mothers, and 58 percent of women in professional and managerial positions would want to stay home. One in five of the women in these categories say they would definitely *not* want to remain home. ("I would go crazy!" one of my staffers says. Another agrees, "If all I had to do was raise a child I would die of boredom.")

Almost two-thirds of the women would return to work by the time their child reached age six. Among working mothers and professional and managerial women, three-quarters would want to return to work by the time their child entered school, and this includes at least 20 percent who'd go back to their careers within the first year. (In a *McCall's* magazine reader survey published early this year, a third of the women aged twenty-five to thirty-four said they had returned to work when their youngest child was under a year old.)

One of our film assistants says she'd want to stay home, "but only for the first couple of years, the most impressionable years. Infants need that security. It's very important that they have at least one of the parents around. I think the guidance should be from the parents." A secretary says, "The young years are so very important for children, and they should have someone steady for them." (I agree, but, as you'll see, that *someone* doesn't have to be a parent.)

Others would work during the child's infancy then return to be with their children during the years two to five: "When they're infants, as long as someone is there to keep them well fed and taken care of, it doesn't mean much to them that their mother isn't there. But when they are older they form attachments. They are aware. It's best to be there at that time with them. To be a steady person." (Again, it's only the *parent* who feels hurt when her child becomes emotionally attached to a sitter or other caregiver.)

Another thinks a child should learn to adapt to its parents' schedule from the start: "I think that once I had the child I would be home for only the first two weeks, just to recuperate. I don't think it's necessary to be constantly around the child. My parents had us work our schedules around them when we were little. We're not the worse for it. Reality is that the world doesn't cater to you. I think the more flexible people are with children when they're very young, then those children can handle changes better when they're adults. It's such a changing world."

Just over half the women in our survey, 53 percent, say the children of full-time homemakers aren't necessarily better off than the children of working mothers. This figure goes up to 65 percent among working mothers themselves, and 70 percent among professional and managerial women.

Here's the sort of information professionals are finding:

- *A nationwide survey of pediatricians in 1983 showed that the majority see no difference in "child development, academic difficulties, or emotional problems" between the children of working mothers and those of full-time homemakers.* Nearly half the doctors surveyed believe that "children whose mothers are employed outside the home function more independently and that children develop stronger attachments to mothers who do not work outside the home," according to the University of Arizona researchers who conducted the survey.

  When they were asked how old a child should be before its mother returns to work, 29 percent of the pediatricians said it didn't matter, 7 percent said three months or less, 26 percent said three years, and 36 percent said when the child starts school. *Only 1 percent said a "mother should never work."*

· Data from the New York Longitudinal Study, which followed 133 people from early infancy into adulthood, showed that *the critical factor in how well a child adjusts is not whether his mother works or not but "how satisfied she is with her choice."*

"If she's happy, she is more likely to have a good relationship with her child," Jacqueline Lerner, of Pennsylvania State University, one of the directors of the study, reported last year. "She will show more warmth and be more consistent with discipline. The child, in turn, will be happier and better adjusted. If the mother is dissatisfied, her relationship with her child won't be as good. Unhappy mothers tend to be more harsh, cold, and rejecting, and their children have more problems in adjustment."

· Research psychologist Sandra Scarr, of the University of Virginia, whose book *Mother Care, Other Care* was published in 1984, has been studying children in day-care centers in Bermuda since the late 1970s. Her research has shown that babies under the age of two don't fare well in large centers, probably because they don't get enough warm, loving attention. In an interview with *Psychology Today,* Scarr noted that these babies are rated years later as "less cooperative, more aggressive, and more active than other children." However, *babies under age two left with a babysitter or in a home-care setting fare just as well as those cared for at home by their mothers.*

"Three- and four-year-olds who are placed in day-care centers actually do better than children who stay at home with their mothers," Scarr told the magazine. "They also do better than children in day-care homes or those with a sitter. The centers provide these older children with peer contact and an educational program. In fact, children in centers with a more structured program, which includes educational activities planned by a teacher, were doing better in intellectual, language, personal, and social development than children who spent their days in free play."

The common wisdom that children get more attention from full-time homemakers has also been thoroughly disproved, Scarr reported. Studies show the average homemaker "spends twenty minutes watching television with her child in the room, thirteen minutes eating with the child sitting beside her, and less than ten minutes a day actually doing something educational with the child. Working mothers spend about the same amount of time in direct interaction with children, reading to them or playing with them, as nonworking mothers."

Scarr also noted that it can be a disadvantage for a child to be around her mother all the time if it results in "an exclusive and very intense relationship with one other person. Preschool children have a better chance of feeling secure and having a healthy emotional life if their whole well-being is not dependent on just one other human being."

I can tell from the comments of women on my staff that these sorts of research findings are already having an impact on our beliefs about how children should be raised. Many of them asserted that children don't necessarily get more love and attention just because their mothers are around all day. And there seems to be wide agreement that the children of working mothers are more independent, self-sufficient, and less "whiny" than children of full-time housewives.

Ironically, one of our secretaries who feels children are better off under the constant gaze of their mothers thinks so because she considers independence an undesirable trait, "It's important to know you're there, you're guiding them, or else they become too independent, too individual." I think the more individual and independent the next generation of children is, the better off we'll be. (For one thing, remember the work of psychologists Maccoby and Jacklin that I mentioned when we talked about math ability: adults with the highest spatial ability are found in "cultures that allow independence to children.")

Other staffers expressed the feeling that it puts a great deal of pressure on a child to make him the focus of a woman's whole existence—especially an intelligent, ambitious, talented woman. "At one time in the past, when mothers were forced into staying home all the time and forced into the role of mothering, they got wacky. They poured all sorts of excessive drive and energy into their children, which didn't help the children at all," one commented.

And listen to one of our managers, who's thirty-five and is raising two young children by herself, "I think some mothers are such full-time homemakers that they suffocate their children. I see my kids as very sociable human beings. They do well outside. To be honest, I feel that I've been around full-time mothers with my kids, and my kids are much different. I like my kids' behavior much better."

Another staffer echoed her sentiments, "I think that if working mothers are happy, they react to their children better. I think kids who are with their mothers all day tend to be namby-pamby and cling to their mothers, who tend to smother them. Children who go to day-care centers or babysitters meet other people. They learn other things, and they have a generally much wider outlook on life. Also, with the mother there all the time, the children tend to let the mother do everything for them and don't learn responsibility until a later age. I don't think you should make the mother the center of the universe," she concludes.

Of course, we helped perpetuate this habit of placing the full burden on the female parent just by the way we asked our question. We could have asked whether a child of working *parents* or a working *father* is worse off than a child with one parent at home full-time. Since 98 percent of women believe childraising should be an equally shared task, any guilt over what a child is missing should be dealt with by both parents.

As we saw earlier, parental behavior is one of those sex-shared abilities where the triggers simply seem to be set at different levels in males and females. Even a male monkey, left alone long enough with an infant, will begin to nurture it and develop a fierce attachment to it that easily rivals "mother love." Nature is full of examples of self-sacrificing fathers, and even complete role reversals in sex and family life. Emperor penguin fathers roll the egg onto the top of their feet almost as soon as their mate lays it, cover it with a paunchy fold of abdominal skin, then stand there on the Antarctic ice warming it for two months. The female, who goes off to sea to feed, relieves him about the time the egg hatches. Female spotted sandpipers fight with each other for territory and mates. As soon as they've laid a clutch of eggs for one male, they take off with another, leaving as many as four jilted males a season with nests full of eggs to care for.

Of course, mammals developed a different strategy, leaving the young dependent on breast milk and giving females the mammaries. Until modern technology provided us with infant formula, we women didn't have much choice about who was to spend the most time with an infant. (I know breast-feeding is going through a popular revival among educated women today, but several generations of Americans grew up hardy and healthy on formula. Women who don't prefer to or can't breast-feed shouldn't feel guilty about it.)

Today our attitudes have changed dramatically. Role reversal is trendy enough to generate popular movies like *Mr. Mom* and TV series like "Who's the Boss?" and "Charles in Charge." That *USA Today* poll last year showed that 90 percent of Americans, both men and women, think fathers should be just as willing as mothers to make career sacrifices to help take care of children.

Like shared housework, however, there's more lip service than reality to shared parenting right now. The nonprofit organization Catalyst surveyed *Fortune* 500 firms last year and found that a third now offer some sort of paternity leave for new fathers. But very few men take it, the survey reported. Ninety-three percent of men and 48 percent of women in the *USA Today* poll said women still have the primary role in raising children. Although 85 percent of the women we surveyed say their partners share equally in "raising" the children, only 64 percent say these men put in equal time tutoring, and only 59 percent do their share transporting them. Psychologists at the University of California at Berkeley found that even in families where fathers were actively trying to share parenting with their wives, fathers' time involvement was far less than their wives'. Fathers were spending an average of twenty-six hours a week with their babies, compared to 121 hours for the mothers.

When things get tough, as they often do in a house with two careers and a baby, couples seem to fall back into traditional patterns. Men are often insecure about their ability to care for their children, and very few can look back to their own fathers as role models (a problem fewer boys of Nina and Kelly's generation will face). Thirty years ago, men tended to hover at the periphery of their families, emotionally aloof, stepping in only to administer discipline. Mothers today don't always make it easy for their husbands to practice and develop a sense of competence in nurturing their children either. Guilty and anxious about going off to work and abandoning traditional roles themselves, mothers may monopolize childcare, reasserting their own competence by belittling that of their husbands.

I believe this is all part of the strain of transition, a tension that will fade as we develop more self-confidence about our new roles. *And the research findings on fathering so far should certainly give men more incentive to get involved with their babies, and working women less reason for anxiety.*

"Everything we know shows that when men are involved with their children, that increases the children's IQ by the time they are six or seven . . . ," pediatrician T. Berry Brazelton told one interviewer. But Brazelton, chief of the Child Development Unit at Boston Children's Hospital and an associate professor at Harvard Medical School, also said "the more interesting evidence to me is that the child is also more likely to have a sense of humor, to develop a sort of inner excitement, to believe in himself or herself, to be more motivated to learn. And these things are, you know, probably more critical to a person's future than anything else."

Stay-at-home fathers whose wives go off to work have children whose scores on developmental tests were way above the average for their age.

These babies thrive, not because fathers are *better* than mothers at child-rearing, but because the working mothers continued to be deeply involved, too. These children simply get a lot more love and attention from both parents combined than other children get from mothers teamed up with traditional fathers. These children continue to flourish even after their fathers return to work. (Much of this is confirmed in a study by Yale University child psychologist Kyle Pruett.)

Such findings, combined with the evidence about children in day care, show that we can expect our new dual-career marriages to produce brighter, more independent, more self-reliant children in the future. I believe it's time to stop romanticizing a past that we can't resurrect and that most of us really wouldn't want to go back to, anyway. The families we're creating for tomorrow will provide us with just the sort of love and support we'll need to flourish in a rapidly changing world.

8

BIRTH TECHNOLOGIES

In the Bible, Sara had her baby when she was ninety. The day when such a miracle actually comes to pass, when a modern-day Sara—retired on her social security pension—has a child, may be very near.

—Dr. Landrum Shettles

ntil twenty-five years ago, about the only certain choice women had in reproduction was selecting *who* the father of their children would be. The Pill added the alternatives of *if* and, within the limits of our biological clocks, *when*, we'd bear children. Tomorrow's choices will be breathtaking.

Contraception freed individual women for the first time to chart their own course in life. *Now science promises to put the very definition of mother, father, family lineage, and even human life in our hands.*

We'll decide not only if and when, but whose eggs and sperm will be used, where fertilization will take place, whose womb the fetus will grow to birth in, what sex it will be, what defects call for abortion or correction, and eventually, what genetic improvements in intelligence, character, or appearance we want to make. All but the last option are available today, and genetic science will probably make enhancement possible by the time women like Nina are ready to think about using it. (One in ten women would use it now, as you'll see.)

I know from our survey that, although many women today are uneasy about how well we'll handle these new choices, you're basically pleased that we have them. After all, the really important work and the real joy of raising a child comes after birth.

Two-thirds of the American and English women we surveyed say they're pleased that women have so many new childbearing options. Only 19 percent of women say they're uneasy about these new choices, and another 12 percent claim indifference.

Forty-one percent of American women think that none of these new birth options are immoral. Thirty percent believe *some* of them are immoral; 27 percent aren't sure; and only 2 percent condemn them all. (About one in ten of the women we surveyed in Japan and South Africa and only 3 percent of the women we talked to in England think these choices are immoral.)

In Australia, England, and western Europe, citizens and governments are already trying to come up with new legal and ethical codes to help us use these novel reproductive powers wisely. The sorts of questions raised by "alternative" or "assisted" reproduction can't be answered by reliance on medieval doctrines: What are the legal and moral rights of three-day-old embryos? Who owns them? Who gets custody in a divorce? Should they be frozen? Will a child adopted as an embryo or conceived with donated sperm or eggs have a right to know who its biological parents are? Should embryo adoption and test-tube fertilization be limited to married couples? When it becomes possible, should genetic screening be used to weed out children with predispositions to schizophrenia or antisocial behavior? Can you require the surrogate mother who carries your child to stop smoking or give up wine with dinner? Does she have the right to change her mind while still on the job, so to speak, and abort your child?

In the United States, the government has so far simply shut its eyes and pretended these new technologies don't exist. Lawmakers are afraid to move away from moralistic rhetoric and acknowledge the arrival of a new age. As a publisher of a science magazine, I come across many instances where important medical or scientific discoveries are hindered or blocked by those in the traditional seat of power. Thousands of lives are lost because one authority or another feared the consequences of change. I'd be the last person to espouse any sort of quackery, but I fault many members of the medical community, especially in the field of obstetrics and gynecology, for not promoting innovation.

"At every crossway on the road that leads to the future, each progressive spirit is opposed by a thousand men appointed to guard the past," is a line written by Maeterlinck that brings to mind the case of Dr. Landrum Shettles, one of the world's most distinguished pioneers in the field of infertility medicine. Shettles envisioned a world of test-tube infants and embryo transplants as early as the 1940s—about the same time that antibiotics were first being introduced. He was decades ahead of others in his field, and his genius for, quite literally, bringing lives into the world was constantly thwarted by those who made the rules. And if a gentler soul or more "progressive spirit" ever existed within the medical community, I'd be hard pressed to find him or her.

Let me cite one story that illustrates my point. In 1973, Dr. Shettles was on the verge of creating the world's first test-tube baby at Columbia-Presbyterian Hospital in New York, where he then worked. An embryo had been produced in a petri dish for an infertile couple who had been unsuccessful in their attempts to have children. But before Shettles could implant the embryo, hospital authorities, fearing, in their ignorance or superstition, that the doctor was creating a monster, deliberately destroyed the embryo. Despite over two decades of dedicated service to Columbia-Presbyterian, Shettles was threatened with arrest and ignominiously dismissed as a result of the incident.

Five years later, the couple whose embryo had been destroyed successfully sued the hospital. Ironically, the first test-tube baby was born later that year, in England, more than five years after Shettles had served as a pioneer in the field. And five years after that, in 1983, the same authorities who had obstructed Shettles' research proudly announced the opening of New York's first test-tube clinic.

I had only one chance to meet Dr. Shettles, during a convention in Las Vegas, but I sensed that this "progressive spirit," the son of a Mississippi farmer, had been forced to fight his entire life for the medical vision that he possessed.

Because the traditional medical community looks askance on new or unorthodox procedures, scientists, physicians, and infertile couples alike are left to make intimate personal decisions with no legal guidelines or safeguards. You've seen the kinds of dilemma that can result on the evening news: a couple refusing to take custody of a retarded infant born to their hired surrogate; frozen embryos "orphaned" when the woman who provided the eggs died in a plane crash; a woman suing a sperm bank for supplying a semen sample that caused her to contract gonorrhea.

Like it or not, our legal system will eventually have to deal with such issues, but I believe women themselves through their personal participation in these new birth technologies will bear the heaviest burden of defining tomorrow's reproductive choices. It's important that women today think about these issues carefully because we *are* carving a path for the women and children of tomorrow.

I'm going to list the alternatives briefly now, then tell you how women today are handling their if-and-when choices before I detail the new birth technologies and the questions they raise. *This is how babies can be made right now—in addition to the old-fashioned way, of course:*

1. If your *husband is infertile,* you can be inseminated artificially with *donor sperm.*
2. If you and your partner are *both fertile but can't conceive* in the normal way—maybe your Fallopian tubes are damaged or his tubes have been vasectomized or otherwise blocked—*eggs and sperm from the two of you* can be removed and joined in a lab dish and the resulting embryo placed in *your womb. This is "in vitro" or "test-tube" fertilization.*
3. If *you are fertile but can't conceive* and your *husband is infertile,* then *donor sperm* can be used to fertilize *your eggs* in the lab dish, and the embryo returned to *your womb.*
4. If *you are infertile* but are able to carry a child, your *partner's sperm* can be used to fertilize a *donated egg* in a lab dish and the embryo implanted in *your womb.*
5. Alternately in that case, your *partner's sperm* can be used to artificially *inseminate another woman,* then the resulting embryo can be washed from the donor's womb and placed in *your womb. This procedure is called an embryo transplant.*
6. If *both of you are infertile* but *you can carry a child,* then you can choose to receive an *adoptive embryo conceived in a surrogate's body or in a lab dish using the donor sperm and eggs of your choice.*
7. If *you are infertile and can't carry a child either,* your *husband's sperm* can be used to artificially *inseminate another woman, a surrogate who will bear the child for you.* Or, *his sperm* and a *donor egg* of your choice can be joined in a lab dish and implanted in a *surrogate's womb.* (If the egg doesn't come from the surrogate, the child will have four parents—your husband as father, the egg donor, the birth mother, and you as adoptive mother.)
8. If *both of you are infertile and you can't carry a child either,* a *surrogate* can bear you a child conceived naturally or artificially

using *donor sperm* and *her own or donated eggs.* (This makes possible the five-parent child—sperm donor, egg donor, birth mother, and adoptive mother and father.)

9. If *both of you are fertile but you can't carry a child*—perhaps you had a hysterectomy but still have functioning ovaries—*eggs and sperm from both of you* can be joined in a lab dish and implanted in the womb of a *surrogate.*

10. If you are fertile but you can't carry a child, and your *husband is infertile, your egg and donor sperm* can be joined and the embryo carried by a *surrogate.*

11. Instead of using *donor sperm or eggs* in one of these combinations because of infertility, a couple may choose to do so because *one or both carries a genetic disease* like Tay-Sachs, thalassemia, cystic fibrosis, muscular dystrophy, and others.

And in the not-too-distant-future, as you'll see, many of these techniques will be available not just to couples with genetic or fertility problems but to women trying to juggle family and career obligations or escape the tyranny of the biological clock.

o   o   o

For the past fifteen years, American women have been waiting longer and longer to start their families. The number of women who put off having their first child until age twenty-five or older more than *doubled* between 1970 and 1982. And among women thirty to thirty-four, first births more than *tripled* during that twelve-year period. Only a little over half of the women of the baby boom generation—women now in their early thirties —had had their first child by age twenty-five. In contrast, among the generation of women now in their late forties, 70 percent had had their first babies by that age. Demographers think the trend is here to stay, and our survey supports their prediction.

Half of the women we surveyed feel that, if the medical risks were the same at any point, the ideal time for giving birth would be between the ages of twenty-six and thirty. The rest were almost evenly split, with 21 percent favoring age twenty-five and under, and another 21 percent favoring ages thirty-one to thirty-five. Overall, only 4 percent of women think it's *ideal* to have children after age thirty-five, even though a much greater proportion of women actually end up doing it.

Among the women with higher incomes and among those who work, especially professional and managerial women, a third would opt for over-thirty childbirth as ideal. And half the women we surveyed who don't have children yet choose thirty-one and up as their preference. More than three-quarters of the women we surveyed who already have children favored under-thirty childbirth. (Ninety percent of the Japanese and South African women we talked to would chose under-thirty childbirth, too. In contrast, more than 40 percent of the English women choose thirty and up as ideal.)

"Educational level is the most important variable affecting the age at which a woman begins childbearing," notes Harvard University economist David Bloom. "The more education she has, the older she will be when her first child is born. *And as the educational level of American women increases, more women are waiting longer to have children . . . Women in high-status, highly skilled occupations tend to be older than other women when they have their first child. In addition, the closer a wife's earnings are to her husband's the more likely she is to delay having children.*"

I think the trend for the future is obvious, because women's educational levels, salaries, and career goals are definitely going to keep rising. We are going to wait to become mothers until our careers are on track, our relationships are stable, and we feel emotionally and financially ready to do the best for our children. "At thirty-five to forty you've had a chance to be selfish about your life and a better chance to not resent your children," one of my executives says. "You've got your life squared away, have your values straightened out. And you're young enough not to be an old parent."

The only reason women today can even make such choices, of course, is due to birth control. According to the National Center for Health Statistics, 55 percent of American women of childbearing age practice birth control today. And the number of unwanted births has dropped by half during the past twenty years. In 1965, two-thirds of all children were born as a result of unwanted or unplanned conceptions. In 1982, only a third of all births were reported as unwanted or unplanned. (That's still an incredible proportion, and I'm sure it reflects the increase in teenage pregnancies. Teenagers are a large proportion of the 45 percent of women who still make no attempt at all to take charge of their reproductive powers.)

Nearly a third of all women who practice birth control use the Pill in one form or another. The rest rely on female sterilization, 22 percent; condoms, 12 percent; male sterilization, 11 percent; diaphragms, 8 percent; IUDs, 7 percent; and rhythm method, 4 percent.

Most versions of the Pill today contain only a third the amount of estrogen in the original ones, and even smaller fractions of the hormone progestin. Newer "triphasic" pills approved for use in the United States in 1984 vary the dose of hormones three times during each menstrual cycle to mimic more closely natural levels. Not only have the side effects been greatly reduced, but women who take these pills for at least a year will cut their risk of ovarian and endometrial cancer in half.

Women in general seem to be fairly satisfied with the birth control methods available. *When we asked about technological breakthroughs that would have the greatest positive effect on their lives, only 7 percent of women mentioned birth control/reproduction. This went up to 18 percent, however, among women who don't yet have children.* The good news for them is that *science has already provided a better answer—a long-lasting, safe, and effective method of birth control that can be reversed at any time.*

In early 1985 the World Health Organization proclaimed the NOR-PLANT System, a timed-release implant produced by Leiras Pharmaceuticals of Finland, "the most important new contraceptive since the Pill." The system consists of six little silicon-rubber capsules the diameter of tiny grains of rice that are inserted by needle just under the skin of your upper arm. You can feel them by running your fingers over the area, but they can't be seen. *They remain effective for five years,* releasing only thirty micrograms of progestin a day (and no estrogen) and causing none of the side effects of the Pill. If you want to get pregnant, a doctor or technician simply removes them.

NORPLANT is already approved and available to women in Finland and Sweden, at a cost of only thirty dollars to sixty dollars, and WHO is seeking swift approval in nations where population control is critical and pregnancy is still a leading cause of death. But it will take another two to three years before the federal Food and Drug Administration allows women in the United States to receive it.

Within a decade, a similar implant may be available for *men.* Researchers at Harbor UCLA Medical Center and in West Germany have been able to inhibit (but not completely block) sperm production in male volunteers by having them wear small pumps that provided constant infusions of a synthetic version of the brain hormone LHRH. But the main problem with this and other male contraceptives so far is that it also kills the sex drive. LHRH is the hormone—you'll sometimes see it called GnRH—that the brain uses to signal the pituitary to set in motion the chain of events that leads to ovulation in women and sperm production in men. Several synthetic versions of it are being tested as female contraceptives, too, but they're impractical for most people because they still have to be taken by injection or as nasal spray.

Some early sex-education pioneers such as Lester A. Kirkendall have suggested that we could "innoculate" children at puberty with a drug that renders them infertile until they themselves decide to reverse it. I think these new contraceptive implants will give us the first tools to do just that, and to make the birth of a child a truly wanted event. Our biggest obstacle now is not technology but our painfully outdated moral codes.

Now back to *having* children. We asked our survey question about the ideal time to have children with the presumption that the medical risks are the same at any age. Historically, of course, that isn't true. The later the pregnancy, the riskier it is for both mother and child. But medical technology, combined with a change in older mothers themselves, has improved the picture dramatically. The women over thirty-five now causing a small boom in the birth rate are largely well-educated professionals instead of lower-income women. They have planned and prepared for this event in their lives, and they can afford the best medical care.

"It's not a matter of being risky or not risky anymore," University of Chicago Medical Center obstetrics chief Atef Moawad told an interviewer. "We understand the risks and we can do something about it now. . . . People are doing it more because they see that it can be done safely."

Health and fitness are what count, as well as good planning and prenatal care. (Here's where women like Nina, who have been active all their lives, will have an advantage over many of us in their mothers' generation.) Moawad recommends that women over thirty spend six months to optimize their diet, weight, and muscle tone before getting pregnant.

Women in their late thirties or older do have a greater risk of complications such as toxemia—pregnancy-induced high blood pressure—stillbirth, premature delivery, and lower-weight babies. But these risks are still very low and preventable with good obstetrical care. The overwhelming majority of women will have no problems. To illustrate, look at the figures for stillbirths collected by epidemiologist Michele Forman, of the federal government's Centers for Disease Control: In women aged twenty to twenty-four pregnant for the first time, the rate of stillbirths is 4.4 per 1,000 births. Among women thirty-five to thirty-nine, the rate almost doubles, to 7.8 per 1,000. But even so that's a minute risk. It means that 992.2 of 1,000 babies born to older mothers will be live births.

The greatest risk older mothers face is giving birth to a child with a chromosomal defect such as Down's syndrome, which causes mental retardation and often life-threatening heart problems. The odds of giving birth to a Down's child at age twenty are one in 1,600; at thirty-five, one in three hundred; and at forty, one in one hundred. *However, with genetic screening and abortion readily available, such births are completely preventable.* (And more than half of American women say they'd want such tests done, as you'll see later.)

The great majority of older women will also have no problem getting pregnant, despite all you've been hearing about declining fertility rates. In the past twenty years, infertility among women in their early twenties has tripled, but the *overall* infertility rate among women fifteen to forty-four hasn't changed. One of every five American couples has an infertility problem of some sort, which is about evenly split between the wife's infertility and the husband's. Physicians can help anywhere from half to three-quarters of these couples conceive, which means that in reality more than 90 percent of couples who want children can have them without resorting to the new technologies.

Several conditions can prevent a woman from conceiving or successfully carrying a child: pelvic inflammatory disease caused by infections, benign fibroid tumors in the womb, or endometriosis, where the lining of the womb spreads outside and attaches itself to other organs like the ovary and Fallopian tubes (often called "career woman's disease" because it progresses over the years and eventually leads to infertility in two-thirds of those who have it). With hormone treatments or surgery, the majority of women with these conditions can get pregnant and carry a child. (A San Francisco surgeon has even transplanted an ovary and Fallopian tube successfully from one sister to her identical twin.)

Some women simply fail to ovulate, a condition that becomes more frequent with age. With fertility drugs like Clomid and Pergonal, 80 percent of women with this problem can get pregnant, although they do face a greater possibility of multiple births this way. And for the 20 percent of women who don't respond to these drugs, science has recently identified another solution: infusions of synthetic LHRH, the same brain hormone that in different doses is being tested as a contraceptive to *prevent* ovulation.

For couples who aren't helped by any of these solutions, we come to the eleven options I listed earlier.

o   o   o

Most women today feel that if they couldn't contribute either their eggs or their wombs to help produce a child, they'd just as soon adopt. *Three-quarters of American women say adoption would be their preference if they were infertile and unable to carry a child.* Only 11 percent would prefer to hire a surrogate mother to bear their husband's child, and 8 percent would choose to remain childless. (Half the women we talked to in Japan, a quarter of those in South Africa, and a fifth of the English would prefer to remain childless.)

That preference for adoption falls way off, however, when women are offered the chance to take part in either producing or bearing the child. *A whopping 88 percent of women say they'd consider trying in vitro fertilization if they and their partners were both fertile but couldn't conceive naturally.* (Two-thirds of the English women say they'd consider it, too. In contrast, about three-quarters of the Japanese and South African women we surveyed were either unsure or answered no.)

Since the birth of the first test-tube baby, Louise Brown, in England in 1978, infertile couples around the world have been clamoring for the procedure. More than a thousand babies conceived in lab dishes had been born worldwide by the end of 1984. By March 1985, the American Fertility Society knew of 115 in vitro fertilization (IVF) clinics in operation in the United States, eight in Canada, and at least fifty in other nations. (You can check with the American Fertility Society at 2131 Magnolia Avenue, Suite 201, Birmingham, Alabama, 35256, to find the name and location of the nearest IVF clinic no matter what part of the world you live in.)

Already the "old-fashioned" procedures that brought us Louise Brown are being replaced by newer approaches, and 1984 was a banner year for firsts: the first baby born using nonsurgical IVF procedures; the first baby born from a frozen embryo; the first births from donor eggs; the first IVF using sperm surgically removed from a man with blocked tubes; the first embryo transplants from one woman to another.

Here's how basic IVF works today: A woman is given Clomid, Pergonal, or hormones to stimulate her ovaries to begin to ripen from two to twelve eggs instead of the usual one. Ultrasound imaging and blood tests for hormone levels are used to track her ovulation and alert the IVF team to the moment her eggs reach the peak of maturity. Then she is given general anesthesia and a telescopic device the thickness of a pencil, a laparoscope, is inserted through an incision near her naval into her ovary. A doctor looks through the scope to identify the little blisterlike follicles containing eggs, then inserts a hollow needle to suction them up.

The microscopic eggs are put in a petri dish or a test tube with a layer of liquid nutrients, and drops of sperm are added. The container is then stored in a body-temperature incubator for a day or so until at least one egg has been fertilized and the embryo has divided to the two- to eight-cell stage. This embryo, or, usually, several embryos, is taken up in a plastic catheter, which is then inserted through the vagina and cervix, and deposited in the uterus.

Two weeks later a pregnancy test will tell the couple whether the embryo has implanted. The best odds when one embryo is implanted are 20 percent, and that's in the most successful clinics. The odds of achieving a pregnancy almost double when three embryos are used, although the chances of multiple birth also increase. (Researchers aren't sure if these odds can be greatly improved, since it's believed that anywhere from one-half to three-quarters of natural conceptions never successfully implant.) Even if the pregnancy "takes," a third of women will miscarry in the first three months. (Again, this is probably close to the normal rate, but heartbreaking for women who have never been able to get pregnant at all before.)

Eventually, out-of-body conception will become a doctor's office procedure instead of a hospital one, and the first steps toward that goal have already been taken in Europe and at the University of California at Los Angeles Medical Center. Teams there have eliminated the surgical part of the egg retrieval process, using ultrasound instead of a laparoscope to guide the needle. In that way, only local anesthesia to the abdomen is needed. So far they've obtained fewer eggs this way, so the chances of success on each try are reduced. But the UCLA team celebrated its first success in 1984, a baby named Greta, born to a thirty-five-year-old California woman.

Cryopreservation, or freezing of embryos in liquid nitrogen, also promises to reduce trouble and expense and boost the success rate by allowing couples to store embryos harvested the first time around for later implant attempts. (Right now the costs per attempt run from $3,000 to $7,000, depending on the clinic.) The freezing process is imperfect now—a third to half of the embryos don't survive it. But the IVF team at Monash University, in Melbourne, Australia, announced its first successful birth from a frozen embryo in 1984, and shortly afterward, the IVF clinic at the University of Southern California Medical Center began the first American cryopreservation program.

The possibility of beating the biological clock by freezing embryos now for reimplantation in your own or someone else's womb later doesn't have much of a following yet, although I believe it will in the future. Only 11 percent of women in general say they'd consider it, and another 19 percent aren't sure. *But among women who are now childless, 17 percent would consider it and 24 percent are still uncertain.* (Ten percent or fewer of the women in South Africa and Japan say they'd consider it. The women we talked to in England were the most enthusiastic of all, however, with 31 percent saying they'd consider it.)

"I wouldn't mind doing this," says one of our secretaries, who is putting off starting a family while she and her husband build their careers. "I eventually plan to have kids myself. I could see this as an option for women who want to pursue a career and don't want interference from a child. By the time they're ready to have kids, they might be in their late thirties, which puts them in a high-risk zone."

Some of my staffers feel the concept is "terrible" or "creepy," and others just imagine too many unforeseeable complications: "What if ten years later down the line I decided I didn't want children, or I hated the father? What would happen to it then?"

Some of these objections will be rendered moot, of course, if scientists can find a successful way to freeze unfertilized eggs instead of embryos. Frozen sperm have been banked for years without causing anyone significant qualms, and if eggs could be similarly stored, a woman wouldn't have to select her future children's father or fathers at the age of eighteen or twenty. No one knows yet why sperm and embryos can be successfully frozen and thawed but eggs are destroyed by the procedure.

Most IVF clinics are also loosening the restrictions that originally discouraged applications from women over thirty-five or couples who needed either eggs or sperm donated. The Australian team started working with donated eggs—usually those left over from another IVF patient—three years ago and reported its first birth in 1984.

All sorts of spin offs of IVF are also providing new ways of getting fertile but reluctant sperm and eggs together inside the body instead of in a dish. If a woman's tubes are open and she's producing eggs but her husband has a low sperm count, intrauterine insemination can be tried before IVF. The woman's eggs aren't removed at all. Instead, her husband's sperm is deposited directly into her womb by using the same plastic catheter that would have been used to implant the embryo if she had undergone IVF. A team at the University of Texas at San Antonio has taken that a step farther with GIFT—gamete intrafallopian transfer. This is a one-step surgery in which the woman's eggs are harvested and both the eggs and her husband's sperm are immediately deposited together in her fallopian tubes. Both of these techniques are too new to say anything about their success rates.

Another first in 1984 was the birth of two babies to women biologically unrelated to them. The transfer of embryos from one female to another is already a multimillion-dollar business in the world of cattle breeding so scientists knew what had to be done. Obstetricians Marie Bustillo and John

E. Buster at Harbor–UCLA Medical Center worked for five years to perfect a safe procedure for humans. It's simple and nonsurgical.

First the menstrual cycles of the prospective mother and the embryo donor are synchronized, using hormones if needed. Then the donor is artificially inseminated with sperm from the prospective mother's husband. Five days later, when fertilization should have taken place and the embryo progressed to the womb, the womb is washed out and the embryo (at the hundred-cell stage or so) is captured in a special catheter the team developed. It is then transferred to the recipient's womb through the cervix, just as an IVF embryo is. The whole process is simple for the recipient but carries a slight risk of unwanted or even tubal pregnancy for the donor, if the embryo isn't recovered or the wash process pushes it back into the Fallopian tube.

Embryo transfer gets a strong but less enthusiastic vote than does IVF as an option for women who are infertile but could carry a pregnancy. *Forty-two percent of women say they would prefer to transplant another woman's embryo, fertilized by their husband's sperm, into their own wombs if they were able to bear a child but not produce eggs. A slightly greater proportion, 47 percent, would still prefer to adopt someone else's child rather than an embryo.* (More than three-quarters of the women we surveyed in Japan and South Africa were either unsure or say they wouldn't consider an embryo transfer, but almost a third of the English women would.)

Many women on my staff say they would definitely want to experience the pregnancy and birth. "I'd want to carry the baby, to give it my environment, to feel the baby stirring," says one of our managers, who has two young children of her own. "The scientific aspects don't bother me," an editor, also a mother, told us. "I would want to carry the child."

Others were decidedly opposed to the idea of carrying another woman's child: "I don't want the trauma of carrying a baby if it's not mine," one of our sales people says. "I don't want stretch marks."

"I'd much rather adopt than go through all the trouble of being pregnant," an executive feels. "Being pregnant is not attractive to me. I'm not that interested in having kids, and there are so many kids that are already born that need to be loved."

"I wouldn't want to take a risk of receiving an anonymous embryo," another staffer says. "I would rather take a child that's already alive. I'm not that nuts about being pregnant. Unless it's my kid, why should I go through all that hassle?"

There also seem to be some fatalists on my staff, and I'm afraid among the rest of the women in the world as well: "If I couldn't conceive myself, I wouldn't want to alter things. If that's the way I am, then I shouldn't tamper with it. I wasn't meant to have kids." Another says, "I wouldn't want to tamper with nature. If I couldn't have children, then I wouldn't want to change that." (If all human beings were that fatalistic, we'd still be living in wandering tribes and waiting for lightning to give us fire.)

As I write this, no embryo transfer services are available to women yet, although Fertility and Genetics Research, Inc., the Chicago company formed to sponser the Harbor–UCLA project, plans to open the first of a network of embryo-adoption clinics in 1986 at the latest. (Check with Fertility and Genetics Research, Inc. at Suite 616, 135 South LaSalle, Chicago, Illinois, 60603, about clinic openings if you're interested in this service. For the present, they're the only ones in the world planning to offer embryo transfers.)

(This company has taken a lot of flack for patenting the special catheter Buster's team developed and for seeking a patent on the whole transfer process. But I expect to see more of this sort of thing if the federal government continues its decade-long ban on providing money for research in IVF and embryo transfer and if scientists are forced to turn to private investors. Gary Hodgen, formerly chief of pregnancy research at the National Institutes of Health, resigned last year over this issue and took a job at America's premier IVF program, at the Eastern Virginia Medical School, in Norfolk. He told a congressional hearing that the denial of support for this research is a breach of national responsibility to "generations of unborn.")

Buster plans to continue his research to find ways of applying embryo transfer to women who don't ovulate at all and so would need to be supplemented with hormones to carry a pregnancy. These might be women with chromosome defects like Turner's syndrome that leave their ovaries undeveloped or women who have experienced premature menopause. *In the future, of course, any technique he develops might be available to women in their fifties or sixties who have gone through normal menopause but still want to bear a child. This would mean the ultimate demise of the biological clock.*

(Endocrinologist John Money even suggests that this kind of hormonal priming may lead to *male pregnancies* some day, if volunteers can be found. There are cases where women have delivered full-term babies by cesarean section from ectopic pregnancies in which the fetus developed in the abdominal or intestinal cavity instead of in the uterus. A man might have an embryo transferred to an appropriate area of his midsection, then take the needed hormones to nurture its development, too. Money says he now suggests that to a number of his classes at Johns Hopkins and asks two questions: " 'Who would take a booking on a trip to the moon, and who would be the first man to carry a pregnancy to term?' And they're scared to death of it. The moon's okay, but to carry a pregnancy . . .")

Of course, if *artificial wombs* were developed neither sex would need to spend nine months carrying a pregnancy. You're not likely to see that very soon, however, because of the opposition to research using embryos or fetuses, although work on bringing mice to term through artificial wombs could be imminent. Besides the federal government's denial of research support, half of all the states ban or severely limit such experimentation. Government-appointed committees in Britain and Australia have recommended that research using embryos be permitted only up to fourteen days, the stage at which the ball of cells develops a "primitive streak," the first feature of what will become the nervous system.

British IVF pioneer Robert Edwards caused a controversy in 1982 when he succeeded in keeping a human embryo alive for nine days outside the womb, a record that still stands. And he and colleague Patrick Steptoe stirred up an even greater furor in 1984 when they suggested it would be useful to implant a human embryo in an animal to study the development process in detail. Zoos and animal breeders, of course, have already succeeded in interspecies embryo transplants—horses have given birth to zebras, mules to thoroughbreds, ordinary cows to wild oxen.

Another technique of modern animal husbandry also seems too controversial to be applied to humans anytime soon. This is the **splitting of embryos into twins or even quadruplets,** a technique Aldous Huxley foresaw in *Brave New World.* For fifteen years, animal breeders have been splitting embryos from prize cattle into twins and giving them to separate females to gestate. The government committee studying IVF in Australia suggested this might even be a way to increase the success rate for IVF where only one egg has been retrieved. Bizarre possibilities can be imagined if the freezing of embryo pieces is ever perfected: a mother might give birth to one child first, then to its twin years later. (Imagine having a younger version of yourself around all the time.) Or a girl might grow up and through an embryo transplant give birth to her own identical twin—her clone.

(That's the only workable way we have so far of *cloning*—reproducing an identical copy—an adult. In fact, American and British geneticists who have been trying to make two-mother or two-father mice, recently believe it may never be possible to take the full set of genes from one of your cells, put it into an egg whose own nucleus has been removed, and get it to guide the development of another you. Embryonic development seems to require a set of genes from each sex. The researchers speculate that genes are conditioned somehow during egg and sperm formation, a conditioning they lose as the embryo grows and cells begin to specialize into their adult roles as blood or eyes or kidneys, etc.)

o   o   o

Artificial insemination by donor sperm (AID) has been available for twenty-five years, and at least a quarter million children in the United States have been conceived that way. But the technique draws less enthusiastic support from women than IVF and embryo transfer. *Half of the women we surveyed would prefer to adopt if their male partners were infertile. Another 38 percent would choose artificial insemination*, and 10 percent would prefer to remain childless. (Half the women we talked to in Japan would prefer to remain childless, while half the English and 60 percent of the South Africans would adopt.)

Several women say they would choose AID in this case even though they'd prefer to remain childless if *they* were the infertile ones, "Because it would be mine. I want to pass on my genes. I'm conceited in that way, but why go through the trouble for someone else's baby, even for my husband? It would be his, not mine." Others believe it would be easier to adopt than to deal with the psychological problems donated sperm might cause their partners.

More than 80 percent of the American women we surveyed, as well as the women we talked to in other countries, would want to know more than the age, race, and general health of the sperm donor if they were to use AID. That's an option they seldom have at sperm banks today, or particularly when they make arrangements through a physician who recruits sperm donors as needed (mostly medical students). It's something I believe will have to change in the future.

Every group of women we surveyed pick the same three traits as the qualities they consider most important in sperm donors: emotional stability, high intelligence, and pleasant personality. After that, in declining order of importance, came good looks, leadership qualities, athletic ability, artistic talent, scientific ability, and financial success.

My staff listed just about every trait you could imagine when I asked what *else* they'd like to know about a sperm donor: They would want him to be sociable, outgoing, generous, well-disciplined, creative, imaginative, thoughtful, and sensitive. They'd want to know his religion, cultural background, geographical location, education, occupation, exposure to environmental hazards, hobbies, hair and eye color, height ("I don't want short kids"), sense of humor, family history ("To give the child a sense of roots"), temperament, "general philosophy," "why he's doing it," and, like the Dewar's Scotch profiles, "last book he read." Some would also want to know his name and to meet him.

And in what professions would women look for men who meet these requirements for sperm donors? The biggest vote by far, almost half, goes to successful businessmen. Lawyers, scientists, and scholars are a distant second, with about 20 percent of the women voting for each of them. Athletes, writers, and teachers make up an even more distant third, with 12 percent of the vote for each of those groups. Following that are artists and musicians, with 7 percent each, religious leaders, with 6 percent, politicians or statesmen, with 4 percent, entertainers, with 2 percent, and actors, at the very bottom, with 1 percent.

But as soon as we put names to those general categories, women's priorities change. The politicians, entertainers, and actors rise right to the top. The late president John F. Kennedy and former newscaster Walter Cronkite take the most votes, with 16 percent each. Actor Robert Redford and the physicist Albert Einstein are close behind, with 13 and 12 percent of the votes, respectively, and Chrysler savior Lee Iacocca gets 10 percent. Trailing behind, in order of declining favor, are Neil Armstrong, Mahatma Gandhi, John D. Rockefeller, Billy Graham, Leonard Bernstein, Henry Kissinger, Pablo Picasso, and John Lennon. *Fully 28 percent of the women we surveyed can find no one on the list they would want as a sperm donor.*

Most of the ten thousand women who turn to the twenty or so sperm banks in this country every year don't really know what they're getting, and the banks and their selection practices aren't regulated in any way. In a letter to the *New England Journal of Medicine* last year, a physician from the Centers for Disease Control said there have been reports of gonorrhea, hepatitis B, and other diseases transmitted to women through AID. A study published in the same journal in 1979 found there was very little genetic screening or even biochemical testing of sperm donors, and only a third of the physicians providing AID services even kept permanent records of donors. Only half the states have even passed laws making the husband of the birth mother the legitimate father of an AID child. (The laws themselves raise another problem. Depending on how they are worded, the laws may take legal fatherhood away from the man who supplies his sperm to a married surrogate so she can bear his child.)

This is just one more area where we need to bring our laws into the 1980s before we can even begin to be prepared for the twenty-first century.

o   o   o

The majority of American women, 59 percent, wouldn't be interested in choosing the sex of their first child. Twenty-four percent, however, *would* want to choose and would want it to be a boy. Another 12 percent would choose a girl, and 4 percent would want a boy and girl, fraternal twins. We didn't ask how many would want to choose the sex of a second child, but I suspect many more people would want to use selection techniques then to get a child of the opposite sex. (Two-thirds of the English women we talked to would also rather let nature take its course, while a third of the women in Japan and South Africa would want to choose boys for their first born.)

Nature alone gives you a 50 percent chance of getting a girl or a boy. The sex selection techniques available now are still in hot dispute, and even their inventors claim to boost your odds to only 75 percent. There are no guaranteed sex selection methods, unless a couple is willing to go through genetic screening and abort a child of the unwanted sex. Today very few couples, except those who carry hereditary diseases like hemophilia that only boys suffer from, have expressed any interest in going through screening and possible abortion just to get a child of a specific sex.

All the sex selection methods that rely on time and temperature and diet will do you little good. *If you want to select the sex of a child you'll have to resort to sperm separation and artificial insemination.* One procedure invented and patented by reproductive physiologist Ronald Ericsson of Gametrics Ltd. in Sausalito, California, promises to give you a 75 percent chance of conceiving a boy. This process, offered at clinics across the country, involves filtering a sperm sample several times through columns of the human blood protein called albumin. This is supposed to leave you with a sample that's predominantly Y-chromosome-bearing sperm. A procedure invented in Belgium and offered at the Philadelphia Fertility Institute filters sperm through a thick gel and is reputed to leave you with an enriched concentration of X-chromosome-bearing sperm that will boost your chances of conceiving a girl.

When researchers at Lawrence Livermore National Laboratory in California used laser-aided cell-sorting technology to examine sperm samples processed by these and other commercial techniques, however, they found no differences in the proportion of X and Y sperm.

We *will* develop much better sex selection methods in the near future, simply because a reliable process would mean billions of dollars to the livestock industry. (The world needs far fewer bulls than milk cows.) Animal scientists are hard at work on new sperm separation techniques. One possibility is the use of monoclonal antibodies—highly specific antibodies developed by new genetic technologies—programmed to seek out and destroy sperm of the "wrong" sex.

These methods will unquestionably be made available to humans, and some people will use them. *But I doubt we are going to have to worry about those old fears of an all-male generation.* In a future where a son or daughter both have an equal shot at making a mark on the world and carrying on the family name, parents aren't going to have a strong preference for one sex over the other. *Besides, they are going to have more important choices to make about the traits and characteristics of their child.*

I can tell from our survey results that women already have a strong sense of "quality control" about the children they bring into the world, and science is going to provide us with many more ways to exercise that selectivity.

Half of the American women, including two-thirds of those who have no children yet, would want to undergo genetic screening if they were pregnant to check the fetus for possible abnormalities. Another third aren't sure and only 15 percent say they would *not* want genetic screening. (Screening has an even bigger following in other countries: two-thirds of the Japanese and South African women we talked to and three-quarters of the English would want amniocentesis.)

Three-quarters of American women would consider aborting a fetus, mostly for moderate-to-severe abnormalities ranging from risk of early heart disease to mental retardation. Thirty-eight percent would consider aborting only for extremely serious conditions such as Down's syndrome, risk of schizophrenia, and diseases that destroy the immune system. Another 34 percent would consider aborting for moderately serious disorders, including blindness, muscular dystrophy, and risk of early heart problems. Only 4 percent would abort for less serious conditions such as asthma, reading disabilities, or diabetes. *Only 23 percent of American women wouldn't consider abortion at all.* That includes a high of 30 percent among homemakers and a low of 15 percent among childless women. (Only 7 percent of the Japanese, 12 percent of the English, and 20 percent of the South Africans we surveyed wouldn't consider abortion.)

For all the noise and violence we're hearing from the antiabortion forces today, it's clear that these people do not represent the majority and should have no right to force their opinions on others. With better birth control information in the future, abortions could actually decline. This will probably happen even though our ability to identify genetic diseases at the fetal level is going to continue to grow, and so will our list of reasons for aborting even a wanted conception. (Just a word for those of you who have had to undergo an abortion: a study released in 1984 by the American College of Obstetricians and Gynecologists shows that abortions, even multiple ones, do *not* decrease a woman's fertility.)

Genetic screening by amniocentesis has been available since the late 1960s, and it has become standard practice for obstetricians to offer the tests to pregnant women aged thirty-five and over. In fact, if a physician doesn't notify a woman of her risks and the availability of the test and a Down's syndrome child is born, the parents can successfully sue for wrongful birth and the child can sue for wrongful life.

In amniocentesis, a hollow needle is inserted through the skin of the lower abdomen into the womb, and a sample of the amniotic fluid that surrounds the fetus is withdrawn. In this fluid are cast-off fetal cells that can be grown in a lab dish and then examined for genetic or chromosomal abnormalities. The major drawback with this process is that it can't be done until seventeen to twenty weeks into the pregnancy, and the testing can take two to three weeks more. This means if an abortion is needed, it has to be done at five months.

In 1983, a new procedure called chorionic villus biopsy was introduced into the United States after more than a decade of use in Russia and China. It is still being safely-tested now, but *many geneticists are already predicting it will revolutionize the diagnosis of birth defects.* The major advantage is that it can be performed at eight to eleven weeks into the pregnancy and the test results can be obtained in one or two days. This means a woman can make decisions about abortion long before the fetus stirs.

The chorion is the outer sac surrounding a fetus, and villi are rootlike strands of fetal tissue that project from it early in pregnancy. To get a sample of fetal tissue to test, a physician inserts a catheter through the cervix into the uterus and removes a fragment of a villus.

Virtually all of the hundred or so known chromosome abnormalities are detectable now by an examination of the chromosomes from fetal cells. By 1981, scientists also had the ability to check the fetal cells for more than 200 genetic diseases such as sickle cell anemia and Tay-Sachs disease. Each of these tests is still time-consuming, however, and offered in only a few medical centers. Therefore, unless a woman or her husband has a family history of genetic disease, chromosome abnormalities are all that a fetus will be tested for today. That's not good enough for the future, however.

All of us carry single copies of some five to ten potentially lethal genes for diseases like cystic fibrosis, muscular dystrophy, or sickle cell anemia. This is called our "genetic load." Only when you marry a person whose genetic load overlaps yours do you risk bearing a child with two copies of the genes for these "recessive" diseases. Today, most couples have no idea what potentially harmful genes they carry until they give birth to a defective child. Then, if it's a disease such as sickle cell anemia, which we can detect, all their future pregnancies can be screened. This is the only practical course right now, but in the future, as we expand our list of detectable diseases from the hundreds to the thousands, we won't have to wait until a damaged child is born to spot potential problems.

Scientists are already building prototypes of automated gene and chromosome analyzers that will be able to examine the DNA of every fetus for hundreds of possible defects. Eventually a genetic profile will be part of the health record of every person, as I mentioned in an earlier chapter. We'll have lists of our own risk factors and the genetic load we bear. When we compare it to our mate's, we'll know just what genetic dangers our children face.

The real goal of genetic research, however, is not just diagnosis and abortion but *cure*. Some cures may only require that we supply a missing enzyme or protein, such as growth hormone to overcome dwarfism, which became available recently through genetic engineering. We can already produce many of these substances by genetically engineering bacteria or yeast to turn them into virtual human protein factories. But cures for other defects will require that we "engineer" individuals by inserting new genes into their cells. Scientists are now preparing to use viruses to carry new genes into children with crippled immune systems and into others with a bizarre form of cerebral palsy, called Lesch-Nyhan syndrome, that compels them to bite and mutilate their own lips and fingers. (Unlike IVF and embryo transfer, human genetic engineering is getting the rapt attention of federal regulatory agencies, and scientists are getting the research money to do the background work that's needed.)

This kind of gene therapy targets the body with virus-carried genes that correct the defect only in certain critical body tissues. A more far-reaching kind of genetic change can be done at the embryonic stage and would alter every cell in the body, including the egg or sperm-forming cells. No one has proposed such experiments on humans yet. This means the genetic change would be passed along to all descendants. By taking a microscopic glass needle and injecting genes into a mouse embryo, molecular biologists are already able to create new strains of mice, including one that carries rat growth genes and consequently achieves twice its normal size.

With human embryos now accessible in lab dishes, the opportunity to experiment is there if we want it. Curing defects in an embryo hardly seems worthwhile, however, even if we could detect them. Some scientists suggest we'll eventually develop a procedure for "embryonic biopsy," stealing a cell or two from an early embryo, then freezing it while enough cells grow to test for genetic defects. (The people at Fertility and Genetics Research, Inc., suggest we'll some day wash all embryos out of our wombs at the five-day stage for genetic testing and reimplantation.) But why try to cure an embryo if we do find a defect? It would be easier to discard it and implant one that tested out healthy.

The real application of genetic engineering to embryos may come when we locate genes that can add a little something extra to the embryo—a second helping of intelligence, kindness, humor, or some other trait we value.

Critics of this research may be surprised to see that 93 percent of American women are already comfortable with the idea of human genetic engineering to the point that they'd consider using it on their children. Fully 83 percent say they'd consider making genetic changes in their child for health reasons only. Another 11 percent, and that includes up to 15 percent of the older, higher-income, and childless women, and those in professional and managerial jobs, would consider making genetic changes in intelligence. Nine percent would consider genetic alteration of personality and emotional characteristics, and 3 percent would think about changing a child's physical characteristics. (One in five women we surveyed in Japan and South Africa and one in four of the English wouldn't consider any genetic changes, but the other 75 percent to 80 percent of those women would give slightly stronger consideration than Americans to changes in intelligence, personality, and physical traits.)

An issue we'll have to face in the future, if genetic enhancement of intelligence or other traits becomes possible, is how to deal with societal ethics and the peer pressure involved. No one wants her child to be left behind. "I would change these traits if it was so common that not to do it would leave the child disadvantaged in comparison to its peers," one of my staffers says. Another agrees, "I would like to change physical traits if it would help, but I'd be scared to fool around with nature. Yet I would do it if it helped the child and gave it an advantage."

o   o   o

I think it's time the United States followed the lead of England and Australia and began to recognize and clarify all the new circumstances of motherhood and fatherhood. And while we're at it, we should do a better job of dealing with all those types of parental relationships that arise from our lifestyles instead of our technology. I'm talking about a child's relationships with stepparents, foster parents, and even grandparents.

Kate Bartlett, director of Duke University Law School's Child Advocacy Clinic, noted that our child custody and responsibility laws are still based on the idealized premise that all children grow up in nuclear families with their two natural parents. And unless these biological parents are judged unfit or abandon the child, their claims usually take precedence. The child may be closer to her grandmother or stepfather, but those psychological ties lose out to genetics. Why should a stepfather have no legal rights in a child's life unless a natural father is willing to give up all of his? Bartlett has called for "custody decisions based on a new doctrine of nonexclusive parenthood" so that a child can maintain important family ties with more than one set of parents at a time.

As birth technologies and alternative family styles blur the significance of genetic lineage, I hope all of us will begin to feel a greater sense of responsibility toward all the children around us, no matter how they came into the world. This is the feeling of extended family I believe will replace the exclusive nuclear family. And I think we and our children will be better for it.

I don't find any reason to fear the consequences of our new ways of making babies, and neither do most American women. *Nearly half of the women we surveyed believe the relationship between women and their children will change for the better in the future and that children will be better planned, more wanted, and more loved. Another third think there will be no changes at all.* Only 11 percent fear that "children will be ordered like consumer goods, and the relationship will be less personal." (More than 80 percent of the women we surveyed in other countries also foresee no change at all, or a change for the better.)

So even when we talk about *Brave New World* scenarios, most women today don't see the future as ominous. Like Kelly, Nina, and Adrian, I believe most women today already look forward to tomorrow's family life and the new degree of freedom and responsibility we'll have in bringing children into the world.

9 TECHNO HOMES

"How old are you?" she wanted to know.

"Thirty-two," I said.

"Then you don't remember a world without robots. There was a time when humanity faced the universe alone and without a friend. Now he has creatures to help him; stronger creatures than himself, more faithful, more useful, and absolutely devoted to him. Mankind is no longer alone. Have you ever thought of it that way?"

—Isaac Asimov, *I, Robot*

There are few limits to what a technological society can do.

—Freeman Dyson

Whether you own a personal computer or not, chances are your home is already host to several little slices of silicon intelligence. They're in your "smart" telephone, video cassette recorder, digital TV, videodisc player, digital dishwasher, programmable microwave oven, automated swimming pool cleaner, music snythesizer, electronic burglar and smoke alarm, and refrigerator that beeps when you leave the door open too long.

Right now you probably don't think of all these separate electronic gadgets as a single system. But you soon will. *The 1990s will be the decade when all our microprocessor-controlled machines and appliances will be integrated into a single household network controlled by a personal computer. More importantly, that's the decade when these home nerve centers will be connected to the outside world,* by satellite or by special optical fiber cables.

As a result, women like Adrian and Nina won't have to spend their spare time writing checks, keeping track of household expenses, planning meals, making lists, or shopping for anything from groceries to new tires for the car. Their computers will do these chores, on command or under standing orders. They'll transfer funds, compose nutritional meal plans, order needed supplies, scan electronic catalogs for the best prices, maintain a preset humidity and temperature in each room, make sure the oven and VCR go on and the pool cleaner goes off at the right times, and call the fire department or police if home sensors detect smoke or intruders. (If this sounds too orderly for you, don't worry. Convenience markets already do a booming business by counting on us to forget the milk or be a little spontaneous in our appetites, and I don't think they're going to go out of business in the future. Computers can't anticipate our sudden whims, but they are good at doing what they are told and I think they'll relieve us of a lot of our daily to-do lists.)

If the women of tomorrow or their husbands or their children want to watch a dance program shown on Chinese TV, examine Van Gogh's paintings, or find information on today's stock prices or tomorrow's flights to San Francisco, they'll simply ask their computers—first by keyboard and later by voice. And when they have babies, and want to be with them, these women will be able to work at home and "telecommute" to their offices without losing professional stride.

Although the terms "electronic cottage" and "telecommute" are already becoming clichés, the reality is just beginning to come together for most of us. Throughout the United States, England, France, and Japan, pilot programs offering computerized home banking, shopping, news, community bulletin boards, and swap clubs are being tested. And thousands of individuals have hooked their home computers into telephone lines by means of devices called modems, which allow them to "talk" to their office computers or search through commercial databases for facts on everything from the pedigrees of North American racehorses to child abuse laws to the nutritional content of chocolate mousse.

The central technology in all this, of course, whether it's a desktop model or a tiny microprocessor, is the computer. At home as well as in the working world, we've entered what's been called the computer or information age. And I was happy to find that *this new age is causing more excitement than uneasiness among women (except, ironically, in Japan).*

An overwhelming 86 percent of the American women say they feel excited about our entry into the computer age. Some of these women must also feel a little ambivalent because, overall, 44 percent express some uneasiness. (In South Africa and England, too, nearly twice as many women say they're *not* uneasy. But in Japan, the proportions are reversed—53 percent of the women we talked to say the computer age makes them uneasy, and only 28 percent feel comfortable or excited about it.)

I know some of you automatically think of adjectives like "cold" or "sterile" when you imagine the high-tech home of the future. But computers are no more cold or unattractive than sewing machines, stereos, or TVs. You don't even have to live with steel and plastic unless that's your taste. Enterprising furniture manufacturers have already responded to the new age by producing computer desks and worktables in every style from French Provincial to Early American. You can even pick a matching console for your big-screen TV.

And that's all the high tech you'll ever need see in tomorrow's home—a video screen of some size and a terminal that will probably be much smaller than today's desktop computers. (By the 1990s some of us will have robots, too, of course. And by the time girls of Kelly and Adrian's generation set up their first homes, robot servants will be as common as dishwashers.) The cables that will integrate all your electronic devices and link them with the outside world will be no more visible than the electrical and telephone wires that snake unseen behind your walls today.

Some people would also like to blame computers for disrupting their family life, in particular turning their husbands into unsociable "nerds" who spend all their free time at the terminal. But a study released last year by New York University showed that home computers don't change the basic social organization of families at all. Instead, existing family patterns shape the use of the computer. If there is already sibling rivalry, then the kids will argue over the computer, too. If the husband and wife have a warm relationship before the machine arrives, it will continue. In fact, if the computer displaces anything, the researchers found, it's TV viewing. So if a person loses her husband to a computer, something was probably wrong with the relationship to begin with. If he hadn't bought the machine he probably would have buried himself in stamp collecting, watching sports, or some other hobby.

A third of the women we surveyed already have a personal computer in their homes, two-thirds are hooked up to cable TV systems, 57 percent have VCRs, and 44 percent have video-game players. As you might imagine, women with children own more of these things than do childless women.

Of the women who don't yet own computers, three-quarters say they want one, and 18 percent say they may get one. Working mothers, more than any other group, want computers, with 82 percent saying yes. Overall, only 7 percent of women say they *don't* want a computer. ***Three-quarters of those who don't own computers expect to buy one within the next one to five years.*** (Interestingly, half of the Japanese women say they *never* want a computer!)

I was surprised to find that even among women who already have computers at home, a third express some uneasiness about them. I think in many cases the machines may belong to their husbands or children and these women have never bothered to learn anything about them. In fact they're probably the same third of computer owners I mentioned earlier who say they *know nothing* about computers.

"I see seven-year-olds using them," one of our young editorial assistants said. "I feel left out, uneasy due to my ignorance." A supervisor said she's uneasy "because my nephews are smarter than I am and I hate it." Another staffer expressed a little discomfort because change is "going too fast and passing me by."

There's absolutely no reason for women to feel helpless about these machines, especially when there is one sitting in the house waiting to be explored. In fact there are strong reasons why women should be more eager than men to harness the potential of computers, especially in the home.

One in five women, and fully a third of the homemakers, tell us that a major technological breakthrough in the domestic environment would have the greatest positive effect on their lives. That's twice the number who say their lives would be greatly improved by a breakthrough in the work environment. (The Japanese women we talked to are almost equally divided between work and home on this.)

I think computers—and the household robots that will follow—*are* the breakthrough these women say they want. ***Computer services have the potential to relieve the time pressures on women trying to juggle the double responsibilities of career and family. But technology alone won't perform any miracles.*** It won't automatically change a woman's role in the family, the way chores are divided up, the relationships between husbands, wives, and children. ***We women have to learn enough about technology to make it work for us.***

Listen to one of the "horrifying possibilities" for the future imagined by feminist Jan Zimmerman in *The Technological Woman: Interfacing with Tomorrow:*

"Women isolated at home, trapped in electronic cages, using cable TV, computers, and touch-tone phones for video shopping and telephone banking. Women reading *Family Circle* magazine on the TV screen to see which recipes they should pull from their home computer file, while daughter Jane plays with her voice-synthesized doll and son Dick plays computer chess. Women forced to do data entry or circuit board assembly from home for piecework pay, so they can work and care for children at the same time."

If women find themselves in such traps, they'll have no one but themselves to blame. Savvy women have the power to decide which technologies they want in their homes and the ground rules under which they'll be used. The world's great libraries and virtually all the books, films, databases, magazines, and journals will be available, and we'll choose our own reading material. If we're doing interesting things with computers, our daughters and our sons will likely follow our lead. Men as well as women can care for children and telecommute if they choose, and the work can range from word processing or designing machine parts to managing institutional stock portfolios. In fact, a good friend of mine who is in banking recently described the success of a new program his bank has for executive women with young children. Under a special plan, these women have the option of staying home part-time and working via computer terminals installed by the bank.

Few people, men or women, want to be isolated at home all the time. By reducing the frenzy of household errands and paperwork, computer systems can actually leave us with more time for ourselves, our families, friends, and hobbies. And we can choose to spend our new leisure time any way we please.

I also believe women of tomorrow are going to use electronics to reassign household responsibilities and help make all family members more competent, self-sufficient, and less dependent on mother. (We saw earlier that virtually all of you want your husbands to pull an equal share of the load around the house.) Many children of working parents already come home to an empty house after school, put the laundry in the washing machine, and start dinner. This sort of independence and worldliness in youngsters alarms some sociologists to the point that they have been predicting the "death of childhood" as we've come to know it in the past century.

I don't think it is something to worry about. None of us wants to see six-year-olds apprenticed to work in taverns and factories ever again or even see them hanging around unsupervised for hours after school. We'll continue to shelter our children from the most brutal realities of the world. But many children of nineteenth-century America weren't any the worse for having to feed chickens and milk cows before school. I imagine they felt more like useful members of their families than some of today's aimless and disoriented young people. The teenagers of 2000, like Adrian and her brother, can play an even larger role in family life by helping with bill paying, meal planning, and other tasks simplified by computer. And they'll learn while doing it.

There is certainly plenty of work to be shared, despite all the labor-saving devices we've filled our homes with so far. Despite what you may have heard, it's a myth that the invention of refrigerators, vacuum cleaners, and self-cleaning ovens has reduced the burden of household chores. Brown University historian Joan Wallach Scott points out that *modern appliances lightened the manual labor involved in housework but didn't cut down the hours. Between 1920 and 1960, the hours homemakers spent on housework actually increased.* And city women spent more time on chores than did farm women, even though the farm women still canned their own food and had more physical labor to do.

Today, married women who work spend twenty-five to thirty-five hours a week on household responsibilities, and full-time homemakers put in forty to fifty hours. (Despite their almost doubled burden, however, even women whose jobs are less than glamorous are so glad to be out of the house that most wouldn't quit work even if they could. *USA Today* found in a 1984 poll that even "if they had enough money to maintain their current style of living without working, only one-third of the women—compared with one-fifth for men—said they would quit their jobs.")

Several factors deserve the blame for our increased workload at home. One is the decline in domestic servants, another is the fact that women have taken over many household responsibilities formerly done by men, and a third is the rise of "home economics" and consumerism and new standards of cleanliness never practised by our grandmothers.

Most middle-class homemakers of the Victorian era had help. "In 1870, 52 percent of employed women were servants," Scott writes. "By 1920 the fraction had decreased to 16 percent . . . In the household without servants, the housewife became the sole domestic worker." (Several columnists, including Art Buchwald, have taken career women to task for hiring other women to do their "dirty work." However, I certainly don't think it's a job to be ashamed of. No one should feel guilty about hiring people to help at home as long as fair wages are paid and the person is shown the same dignity any employee expects. Men certainly don't feel guilty about hiring plumbers and auto mechanics to do what used to be their chores.)

When the automobile replaced the horse and buggy, women took over the driving and were left to shuttle kids to school and run the family errands that men used to handle, Ruth S. Cowan pointed out in *More Work for Mother*. Indoor plumbing, gas, and electricity relieved men of chopping wood, pumping water, and hauling kerosene and gave women more fixtures *to clean*. Men turned the repairs they used to do themselves over to plumbers and electricians, and women were left to summon and wait for them (and deal with the inconvenience and mess in the meantime).

From the 1890s on came the rise of the home economics movement that "portrayed women as scientific managers of the health of the household," Scott notes, and placed new emphasis on the "principles of childrearing." Standards of cleanliness became increasingly elaborate as magazine articles and ads began to glorify spotless homes. Thousands of new cleansers, polishes, detergents, toiletries, paper goods, cleaning tools, and kitchen gadgets flooded the market. Supermarkets, filled with tens of thousands of choices in fresh, canned, and frozen foods, increased rather than shortened the time needed for meal planning and grocery shopping. We became consumers. We traded our washboards for washing machines, but we bought more clothes and started washing them after each wearing. (Heaven forbid your teenager should appear at school in the same outfit two days in a row!) We stopped paying cash, opened charge and checking accounts, and found ourselves with monthly bills and checks to write. Men's work hours shortened and wages increased, so families began to go to movies and to entertain more. Women became social directors.

None of this is bad in itself. I'm glad we all bathe and wash our clothes more often and have more sanitary homes, abundant food choices, and leisure time to entertain. I certainly wouldn't choose to return to the 1890s. But *somehow along the way women not only took on more household burdens but also let society get away with tying our competence and self-worth to the condition of our homes*. Even today's successful women executives and physicists probably feel a little twinge of guilt if their homes aren't up to snuff and the family isn't getting homemade muffins every morning. Men feel no such twinges. The best of them today are willing to "help out" or even do their full share, but virtually none of them suffer any self-doubts for having dust on top of the refrigerator or taking the children to a fast-food place for supper.

The next generation of women is going to be less compulsive and possessive about household duties. We'll organize our lives so that we spend time on the things we're best at and with the people we care about. A woman of tomorrow will be the best biochemist or chairman of the board she can be during the day, spend time with her partner in the evening, indulge in her hobbies, and ride a bicycle or play games with her children if that's the way she enjoys spending her time. If she has to eat out, hire a sitter, send the clothes to the laundry, and buy her "homemade" cookies at Mrs. Field's in order to find time for the things she values (and this can certainly include baking homemade goodies if a woman gets pleasure from doing it), she won't feel a glimmer of guilt.

Computers will help. They can't take over the dusting and sweeping yet, but as we've seen, those aren't the most time-consuming chores in a modern household anyway. Let's look first at how women today expect to use their home computers.

o   o   o

The biggest role women see for computers right now is using them to help teach their children. I agree that for most families this is probably the best reason to have a computer today. *Forty to 60 percent would also use it to do family accounting and bookkeeping, file personal data like addresses and recipes, call up databases for information, and write letters and other text. About a quarter of women expect to play video or mental games or shop from home with their computers, and only 16 percent expect to use them to work at home and telecommute to the office.* (The Japanese women we talked to see almost no use for home computers, but half would play games on them if they had them.) I'll take a closer look at each of these areas, because I think our expectations about the usefulness of computers are going to change in the next decade.

Many of the tasks people use computers for today are fairly mundane, simply substituting the machines for what used to be done with paper and calculators. *Sixty-one percent of the women we surveyed say they would use their computers for family accounting and bookkeeping,* and that figure goes up to 71 percent among the younger age group. However, among the women who already have computers, only 52 percent say they use them for these tasks. (Half the South African and English women we talked to, but only nine percent of the Japanese, would use computers to keep family accounts.)

Fifty-eight percent expect to use computers to file things like addresses, recipes, and shopping lists. Only 44 percent say they'd use their computers as word processors, although 53 percent of women who already have computers use them this way. (Two-thirds of the English, a quarter of the South Africans, and only 7 percent of the Japanese would use them for word processing.) *Only 28 percent of women are interested in using the machines for playing video or mental games,* and that figure is about the same for women both with or without children. (Less than a third of the women in the other countries we surveyed were interested in computer games, with the exception of the Japanese, as I mentioned, who seem to feel that's about all home computers are good for.)

The least popular of all the possible uses we mentioned for computers is working at home and telecommuting with them. Only 16 percent of American women are interested in doing this, and that includes a high of 21 percent of childless women—not the group I would have expected to favor it the most. (In contrast, half of the women we interviewed on my staff and in England would like to telecommute, compared to 17 percent of the South Africans and only 7 percent of the Japanese.)

In answer to another question, *two-thirds of the American women say that if they had a choice about where they did their jobs, they'd split the working time between their homes and offices.*

The word "telecommute" was coined a dozen years ago by Jack Nilles, director of the University of Southern California's Information Technology Program. He figured that by the year 2000, about 10 million of us would be spending part of our time working at home and part in the office. (There aren't any reliable figures, but so far the numbers seem to be in the tens of thousands, not millions.) Five years ago, futurist Alvin Toffler made a stronger prediction, proclaiming, in *The Third Wave,* that executives and secretaries alike would retreat to their homes to work, reversing the 200-year-old pattern of the Industrial Revolution, which had shifted economic life away from the home.

Our survey shows that John Naisbitt was more correct when he foresaw in *Megatrends* a very limited future for telecommuting: "Yes, it's fun for a while to escape the daily grind. No doubt about that. But after a time, most miss the office gossip and the warm interaction with co-workers . . . Alone in their electronic cottages, they feel a high-tech isolation . . . My own sense of it is that not very many of us will be willing to work at home."

One of my copywriters says, "I freelanced when I first started, but it was too lonely. I'd like to work at home, but I'd want to be able to come to the office occasionally, too." An editor notes that she "tried staying at home and working. I hated it. I got bored to death." Another thinks, "If I were to have a family I would want the flexibility of being able to stay at home, but I also need the interaction with other people." (Not everyone feels this need. "I like my privacy," one of our sales people says. "I came from a family of eleven children. I was socialized enough." And another feels she'd just as soon get her socializing in at her health club instead of at the office.)

I think working at home appeals mainly to people like computer programmers, freelance and technical writers, designers, architects, and consultants. These are usually self-motivated people, who tend to go off by themselves and work day and night when they are absorbed in a challenging project anyway. (Most studies show people put in longer hours when they work at home, and some even spend full days at the office in addition to the time at home.) Some handicapped people and parents of young children might also choose to work at home, at least part time (although I can't imagine anything more distracting than trying to work and tend a toddler at the same time).

But most careers, especially executive and professional ones, will always require a lot of time in the office, lab, or factory. Certainly, any woman who wants to move up in the executive hierarchy today can't afford *not* to be there to make her presence felt and her voice heard when it counts.

Some people have legitimate fears that women in lower-status clerical jobs like data entry could be exploited by companies that force them to work at home in "electronic sweatshops," at machines that count keystrokes per minute, and pay them piecework rates. Nevertheless, I think the AFL-CIO was wrong when its leaders voted two years ago to try to get computer home-work banned. We're going to have to adjust our wage and employment laws in the future to protect the most vulnerable workers and still allow independence and flexibility for telecommuters who can take care of themselves in the job market.

Now, we get into more futuristic uses of computers when we turn to electronic shopping and use of databases. These are the sorts of things that I predict are going to bring many of those computers that were purchased only as status symbols back out of the closets and into daily use. *Almost half the women we surveyed in the United States would use their computers to gain electronic access to medical information, catalogs, directories, encyclopedias, and other data.* (Eighty percent of my staff, half the women we talked to in England, a third of those we interviewed in South Africa, but only 7 percent of the Japanese expect to use computers this way.)

If I were a mother right now, I'd forget about encyclopedias and buy my child a computer, a modem, and a membership in a multipurpose database. For adults and children both, quick access to information is probably the most important thing a computer can provide today, and it's the one thing computer makers advertise the least. The *Omni Online Database Directory* (published with Macmillan) includes reviews of more than a thousand databases that contain information from 50 million books and 100 million periodicals, all of it available on your home computer screen simply by dialing a telephone number and punching a few keys. And more databases are being created every year.

If you're a professional in chemistry, nutrition, city planning, engineering, law, marketing, insurance, or dozens of other fields, there are specialized databases carrying the latest technical material in your area. Other popular computer networks like The Source offer an eclectic mix of worldwide ski reports, nationwide restaurant directories, business and stock market news, bulletin boards, classified ads, barter and trade clubs, games, electronic mail services, travel services, national and international news commentaries, UPI wire service news, and hundreds of other services. (I use the on-line restaurant directories for help when I have to take a client to dinner in Nashville or some other city I don't travel to very often.)

Only 22 percent of women we surveyed say they would want to shop from home by computer, but I know this proportion will go up as home banking, shopping, and information services proliferate in the 1990s. (Fully a third of the English women are interested in this service, as are half of my staff, but fewer than 10 percent of the women we talked to in South Africa and Japan.)

When I say shopping, I don't mean shopping for clothes and shoes and things most of us enjoy selecting in person. (Although, if you already buy most of your clothes by mail from catalogs, this would be just the thing for you.) But I'd much rather call up a *Consumer Reports* review of microwave ovens on my personal computer, pick out an oven, compare prices from electronic catalogs, and have one delivered than trudge all over the city dealing with shop assistants who know less about microwave ovens than I do.

Computer shopping, banking, and other consumer services are already available in some parts of the country, but they won't really flourish until more of us come "on-line" to use them. Consultant Richard Adler, of the Institute for the Future, in Menlo Park, California, compares the state of computer services now to the early days of radio. "Radio was invented in the nineteenth century," he told one interviewer. "But it took twenty years before anyone came along and invented broadcasting. And then it was another five years before anyone thought of advertising on it." (And with advertising, the cost of these new computer services to subscribers could be as low as $15 a month.)

The services are called *videotex* if they are offered through telephone lines or TV cables, and *teletext* if the signals arrive by broadcast. With teletext, however, you can only receive information. Videotex is two-way, or "transactional" as the industry people call it. You can use it not only to look at airline schedules and video catalogs but to book reservations, order merchandise, and pay for it electronically by transferring money from your account or using a credit card number.

Through videotex pilot programs like Antiope in France, Prestel and Oracle in England, Telidon in Canada, Viewtron in South Florida, Gateway in Southern California, and Keycom in Chicago, subscribers can receive up-to-the-minute news, sports and weather reports, stock quotations, educational programs, and travel information on their home TV screens as well as shop and bank using their telephones and special terminals. Eventually anyone with a modem and computer of any sort should be able to subscribe. For instance, the first clients of Gateway had to buy or lease terminals from the telephone company, but soon personal computer owners will be allowed to hook into the network with their own equipment.

The U.S. programs are being sponsored by large banks, TV networks, publishing companies, and other major corporations like AT&T, Knight-Ridder and Times-Mirror newspapers, CBS, and Chase Manhattan Bank. (Other institutions like Chemical Bank, in New York, and Bank of America, in California haven't waited for full videotex services to gain popularity. More than ten thousand Bank of America customers have been able to pay bills and transfer funds from one account to another by personal computer and phone line since 1983.) In 1986 IBM, CBS, and Sears are expected to team up to launch the biggest videotex offering yet. So there's no lack of money on the supply side. And everyone expects the demand to be there, too, as soon as people realize how much time these systems can save them.

The Cleveland-based forecasting firm Predicasts figures that by 1995, 20 percent of American homes will be hooked up to videotex services and fully two-thirds will have teletext available. A National Science Foundation report suggests that by the year 2000, about 40 percent of our homes will have videotex.

Two-thirds of American women say they'll use their computers to teach their children and to learn alongside them. This includes 86 percent of the working mothers in our survey. (More than two-thirds of the women in England and South Africa, but only 11 percent of the Japanese, would also use their computers this way.)

For two reasons, this *is* the most important thing you can do with a home computer and all the on-line services it provides now. The first is that your children need to grow up to be comfortable with computers and aware of what the machines can do. The second reason is that *the public school system in this country is a disgrace, and parents really have no choice but to take on more of the responsibility of educating their own children.*

"We've got seventeen million people in the United States who can't read at all," futurist Marvin Cetron, of Forecasting International, told a gathering recently. "We have forty-seven million who can't read at the third grade level, who can't draw an analogy, can't draw an inference, don't know what a percentage is, a ratio. They can't solve a problem . . . It's a shame. It's the first generation whose SAT scores were lower than those of their parents."

We've had plenty of studies telling us how bad the schools are and outlining solutions—eight major reports in 1983 alone. They call on us to lengthen the school day or year or both, pile on more homework, train better teachers, pay teachers more, and make the students sit through more English, math, computer, and science courses. But even if these remedies were implemented (and the record of the past few years isn't promising) they'd still leave us with essentially the same school system we've had for a century.

"Teachers would still be standing or sitting in front of some twenty to thirty-five mostly passive students of the same age and giving out the same information at the same time to all these students, regardless of their individual abilities, cultural backgrounds, or learning styles," writes George Leonard, author of *Education and Ecstasy* and critic of the latest reform proposals. He believes that piling on more of the same will only worsen the morale of teachers and children. What we need, he adds, is to start "individualizing education as soon as possible, in every responsible way possible."

Leonard thinks computers will be the driving force in this effort, especially if we develop a new computerized curriculum "to teach students more than just how to use computers." (Not that teaching computer programming itself should be discouraged, although most people won't be programming their own computers any more often than they repair their own cars. Columbia University psychologist Eugene Galanter, who started The Children's Computer School in New York in 1980, has pointed out that since rhetoric and military arts disappeared from our curriculum, children have been given no training in operational logic, "the logic of planning." "Programming," he says, "can provide this.")

"Given the will and imagination, it will soon be possible to use computers as the *primary* educational information-delivery system for most of the basic cognitive material now presented in the classroom," Leonard writes. "This will free teachers to serve as tutors, as seminar leaders, and as lecturers for special occasions."

This is the beginnings of the same sort of vision Gerard K. O'Neill gave us in *2081: A Hopeful View of the Human Future:* "In my ideal school of the future, children would assemble each afternoon for sports, music, and club activities that require group interaction. The mornings would be reserved for individual study, probably at home. The child would be in a private room in one-on-one interaction with a "tutor," the realistic holographic presentation of an actual human being, one of the rare, inspiring, one-in-a-thousand, superbly gifted teachers. Brief lectures, personally directed to the student and with lots of eye contact, would be aided by all possible tricks of costuming and special effects, but those lectures would have been staged as carefully as a dramatic movie and would have been preserved on videodiscs. With computer-generated responses, apparently coming from the personified tutor, there would then be an amusing rapid-fire give-and-take, highly involving, in which the tutor would devote all his attention to the student, teasing out answers, rewarding and scolding, and always stimulating thought and reinforcing memory."

In case you fear that technology can't do the job a real live teacher can, Andrew R. Molnar, of the National Science Foundation, has compiled studies showing that *computer-based instruction is more effective in boosting achievement and also leaves students with better attitudes and takes only about two-thirds the time that conventional teaching methods require to get across the same material.* This holds true from elementary school through college. And combining TV with computer lessons seems to be even more effective. (The NSF's 1983 report on the schools called for "making maximum use of new computerized information technology in teaching.")

Positive results are already coming in, too, from pilot programs that combine computer instruction with a technology O'Neill mentioned—optical videodiscs. You may already own a videodisc player hooked up to your TV to show movies or music videos. The system uses lasers both to read and inscribe information on plastic discs that look a lot like phonograph records. The discs hold many times as much information as do videotape or the floppy discs now used in computers. In fact, whole medical or engineering libraries can be encoded on today's discs. One disc now available at home-video stores contains more than 1,600 paintings, sculptures, drawings, and prints from the National Gallery of Art, along with information about the artists and their work.

When videodisc players are connected to personal computers instead of TVs, educational programs can be devised that let the student move at her own pace, switching around to any spot on the disc to call up text, lectures, illustrations, or video presentations. (This is the sort of technology I imagined Kelly using for her art history lectures, although since videodisc is available now she'll undoubtedly be using something that in forty years will be much more sophisticated.)

Almost everyone who understands these new technologies realizes that we can turn education around if we use them properly. But as Molnar says, many schools "are not taking the information revolution seriously." Our schools are pouring money into computers, of course, but few teachers know what to do with them and even fewer good software programs are available right now for children to use. Most computers in the schools today serve as little more than electronic workbooks or flash cards, letting students drill and practice on screen instead of on paper. (And some of the game programs are simply electronic babysitters.)

"Adding computers to the classroom without restructuring the U.S. educational system and its curriculum or without retraining . . . teachers will more likely create computer anxiety than productive thinking and problem solving," Molnar and Dorothy K. Deringer of Atari believe. "The goal of computer literacy offers a new way of thinking about thinking. Certainly, *the existing tendency toward counting computers rather than making computers count must be changed if computers are to have an impact on education.*"

But who knows how long this effort will take? I hope the schools will be *very* different when Kelly's and Nina's children are old enough to attend, but that's too long to wait if you have children now. With a computer at home, and a little effort spent learning which programs to buy for it and which databases to subscribe to, you can help make up for the deficiencies in your local school system. Innovative programs are available that allow children to compose music, create animated stories, assemble machines and factories on screen, make simulated trips across the Oregon Trail, "perform" genetics experiments, and play the part of a dinosaur trying to survive ecological change.

You can find reviews of programs in most computer magazines. Or ask your school or public library—they may have copies of evaluations provided by a nonprofit group called Educational Products Information Exchange Institute (EPIE), based at Columbia University's Teacher's College, which reviews software for nearly a fourth of the nation's schools. (I've been talking about children, but there are plenty of adult and professional education programs available, too. You can even take courses from major universities by computer and get college credit through the Electronic University program developed by TeleLearning Systems, Inc. Contact them at 505 Beach St., San Francisco, California, 94133 for details and a list of course offerings.)

All of what I've said about the importance of home computers is doubly true if you have daughters. Studies show that 93 percent of home computer users now are males. And boys greatly outnumber girls in the video arcades, computer camps, and even school computer classes. (More on this later.) The vast majority of future jobs are going to require at least some use of computer terminals, and the earlier girls get familiar with these machines, the more self-confident they're going to be in choosing careers.

o   o   o

Information technologies are going to become even more valuable and widely used when *all* of our homes are linked into a computerized communication network and our "smart" telephones merge with our computer terminals. The copper telephone cables that snake across our country from telephone pole to telephone pole or underground, carrying conversations in the form of electrical current, are being replaced by cables of hair-thin optical fibers that transmit voices, data, or video signals as pulses of laser light. Light beams carry a dozen times more information. (Today's phone system would be swamped if all of us suddenly went on-line with our computers.)

At Carnegie-Mellon University, in Pittsburgh, IBM is helping turn the campus into a miniature version of the city of the future. Soon, optical fiber cables will connect the more than 7,000 desktop computers on campus to each other and to a central campus data bank. University officials say that when the system is in place, students can write out their assignments at their own computer terminals, then push a few commands to transmit the work to their professors' electronic "mailboxes." Faculty members will call up these assignments on their screens, grade them, add their comments, and send them back electronically.

Bell Labs already has a prototype of a telephone terminal that would connect nicely into such a system. It is called EPIC, and is essentially a computer terminal with a built-in telephone handset and speakerphone. Unlike the memory telephones you can buy today that store a short list of numbers and dial them automatically at the push of a button, EPIC will tap into electronic directories nationwide in search of any number you ask for, then ring it. You can instruct EPIC to route incoming calls to other telephones, flash the number of the caller on the screen, or not bother ringing at all when calls come in from people you want to avoid. You can also hook it up to your microprocessor-controlled household alarms and instruct it to dial the police or fire departments automatically if trouble arises. And its computer can also be instructed to control your appliances, thermostats, and lights. (You can already buy a home appliance control system that will hook up to your present telephone—the X-10 Inc. system,

General Electric's HomeMinder, or Mitsubishi Electric's Housekeeping System. Mitsubishi's systems are already in wide use in Japan, and in the United States, one of the nation's largest homebuilders, Ryan Homes, is installing GE HomeMinders in all the new houses it builds. The National Association of Home Builders sees this as the wave of the future. Its research arm is now developing standards for "Smart Houses" in which home control systems are installed as standard equipment.)

Eventually we won't even have to type on a keyboard, or touch symbols on a touch-sensitive screen, or point to commands with a joystick or "mouse" to make our wishes known. We'll simply talk to our computers, or gesture, or even "think" what we want them to do. A research group at the University of Missouri and Rush-Presbyterian St. Luke's Medical Center, in Chicago, are working to get a computer to respond to the brain waves people emit just before they speak.

Devices that recognize human speech are already available, but Richard A. Bolt, of the Massachusettes Institute of Technology, notes that they "hear" with only about 65 percent accuracy unless a speaker is trained and uses specific words. Talking with a dumb machine can be frustrating. And since Bolt's specialty is human-machine interaction, he believes making computers truly "user friendly" means making them "as easy and as interesting to talk to as another person."

Bolt and his colleagues at MIT have created a Media Room where the room itself becomes a computer terminal. A person enters and puts on a special microphone and wristband connected to voice-recognition and magnetic locating devices. With these, the computer collects information about where the person is pointing as well as what she's saying while she asks it to create objects and move them about on a screen. If the person also wears a special pair of glasses, the computer can get more information by following her gaze as she looks at the screen while talking. And if the computer weighs all that information and still can't draw a reasonable conclusion about what the person wants, it asks her a pertinent question in a synthesized voice. Even with its occasional fumbles, the system is acceptable to users, Bolt says, because people can feel that it's "doing its best."

Some day, he believes, personal computers will interact with us the way we do with one another, watching our eyes and our gestures and listening to our voice to determine if we want quick, brief answers to our questions or book-length discourses, and sensing when our attention has wandered. The technology for doing this already exists "at varying levels of refinement," he writes. The most difficult part is developing the software programs that allow the computer to interpret what it sees and hears and to choose an appropriate response. When these are available, he believes, *then computers will provide the sort of convivial company that we'll all be glad to live and work with.* An early science fiction vision of this is "Albert Einstein," Robin Broadbent's marvelous holographic computer program in the "Gateway" series by Frederick Pohe.

(Even your dishwasher may respond to verbal commands someday, although industrial designers at General Electric found that people were uncomfortable when experimental dishwashers spoke back to *them*—"close the door," "use more soap." And I'll tell you later about automated typewriters that listen and type directly from speech, eliminating the need for a human typist.)

The kind of programs Bolt is talking about fall in the realm of *artificial intelligence.* And the kind of system he's predicting is the *fifth generation* computer that all the world's industrial nations are racing to develop by the early 1990s. Japan, the United States, England, and the Common Market nations have all launched major research efforts to develop computers many thousands of times more powerful than today's, machines "smart" enough to take verbal instructions and make both common sense and expert judgments. These computers, like the human brain, will perform thousands of operations simultaneously—a procedure called parallel processing—instead of one operation at a time in sequence, as today's computers do.

Computers this powerful will not only be able to tap into databases of medical information for us but will be able to diagnose our ailments as well. We'll simply discuss our symptoms as we would with a human doctor, and an "expert system" will sift through its memory for all the current knowledge in the field and apply the same basic assumptions human experts use to come up with a diagnosis. Actually, expert systems are the simplest form of artificial intelligence (common sense is much harder), and several are already being used to help doctors and hospitals make difficult diagnoses and aid geologists in locating underground oil reserves. Some computer experts think we'll all have access to such systems through our personal computers within five years.

And the subject of fifth generation computers brings me to another childhood dream—home robots. The development of really useful household robots depends on the power and intelligence we can put into that next generation of computers.

o   o   o

The world is already full of robots today, about sixty thousand of them, but seeing them is a disappointment for most people. They don't walk or talk like C3PO or bleep with emotion like R2D2, the *Star Wars* androids. Most are simply giant mechanical arms, their movements precisely programmed by computer brains and repeated continuously until the program is changed. They weld and spray-paint cars and appliances on factory assembly lines, shear sheep, slice sushi, aid in brain surgery, and grab errant satellites to be pulled into the Space Shuttle cargo bay. A more complex one, called "Galileo," is going to visit Jupiter in the latter part of this decade. Few people realize that Voyagers I and II, Mariner, and other space probes are in reality robots and that the work done by NASA on these and future probes is of vital importance in keeping America ahead in the science of robotics. Robots with camera eyes inspect welds inside reactor vessels at nuclear power plants, patrol prison corridors, and grade the fat content of bacon on the packing line.

I've wanted a real "live" robot ever since I read Isaac Asimov's *I, Robot* as a child. And five years ago we had a little automaton called *Omnivac*, which was developed to help us promote the magazine. Unfortunately, the technology that would allow it to roam about in crowds and converse a bit with people it met was so complex and cumbersome that we abandoned the project after a few conventions.

Much to the surprise of scientists and science fiction writers alike, mobility has turned out to be harder to program into robots than have simple automated speech, hearing, and vision. When you think about it, a great deal of brainpower—or computing power—is required to navigate through our cluttered world, watching, listening, and feeling for obstacles and making judgments about how to move around them without running off curbs, through sliding glass doors, or over the cat's tail. It requires what we call common sense, and as I mentioned, this has proved to be a lot more difficult to quantify and feed into computer memory than all our high-level knowledge on blood diseases or mineral deposits or chess strategies.

Researchers at Carnegie-Mellon University, under the leadership of Hans P. Moravec, have developed several robotic rovers with names like Pluto, Neptune, and Uranus that can pick their way *very* slowly through an unfamiliar obstacle course, using wheels for mobility, TV camera eyes, and powerful computer brains to choose their paths. But they can move only a few feet at a time, pausing for awhile to take new bearings and ponder the trajectory of their next roll as they zigzag around objects in their path. (Walking on two legs requires an even more incredible degree of sensory and motor coordination, so you won't see robots that look like C3PO anytime soon.)

The first generation of *personal robots* hit the consumer market only four years ago, and they're still little more than mobile conversation pieces. Most are shaped somewhat like a fireplug or canister and range in price from $1,000 to $6,000. Heath Co., RB Robot Corp., and Androbot, Inc., were first into the market, but by last year about two dozen companies were offering personal robots. (You can check with the National Personal Robot Association at P.O. Box 1366, Dearborn, Michigan, 48121, for information or schedules of robot shows and expositions in your area.) Most can be programmed to talk but can't hear (although several companies were promising to offer add-ons in 1985 that would allow their robots to respond to voice commands). They are blind but can follow a set path from one point to another once you "teach" it to them, and they'll stop when sonar and infrared sensors tell them they're about to run into something (so you don't have to worry about dogs or children crossing the robot's path.)

"It's the next generation of computers that will give robots the brain-power to be able to navigate in the home environment," Michael N. Forino, president and founder of Hubotics in Carlsbad, California, told us. And he thinks robots will become the command center of the household intelligence network, not desktop computers. "We've spent a lot of time and effort automating the factory, and next we started automating the office. The next major market is the home," he believes.

In a report last year, Future Computing, Inc., predicted the market for home robots would start to boom in 1990. By then, we should be able to buy *useful* home robots for about $2,000.

Not that today's personal robots are completely useless. Hubotics' Hubot, for instance, has a built-in AM-FM radio, a tape deck, a computer screen "face" that also serves as a black-and-white TV, and an onboard personal computer with a keyboard that pulls out from his midriff so that you can sit in front of him and write. If you tell him to, he can roll to your bedside at 6 A.M. and wake you up with whatever greeting you prefer. And with a vacuum attachment in his base he can clean the floor in his path.

"It's not going to sweep under the beds, but if you have to work and company is coming that evening, you can program it to turn on at four and run over the well-traveled areas," Forino says. He thinks today's personal robots are an evolutionary first step. "Look, I think of the dishwasher as a robot. It replaces you for jobs that are mundane. You can't buy or sell a home without a dishwasher now. We're where the dishwasher was fifteen years ago. As robots get into the home, people will want the convenience, just like we want TVs with remote control. You don't need it, but a year after you get it, you don't see how you lived without it."

Our survey shows women are ready for it. *Seventy percent of them are interested in owning a robot to help around the house.* Among women who already own personal computers, 77 percent would like a robot helper. (And yet, as I reported earlier, a mere 6 percent of women say they have some familiarity with robotics, and only a quarter of women are even interested in learning more. Of course, you aren't really going to need to know much more about the inner workings of a robot to use it than you do about the circuitry of your TV set. But I do think we're going to have to develop a greater curiosity about technologies that affect us if we hope to fit them into our lives in the most effective ways.)

There is no question about the number one duty women want to assign to their home robots in the future—housecleaning. Overall, 86 percent of women say they'd let a robot help with the housecleaning. (Women in England and South Africa felt just as strongly about this, but in Japan only 38 percent of the women we surveyed would be willing to let a robot help clean.)

"I'd have the robot clean the cat's litter box," one staffer says. "Wouldn't that be great?" Another is vehement in her dislike for housecleaning: "I hate cleaning the house. I absolutely hate it with a passion. I would have no compunction about letting a robot do the housecleaning. I get no enjoyment out of it. It is the most disgusting, boring chore that God put on this earth." But I did see some of that old possessiveness about housework showing up in a few answers: "I wouldn't trust a robot to clean my house, cook, or garden. It wouldn't do as good a job as me," one of our young managers told us. (She was just about to get married when she took that survey, so she may have had reason to change her mind by now about how perfect a house needs to be.)

The next most popular job for robots is serving as burglar alarms. Three-quarters of the American women, two-thirds of those in Japan and South Africa, and 86 percent of the English would let their robots patrol their homes. (This was the *only* task that a majority of the Japanese women we interviewed say they'd let a robot do.) Actually, this is one of the few jobs most of the home robots now on the market *can* do.

Doing the laundry came in a close third. Two-thirds of American women would turn that chore over to robots. Half would let the robot do the gardening, and 43 percent would send it into the kitchen to cook. (Even half of the English women and 42 percent of the Japanese would turn their cherished gardens over to robots, but only 17 percent of the South Africans would. Half of the English would also let the robots cook, but only 10 percent of the Japanese and South Africans want the machines in their kitchens.)

Thirty percent of American women would let robots help plan their personal finances, including 39 percent of all professional and managerial women (so would a third of the Japanese and South Africans and 40 percent of the English women we interviewed.)

For the home tasks that demand personal intimacy or understanding —maternal support and affection-oriented duties—women seem unwilling to have a robot step in. Only a quarter of American women say they'd let a robot help teach their children. (Sixteen percent of the English and only 7 percent and 4 percent of the South Africans and Japanese, respectively, would want the robot to teach their children.)

A mere 1 percent of American women think they would let a robot wash their babies or change their diapers. (The women in South Africa are equally against this use of robots, although 4 percent of the Japanese and a full 12 percent of the English would let robots tend their babies. As it turns out, the Englishwomen we talked with are more accepting of robots on almost every count.)

A few women figure they'll eventually get used to many things that make them squeamish now. "I think everything will eventually be taken over by robots, even washing and changing the baby," a production manager says. "I may not want to now, but if I'm used to it by then, I would probably do so." She'll have plenty of time to get used to it while researchers perfect the judgment and refine motor skills of robots.

Only 9 percent of American women—including 12 percent of those between the ages of twenty-five and thirty-four—think they would want a robot as a pet or companion. (A similar 9 percent of the English and Japanese, but only 3 percent of South Africans, could see robots this way.) Actually, Future Computing predicts that "the first home applications will be as playmates for children and companions for the elderly."

"C'mon, robots haven't any feelings," one of our secretaries says. Well, neither do cars, but we couldn't possibly have had a greater love affair with any machine than we've had with the automobile. We'll personalize and romanticize and mythologize our robots just as we have our cars, and write songs about them, too. I can just imagine what "keeping up with the Joneses" will be like when robot-customizing kits and fancy new attachments begin to come on the market: more adroit and sensitive mechanical arms, add-on chips to increase "brainpower," software programs to "teach" your robot the latest song-and-dance routines, or expert systems designed to ask or answer just about any silly riddle a six-year-old can come up with. We've always humanized our technology rather than let it dehumanize us. And if you think the next generation will have any trouble keeping company with robots, just remember that robots rival Cabbage Patch dolls as the hottest toys on the market.

I've never forgotten Asimov's tale of eight-year-old Gloria and her nurse-maid robot, Robbie. I wasn't much older than Gloria when I read it for the first time, and I envied her terribly. Robbie couldn't speak but walked on two legs, played hide-and-seek tirelessly, and listened patiently to Gloria's childish fantasies. When he wrote the story in 1940, Asimov put the date of Robbie's creation at 1996.

The real robots of 1996 won't move about as nimbly as Robbie, but they'll watch, listen, speak, and respond with an "intelligence" that might startle adults who don't understand how it was created. I'm sure children like Nina and Adrian will accept these creatures without questioning, however, and delight in their company. As computing speed grows ever faster, we'll teach our robots to be delicate with their "hands" and move about in our world without bumping into things. And that's when the last fussy woman will overcome her resistance and hand the robot the vacuum cleaner.

IV | AT WORK

IN THE WORLD

10 WOMEN'S WORK

... an intelligent, energetic, educated woman cannot be kept in four walls
—even satin-lined, diamond-studded walls—without discovering sooner
or later that they are still a prison cell. No home offers scope enough today
for the trained energies of an intelligent modern woman.
—Pearl S. Buck, 1938

In the heart of California's Silicon Valley, Apple Computer has created a glimpse of tomorrow, a futuristic factory where machines build machines with minimal human help. Just the sort of place that could use a woman's touch? Defying all tradition, that's exactly what this plant has. The feminine touches, however, don't exactly fit the clichés.

If you hang around the burn-in towers where four thousand newly assembled Macintosh computers, their screens aglow with test patterns, are being put through their paces, you're likely to run into the factory chief herself, thirty-two-year-old Debi Coleman. "I can't stay in my office for eight hours without going to the floor. It's physically impossible," says Coleman, a kinetic "part technocrat, part New England housewife" who never forgets that even with all the machines, her factory is full of people.

"There are six hundred people out here whose faces I know. I get a kick out of that. People are always kidding about my mother image. But I don't kid myself about it. I like it," says Coleman. "The effective mother is communicative, supportive, and affectionate, but not stifling, overwhelming, and bossy. And that's what effective management is. You've got to walk that line."

Her style may sound "soft" but her results aren't. Coleman got the Mac plant up to full production nine months after start-up, a goal many other factories take years to reach, and doubled its capacity four months later.

Past the towers at the end of the conveyor lines, assembly manager Joane McManus, thirty, watches proudly as finished Macs are automatically popped into cartons by a mechanical boxer and handed off to a robot for stacking.

"You know what I like about this?" she asks. "I'm a very straightforward person. I like to be able to go out at the end of the day and see what I did. I like to go out and say, 'okay, we made a thousand today.' I can count them. Manufacturing is just perfect for people like me who are very action oriented . . . You've always got to know what's standing in the way of running a record ship. Why aren't we moving at one hundred percent today? What can we fix that's keeping us from meeting our goal?"

Action oriented? What about those stereotypes of woman the communicator and man the action-taker? "All those stereotypes are being broken," McManus says. "I'm glad I live in the eighties because if I'd lived a generation before, a lot of these things would've been much more difficult for me to accomplish . . . My mother's goal for me was to marry a stockbroker, join the Junior League, have 2.3 children, and drive around in one of those station wagons with the wood paneling on the side."

Even in the 1980s there aren't many factories with women overseeing the production lines. But as American factories increasingly turn to automation to boost productivity, muscle power is becoming obsolete. "I feel I have a lot of power because I get a lot of things done," McManus says. "And here I'm allowed to do a lot of things."

Look along the conveyor belts at the men and women adding the screens and disk drives—about 15 percent of the Mac is put together by people —and you'll notice that this assembly line isn't a "female ghetto," as are most. All the workers know that the job they are doing today won't last forever, and many are already training to tend the robots that will take their places.

Move on and you'll run into more women—the program manager, the safety engineer, process engineers, and senior buyers who negotiate for everything from computer chips to robots. And of course, there are still more women in executive, financial, personnel, and secretarial jobs, too.

I've described the Mac factory to you to illustrate a much bigger point: *There is not much in today's workplace that the right woman can't do. In fact, there is almost nothing women aren't already doing, if only in small numbers.* And in the process, they are trouncing the old stereotypes of female nature. Yes, we can bring humane, people-oriented values to the workplace. But we can also bring brains, ambition, self-confidence, vitality, creativity, and our own unique vision and style. *The same electronic revolution that is making plants like the Mac factory possible is also bringing on the biggest shake-up in the working world since the Industrial Revolution.* It's reaching into offices, banks, supermarkets, and schools. It will open up career horizons for multitudes of women, drawing us out of the low-wage "pink-collar" ghettos and into thousands of new jobs and activities. Some of these may sound too unfamiliar to interest you—laser technicians, telecommunications consultants, videotex advertising and sales specialists, bioengineers, and mission controllers.

But *women cannot afford to be indifferent or unprepared because many of these pink-collar jobs that the majority of us still depend on will be eliminated along with the blue-collar assembly-line jobs.* For instance, one prominent forecaster expects the elimination of fully *half* of all clerical and stenographic jobs by the end of this century—fifteen years away. Executives, designers, writers, artists, and teachers will still be with us, but the way they do their jobs will change dramatically. Shortly, I'll provide you with some advance intelligence on tomorrow's workplace because I think the girls of Kelly and Nina's generation are going to have a marvelous array of career choices. But first I want to take a look at where women are now and what sorts of career goals appeal to them today.

o   o   o

American women have been pouring into the work force in record numbers for more than a decade now, claiming two-thirds of the new jobs created during the 1970s. *By 1979, working women became the majority, and today 54 percent of us work outside our homes* (compared to 77 percent of men). Forty-four percent of all American workers are women. We earn a third of all wages, about $500 billion a year. Because of us, almost half of American families earn more than $25,000 a year. Little more than a quarter of the families were that well off twenty years ago.

"Because a rapidly expanding labor force is a principal element in propelling an economy onto a fast-growth track, the influx of women into the job market may be the major reason that the United States has emerged so much healthier than other countries from the economic shocks of the

1970s," *Business Week* proclaimed recently. "Real gross national product has risen faster in the United States than in all other major industrialized nations, with the exception of Japan, during the past decade."

The government's Bureau of Labor Statistics predicts 60 percent of us will be at work within another decade. Less conservative forecasters, however, are betting that within just five years, two-thirds of us will be on the job. There appears to be no support at all for the hopes of some traditionalists that women-at-work is just a temporary fad.

Three-quarters of American women tell us they expect to be working outside their homes most of their adult lives. Ninety percent of the women who are working now, mothers and childless women alike, expect to continue. And even 38 percent of the housewives and unemployed women expect to have a job most of their lives. (In contrast, only half the women we talked to in England, 35 percent in Japan, and 27 percent in South Africa expect to work most of their lives. While American women have been flocking into the job market, the proportion of Japanese women who work has actually declined since 1970, from 49 to 47 percent.)

Most women won't be working only because of financial necessity. When we asked their reasons for planning to spend most of their lives on the job, half these women (including two-thirds of the women staying home right now) say, "to get out of the house and stay active"; 47 percent want to provide financial help for their families; 39 percent will work for personal financial gains; 34 percent to get ahead in a chosen career; and only 26 percent out of financial necessity. (Three-fourths of the South Africans, 55 percent of the English, and only 7 percent of the Japanese who plan to work will be doing it because of financial necessity. Two-thirds of the English, a third of the Japanese, and 13 percent of the South Africans say they'll work to achieve career success.)

My own staff added some other reasons: "Personal growth and peace of mind"; "To have a sense of purpose"; "To keep away boredom"; "To keep from concentrating on myself. I'd start worrying about wrinkles if I were home all the time." (And, as we saw earlier, statistics show they would probably be more depressed, less healthy, and have a shorter life span if they spent it at home.)

Other surveys also show just how serious women are about working. Almost 90 percent of the women polled by *Glamour* magazine last year said they consider an exciting and stimulating job either moderately or very important in their lives. Some 57 percent of career women contacted by SRI International said they'd continue to go to work even if they could be paid the same money for not working. And remember the findings of the

USA Today poll, that two-thirds of American women would keep right on working even if they could maintain their current lifestyle without the paycheck.

Even the women we look up to today as role models for our daughters are professional women. In our survey, Geraldine Ferraro, Sally Ride, Supreme Court Justice Sandra Day O'Connor, and England's Prime Minister, Margaret Thatcher, were the top choices as role models for today's young women. Behind them came India's Mother Teresa, surely the ultimate embodiment of female self-sacrifice, with 13 percent; newscaster Barbara Walters with 10 percent; First Lady Nancy Reagan with 9 percent; Estee Lauder and Jane Fonda, 8 percent each. (Women in the other countries we surveyed picked Thatcher and Mother Teresa as their top choices. In England and South Africa, the British prime minister got about 40 percent of the vote to Mother Teresa's 20 percent. In Japan, Mother Teresa won out by 40 percent over Thatcher's 35 percent.)

Clearly, both our intentions and our selection of role models indicate that we're not just making a cameo appearance in the workplace. The forces driving us out of our homes go back beyond the turn of the century, to the time when Americans left the farms and moved to the cities in large numbers. I mentioned this earlier, but let me recap them briefly: Children ceased to be economic assets, so families grew smaller. Women's educational levels increased. The growth of commerce fed a demand for more clerical and service workers than the male work force could supply. The first to heed the call of the office were young single women—the same group that in the nineteenth century had been drawn into mills and factories. By the 1940s, the job market began to tap married women with grown children, and, finally, after World War II, mothers with children at home.

Today's pink-collar jobs were created to suit nineteenth-century stereotypes of feminine nature, historian Joan Wallach Scott has noted. Women were expected to quit when they married, so assigned tasks were kept simple and repetitive, the kind easily learned by a high-turnover work force. And besides that, boring work was thought suitable for the supposedly passive, patient, careful, pleasant female temperament anyway. (And for our nimble fingers: "It was said that women's fingers raced as deftly over the typewriter keys as if they had been playing the piano," Scott writes.)

Earlier in the nineteenth century, before the invention of the typewriter and the arrival of the paperwork blitz of expanding commerce, clerical work had been done by young men apprenticing for partnerships or even inheritance of the business, Scott says. The archetype, of course, is Bob Cratchit, Scrooge's much-abused apprentice in *A Christmas Carol*. "As the volume of paperwork increased, however, clerical work was separated from administrative work and from advancement in the executive hierarchy," Scott writes. That's when it was handed over to women. "In the U.S. Census of 1880, only a few women were listed as office clerical workers. By 1910, 83 percent of all stenographers and typists were women; the proportion was similar in France and England. The feminization of clerical work has continued: in 1980, 97 percent of typists in the U.S. were women, as were 89 percent of stenographers."

The same pattern holds for other "women's work" created within the past century. Ninety-nine percent of secretaries, 95 percent of registered nurses, 94 percent of telephone operators, 87 percent of waitresses, and at least 80 percent of elementary school teachers, bookkeepers, cashiers, receptionists, and bank tellers today are women. And the Bureau of Labor Statistics say men aren't making any perceptible move into these fields. We, however, have been making some effort to get *out* of them.

We've seen a lot of wonderful "firsts" in the past decade as women have begun to break out of these all-female categories—the first astronauts and generals, a Supreme Court justice, and a vice-presidential candidate. What's even more important is that these firsts are being followed by thousands. Our progress can now be measured in statistics instead of anecdotes:

- *In the decade from 1970 to 1980, women's share of all executive, administrative, and managerial positions rose from 18.5 percent to 30.5 percent.* About half the personnel and labor relations specialists and the managers in health-related fields are women. And we hold a third of the management positions in public administration, finance, education, and real estate. (However, very few women —fewer than a thousand nationwide—have advanced to senior management levels in major corporations yet.)
- *During the same period, the percentage of women in professions like law, architecture, and engineering at least doubled.* For instance, the proportion of women attorneys rose from 5 to 14 percent. That will continue to increase in the future because a third of the law school graduates today are women. Nearly a third of entry-level medical students are female, and 16 percent of physicians are women, double the percentage of 1970. In contrast, only 1 percent of bachelor's degrees in engineering went to women in 1970, and only 6 percent of today's engineers are women. (I'm going to talk at length about our progress in science and engineering

in the next chapter because I think these are the key areas from which we can really influence the future.)

· *Amazingly women now outnumber men in American colleges and universities.* From 1972 to 1982, college enrollments went up 27 percent, and women accounted for four-fifths of that increase. (We're 52 percent of students now.) Most of these new students were women over twenty-five. "In fact, the increase in the number of older women alone constituted 44 percent of the total growth in the number of persons enrolled in college over the decade," the Census Bureau reported. Men still slightly outnumber women in graduate schools, however.

· Even though men aren't moving into women's fields, *more men are working elbow-to-elbow with women today in sex-integrated occupations.* In 1970, more than half of all men worked in blue-collar fields that had (and still have) less than 10 percent women—truck drivers, carpenters, auto mechanics, farmers, construction workers, welders, electricians, and machinists. But job opportunities in these areas are down, and by 1980, little more than a third of men worked in them.

Despite this progress, more than half of working women are still clustered in overwhelmingly female occupations. The top five jobs in terms of the numbers of women they employ are secretary, elementary school teacher, bookkeeper, cashier, and office clerk.

After looking at the list of career choices that women find most appealing, however, I can see it's going to take a dramatic change in attitudes before any great percentage of us move out of pink-collar categories. As I mentioned earlier, 29 percent of women overall choose motherhood as the career with greatest appeal, even though today it's hard to make that job stretch for a lifetime. *Among women who don't already have children, 34 percent pick business executive as the most appealing career, and, overall, a quarter of women list that as their number one choice. Close behind is interior designer, which 21 percent of women find most appealing.*

After that come *teacher*, 15 percent; *writer/editor*, 14 percent; *medical doctor*, 13 percent; *fashion designer*, 10 percent; *lawyer* and *nurse*, 8 percent each; *astronaut/pilot, scientist, computer programmer, politician/ stateswoman, and athlete*, 6 percent each; *mathematician*, 3 percent; *policewoman and secretary*, 2 percent each; and *engineer and military officer*, 1 percent each. (The Japanese are even more traditional in their career choices, putting wife and mother first, secretary second, and interior designer third. The South Africans put interior designer first, fashion designer second, and motherhood third. Motherhood fell to fourth place among the English, with business executive placing first, writer/editor second, and interior designer third.)

There are some jobs on the list that didn't get any votes at all—combat soldier and fire fighter—and I certainly agree there's not much future for women there. In fact, as I mentioned earlier, *37 percent of women believe women are unsuited to be combat soldiers even if they are given the proper training.* It's surprising this figure wasn't higher, actually. It means nearly two-thirds of American women think women *can* do the job with the right training. Only 13 percent say women are unsuited to be *fire fighters,* even with training; 8 percent say *military officers;* 4 percent say *policewomen;* and, incredibly, 1 percent even say *politician/stateswoman.* (A third of the English, 40 percent of the South Africans, and 60 percent of the Japanese believed women are unsuited for combat, even with proper training. A third of the Japanese also consider women unfit to be military officers or fire fighters.)

We didn't even ask about manufacturing or technical jobs, but I think I can tell from this list where they would fall. Women want their daughters and other young women to emulate Ferraro, Ride, O'Connor, and Thatcher, but they don't seem to be willing to stretch their personal horizons. *I hope the women of Kelly and Nina's generation will be more willing than women today to tackle the rewarding and innovative careers that technology is opening up to us.* There are several good reasons why they should:

The most important reason to break down the distinctions between men's and women's work is that *it's our best shot at closing the wage gap between the sexes.* As of 1984, working women overall earned sixty-four cents for every dollar men received. Among professionals, women still earn only seventy-five cents on men's dollar. But in scientific and technical professions like engineering, medicine, and computer programming that goes up to eighty cents or higher.

Second, as I mentioned, *new technologies are going to make a lot of pink-collar jobs obsolete. The days of bookkeepers, cashiers, and office clerks are definitely numbered, and secretaries will have to sell employers on their organizational skills to keep their jobs.*

You can get some idea of what the future holds by looking at younger women, who tend to be better educated and less locked in to traditional female jobs. The Census Bureau found that by 1982, the wages of women aged twenty to twenty-four had moved to within 13 percent of those of men their age. *And by 1983, women engineers graduating from college were getting* better *salary offers than their male peers.* All the forecasts also show that these young, highly trained professional women will interrupt their careers briefly, or not at all, for motherhood and family obligations.

"If there is any one decade when it pays to work hard and to be consistently in the labor force, it is the decade between twenty-five and thirty-five," economist Lester C. Thurow, of MIT, has written. "For those who succeed, earnings will rise rapidly." And yet that's the decade "when women are the most apt to leave the labor force or become part-time workers to have children. When they do, the current system of promotion and skill acquisition will extract an enormous lifetime price."

The third reason for breaking out of the pink-collar world has a lot to do with why I wrote this book in the first place. The jobs that technology is opening up provide us with our first solid opportunity to be "where the action is," to help share in the excitement and challenge of shaping tomorrow's world.

o   o   o

By now all of us have heard or read that *western culture has entered a new era, variously called the information or postindustrial or superindustrial society.* The United States actually passed unheralded into this new age thirty years ago. The mid-1950s marked a turning point in *what* the majority of Americans do for a living, and today we're seeing a revolution in *how* we do it. Because of this, the very qualities required of both workers and executives have changed. And it just happens that women are abundantly endowed with the qualities business and industry now need.

The United States began as an agricultural nation that then evolved into a largely industrial nation by the beginning of this century. Today's postindustrial age dates from about the mid-1950s, when a majority of Americans stopped manufacturing goods or building things for a living and the United States became a predominantly white-collar nation.

Today, 70 percent of American workers discover, produce, collect, manage, or communicate information or services for a living. John Naisbitt points out in *Megatrends* that the traditional service sector—fire fighters and police, hairdressers, dry cleaners—has held steady at about 10 percent of the work force since 1950, although the jobs have shifted around. There are fewer maids and more fast-food workers today.

"The real increase has been in information occupations," Naisbitt writes. "In 1950, only about 17 percent of us worked in information jobs. Now more than 60 percent of us work with information, as programmers, teachers, clerks, secretaries, accountants, stockbrokers, managers, insurance people, bureaucrats, lawyers, bankers, and technicians." In that category he'd also include most other professionals, from engineers, scientists, and physicians to architects and writers.

Most of us aren't doing the same kind of work our grandparents did. *Even the way information workers do their jobs is changing because of breakthroughs in computer and communication technologies.* These are transforming not only the office, bank, and supermarket but the factory as well, turning it into an increasingly white-collar preserve.

Blue-collar workers have been called dinosaurs, and their extinction is at hand (Naisbitt predicts a drop from 16 percent of the work force to only 3 percent or 4 percent by 2000). This is no time for large numbers of women to try to cash in on fat hourly wages as lathe operators and machinists. Those jobs are simply not going to last. Computer-driven robots are already machining tractor parts, jet engines, dishwashers, and lawn mowers as well as plugging chips and resistors into computer circuit boards in American factories. Systems called CAD and CAM—computer-aided design and computer-aided manufacturing—are helping technicians and engineers simulate and test new products and organize, schedule, and manage the production process for maximum efficiency.

In old-line smokestack industries that haven't retooled ("sunset" industries, Naisbitt calls them), America is losing out to more automated nations. "In 1980, Japan became the number-one automobile maker in the world," Naisbitt writes, ". . . exceeding U.S. production by an almost unbelieveable 40 percent."

"A robot replaces six workers," forecaster Marvin Cetron told an audience recently. "So why do we want it, with all the social problems it brings —welfare, unemployment, retraining? It's because of a thing called quality. When you use a robot, you don't get 15 percent scrap. You get less than 1 percent scrap. When you're using a robot, you use only 60 percent of the paint when you spray. When you're using robots, you're not dealing with a sixty-fourth or a thirty-second of an inch on tolerances. You're using laser dimensionality—[to an accuracy of] a thousandth of an inch.

"Obviously, a robot-made automobile is nine times better than a Wednesday car. You know, Monday the worker comes in a little hung over . . . Friday he puts four of the five bolts on and the car falls apart. But Wednesday is the best we produce . . . A car built by a robot is nine times better than that car," Cetron proclaims.

But what happens to the six workers? "What you do is you take the four oldest workers, you have them work a twenty-hour workweek; they get paid for a forty-hour workweek so they can buy the products, and you're getting a 50 percent increase in productivity," he proposes. "As they retire—and the average age is fifty-four in the auto industry—you're getting even more increase in productivity."

(Cetron predicts robots will cut the workweek to thirty-two hours by 1990 and to twenty-five hours by the year 2000. Nobel prize economist Wassily Leontief doubts this, and so do I, even though a study conducted by the Austrian government showed that that country could automate its industries to the maximum and still keep unemployment down to 2 percent by reducing the workweek but not the wage. Leontief said, however, that the real hurdle will be getting Americans to set aside the work ethic: "We are ready to relax on sexual morality, but we are not ready to relax on work morality, which, even slightly loosened up, would make things much easier. We refuse to pay money to support people. Policies that provide income to nonworking people are considered immoral.")

Cetron continues, "The two youngsters, you have them out there installing robots, scheduling robots, fixing them, selling them, marketing them, and exporting them all over the world. Robots will create more jobs than they destroy, the same as the computer did, but you've got to train people in advance, and we're not. Our training is absolutely abominable in our country."

I know there's a great fear in some quarters today that technology will put people out of work. *Technology will make some jobs obsolete just as it always has, but in the end it will create more opportunities than it eliminates*—just as it always has. And the new jobs will be much more interesting than the old ones. A survey of workers conducted by Daniel Yankelovich's nonprofit Public Agenda Foundation has found that technology actually *improves* 80 percent of jobs it touches.

"I think most automation is justified in typical male terms of return on investments, etc.," Debi Coleman says. "I'm determined to automate for two major reasons. One is for process control. And the second is to eliminate dull, boring, repetitive tasks, which I despise. For almost every production worker that you displace, you create a programming or equipment support job which is higher paying, much more creative, and much more challenging." (And her plant makes training programs for such jobs available to employees right on site or at a nearby college.)

Most of these new factory jobs, of course, are white-collar jobs, information jobs. At the Macintosh plant, these white-collar and support jobs outnumber direct labor by four to one.

I'm going to talk about the office next, because that's where most women are now, but first I want to make one more comment about technology and the jobs it creates. All the things I've pointed out so far are the obvious ones, the tasks required to tend the machine that's doing your old job. But automation always changes the way we live, work, and play in a fashion that even the most prescient futurists seldom foresee. Henry Ford might have imagined that his automobile would create jobs for automakers, highway engineers, car salesmen, mechanics, and gas station operators. I doubt he could have guessed that newly mobile Americans would use his invention to move to the suburbs, build shopping malls, and create drive-in restaurants, movies, and banks. That one bit of technology has transformed our culture in ways that created millions of new jobs you wouldn't think to trace back to the automobile.

And who could have imagined when those first room-size computers were being built back in the 1940s that thousands of people would be making good livings building and selling desktop-size machines, creating games and other software programs, holding workshops and classes, writing users' manuals, designing furniture to hold them, and even creating special lines of "user friendly" greeting cards and chocolate bars in the shape of integrated circuits to sell to computer buffs. (I can hardly wait to see what sort of "peripherals" people will think up when home robots catch on in the market.)

And that's barely the beginning. As commerce goes electronic, and our homes and businesses tie into videotex and other communications networks, we're going to need new sales, advertising, marketing, research, programming, and education specialists to create innovative on-line services. If you're in marketing or one of these other fields, I urge you to begin reading all you can about videotex and teletext to see if there's a place where your ideas and talents can help to pioneer a new medium.

Now back to the office of the future. "An anthropologist visiting an office today would see much that he would have seen twenty-five years ago," writes information-systems specialist Vincent Giuliano. "He would see people reading, writing on paper, handling mail, talking with one another face to face and on the telephone, typing, operating calculators, dictating, filing, and retrieving files from metal cabinets. He would observe some new behavior, too. He would see a surprising number of people working with devices that have a typewriterlike keyboard but also have a video screen or an automatic printing element."

This of course, is the computer. The person sitting at it could be a stockbroker checking the current markets, analyzing trends, or looking over a customer's portfolio. It could be an attorney or law clerk searching through an electronic database for court decisions. Or it might be a secretary typing or editing letters (word processing). It's this last scene that's going to change in the future, along with the handling of mail and paper, the dictating, the filing and retrieval, and even those metal file cabinets themselves.

One step toward this future will be the linking of office computers into "electronic mail" networks, something that many large corporations have already done. But the key step in transforming the office will come when computer keyboards are eliminated, along with the manual labor (typing) involved in entering data into a computer. *By 1995 most large offices will be able to operate without paper, without typists, and without file clerks. Executives and account managers will dictate directly to their computers. Even the mail that still arrives in paper form instead of electronically will be scanned and fed into computer memory systems automatically.* The two major technologies that will make this possible are the *voice-activated typewriter and the electronic text reader.*

Optical character-recognition systems or electronic text readers already on the market eliminate the need to use a keyboard or to type information into the computer. A company can use the machines to scan all of its old files, its library materials, or any new information that comes in and feed it directly into electronic storage banks (or eventually videodiscs) for easy on-screen retrieval. (This is a good technology for you to keep up with if you're a file clerk now. Become enough of an expert at what can be done with the machines and your boss might just ask your advice when shopping for one, and then put you in charge of the file conversion and later the management of the databank.)

Voice-activated typewriters or word lexicon machines should be commercially available any day now. By mid-1985, IBM was already showing its prototype machine around. So was Kurzweil Speech Systems. These computers recognize speech so efficiently that an executive can dictate letters directly to them and see the results appear on the screen with 95 percent accuracy or better. Mistakes can then be edited out by spelling and grammar-correction programs already on the market. A team at Duke University has even designed a system that edits by voice command, allowing the user to say "delete the third sentence" or "put this paragraph last" and watch as the machine does it.

Today's models of the voice-activated typewriter are still fairly slow and not nearly as "easy to talk to" as they will eventually become. This will be one of the major applications of the "fifth generation" computers I talked about in the last chapter, although very usable voice-activated machines will be on the market long before artificial intelligence is perfected.

Once the material on the screen is corrected, you can then push a button to print out a copy. Or more likely, just tell the computer to transmit it electronically by telephone line, directly to the "mailbox" of a client across the country. And at the same time have it file a copy in electronic storage.

(Just a word about the concept of a "paperless office." So far computers, high-speed printers, and copiers have actually generated a record blitz of paper, and this isn't likely to end soon, even if it's technologically possible. Until our whole society is on line, we'll always have to print and mail certain documents. And as long as you're making one copy, technology makes it tempting to make fifty. One attorney told me about a senior colleague who never used to name more than six defendants in any lawsuit because that's all the carbons his long-time secretary could type at once, and she refused to type anything twice. After he bought her a word processing system he began to go after dozens of defendants at a time.)

If you're an executive or professional or account manager, tomorrow's advanced computer systems will make you more self-sufficient and put incredible amounts of information at your fingertips. If you're a secretary, file clerk, or stenographer whose work is confined to typing, word processing, or filing, it's time to start to get some training in a new field, or see that your boss begins to value other contributions you make to office life, such as your behind-the-scenes "people skills" that provide continuity and keep the office running smoothly.

Bookkeepers and corporate accountants, too, face obsolescence as the "books" are kept electronically and the boss can call up an up-to-the-second cash flow on the screen anytime. (This doesn't mean there won't be any bookkeepers or file clerks around in 2000 who keep accounts and file by hand. After all, there are still offices today where people are expected to type on manual typewriters. But they aren't exactly the most progressive and high-paying places to work, and I hope most women won't aim that low.)

Most bank tellers can already see from the mushrooming network of automated-teller machines (ATM) and computer-banking services that they should be training for a different job. (Banks were actually surprised at how quickly ATMs caught on with customers. Obviously, most people would rather forgo the "personal touch" if it means standing in a long line to cash a check.) The financial services companies are hungry for technology experts to help them organize new on-line services, so if I were a teller now I'd be busy learning a communications or data-processing specialty.

Telephone operators are already on the wane as computerized switching allows callers to be connected automatically. Travel agents may survive to the turn of the century. But by that time, most of the people with the money or the business mandate to travel will also have videotex services that allow them to make their own airplane and hotel reservations directly. And ticket agents at airports, train stations, and movie theaters are already being replaced by automated cash or credit-card-operated dispensers.

In major supermarkets and department stores, cashiers already do little more than push purchases across laser scanners that read the price code, signal the amount to the register, and automatically adjust the store's computerized inventory. By the 1990s, some of these stores will offer customers the convenience of using their home computers to transmit shopping lists directly to the store's warehouse computer. The grocery order will be packed for delivery and the customer's payment transferred electronically from her checking account to that of the store. On-line videotex catalogs offering tires, appliances, and many other goods will operate in a similar way.

Our survey shows *the vast majority of American women realize that bank tellers, ticket agents, and file clerks are being made obsolete by new technologies.* Eighty-one percent say bank teller jobs will disappear; 73 percent say ticket agents; and 68 percent file clerks. *A third also believe fast-food workers will become obsolete.* This will take longer. But since the Japanese already have robots that can slice and serve sushi, I can't believe automating a hamburger assembly line will be terribly difficult.

Only about one fourth of women seem to know what's in store for machinists, welders, draftsmen, and miners. Twenty-nine percent say machinists will become obsolete, 28 percent say miners, 27 percent say draftsmen, and 21 percent say welders. Draftsmen who want to survive past the mid-1990s had better start now learning something about the computer-aided design systems that architects and engineers are already using to analyze possible buildings or product designs and draw up the plans. *Nineteen percent of women think secretaries will become obsolete; 13 percent say factory foremen (you don't need foremen when the work crew are robots); 9 percent say combat soldiers; and 2 percent fire fighters*—robots are the perfect choice to carry hoses into a raging inferno. *More than 80 percent of American women who are now working say they aren't concerned that their own job will become obsolete in the next decade or two.*

The National Task Force on Education for Economic Growth has predicted that as many as twenty million Americans will need retraining by the early 1990s as their skills become obsolete.

Among women who aren't working now, nearly two-thirds say they're willing to go back to school or enter a training program to become more employable. Another 11 percent are already doing it. (That last figure includes a quarter of homemakers with household incomes above $50,000.) Only 4 percent say they aren't willing, and 22 percent aren't sure.

It's encouraging to see that most women are willing to get whatever education and training it takes to go after tomorrow's jobs. The key thing we have to do now in order to make sure we share equally in the rewards (particularly wages) and challenges of the workplace is to expand our vision of women's work. (You can't rely on the U.S. Labor Department's projections to tell you where the best jobs will be in the future. The agency only makes employment predictions about job categories that already exist. For projections on future jobs see books like *Emerging Careers: New Occupations for the Year 2000 and Beyond* by Norman Feingold and Norma Reno Miller or *Jobs of the Future* by Marvin Cetron with Marcia Appel.)

Even though I've been talking about technology, I don't want you to think that all of tomorrow's opportunities will be high-tech jobs per se. Computers will open up new possibilities for many people in traditional fields, including artists, musicians, writers, and teachers.

Technology is already providing musicians with synthesizers and electric keyboards that capture sounds as complex as those of a concert piano. But that's just the beginning. Experimental computer systems like those at the University of California, San Diego's Computer Audio Research Laboratory are allowing composers to exploit a universe of sounds unreachable by any known musical instruments. (Francis Bacon prophesied such a future when he wrote *The New Atlantis* in 1624: "We have also our sound-houses, where we practice and demonstrate all sounds, and their generation. We have harmonies which you do not, of quarter-sounds, and lesser slides of sounds. Divers [diverse] instruments of music likewise to you unknown . . . We represent and imitate all articulate sounds and letters, and the voices and notes of beasts and birds. . . .")

Artists have just begun to explore the world of computer-generated imagery and animation. Educators, as I pointed out before, could use the new information media to transform the nation's classrooms into places of real excitement and learning for a change. I hope that poets, artists, writers, directors, musicians, and teachers will pool their imaginations to create much more exciting programs to offer us in our new leisure time than the boring fare currently available on network television.

There is another career option increasing numbers of women are taking advantage of—entrepreneuring. *For every dozen women who work for someone else, there's a woman out there working for herself. Between 1977 and 1980 alone, the number of businesses owned by women jumped by 33 percent.* Today we own one quarter of all the nation's small businesses, ranging from law firms, insurance agencies, and computer software developers to beauty shops, boutiques, and restaurants. Obviously, most fall into those latter categories, but as more women gain technical and professional educations the proportions are going to change.

The very fact that women are going off to work in steadily increasing numbers also means that services like quality day care, take-out food, and dry cleaning will be in demand as families with two working parents continue to buy services that mothers used to provide for free. More people will also be willing to pay for personal services like fitness consultants, nutrition counselors, wardrobe organizers, caterers, and gift-shoppers.

In this sense, modern homemaking skills aren't going to be abandoned. In fact, they may even gain a great deal of respect as they become marketplace commodities that people must purchase. The woman who opens a lucrative cookie-baking franchise or hosts paying customers in her own restaurant is going to get a much bigger boost to her self-esteem than she'd ever get facing a chorus of "What's for dinner?" from husband and children. I think she's going to feel less like one of the kitchen appliances and more like an accomplished and competent human being. And that's what being a woman of tomorrow is all about.

We are entering an age of rapid change where none of us can be sure the job we are doing today will be relevant in ten years. The people who thrive will be the ones who keep on learning, reading, and asking questions, who anticipate new directions not only in technology but in lifestyles. I believe women now have the power to influence change instead of simply reacting to it, if we'll just keep our eyes on the future.

OUR MINDS, OURSELVES

The urge to know has evolved from an instinct to a profession.
—Astronomer Harlow Shapley

Knowledge is Power.

—Francis Bacon

Knowledge is the most precious commodity in the information age, and I believe the really promising careers for a woman of tomorrow lie in the search for new knowledge—science—and the application of knowledge to human needs—technology.

The doors are wide open now, and everywhere you look women are pushing against the frontiers of ignorance. They are descending in subs to hot springs in the deep seabed to scout for rare minerals or learn how living creatures survive in a pressure-cooker environment; performing vital experiments that will allow us to manufacture new medicines and novel alloys in the weightlessness of space; probing the DNA of hundreds of people in search of genes that cause muscular dystrophy, cystic fibrosis, and other devastating diseases; peering into the brain for the chemistry of mood and memory and into the heart of the atom for the ultimate building blocks of matter and the forces that created our universe.

For the first time in human history, we women have begun to take our mental and intellectual capabilities seriously. In growing numbers, we're becoming thinkers as well as nurturers. This doesn't mean abandoning the sense of nurturing, helping, and caring that's been our forte for so long. Instead, *I think women are forging new ways to care, applying their concern along with their intellect to much larger human goals. After all, science and technology can be the ultimate "helping" professions in the hands of people who care enough to try to create a better world.*

But, despite the new crop of female faces appearing in the nation's labs, *women's progress in science will level off soon unless the girls of Adrian and Nina's generation make very different choices than women today.* I'll show you the progress women have made, and the obstacles that remain. Most of them, as you'll see, are within our power to change. Next, I'll look at why more women ought to be involved in science and technology, and what fields interest today's women the most. And finally, I'm going to tell you about women's role in the grandest dream of all, pioneering space, the high frontier.

o   o   o

Between 1972 and 1982, the number of women in science and engineering doubled, but we still represent only 13 percent of the overall work force in those professions. The figures look much better for some areas of science than others, however. According to the nonprofit Scientific Manpower Commission, women are now 57 percent of all psychologists, 41 percent of life scientists, 30 percent of mathematicians and computer specialists, 23 percent of chemists, 18 percent of geologists, but only 6 percent of engineers.

If you look at the recent college graduating classes, you can see just how much those proportions are going to grow in the future. In 1970, women were earning barely 1 percent of the engineering degrees. By 1985, more than 16 percent were going to women. In computer sciences, women's share of the bachelor's degrees rose from 13 percent to 30 percent during the 1970s. Our share of master's degrees more than doubled, from 9 percent to 21 percent, and our share of Ph.D. degrees jumped from 2 percent to 11 percent. In the biological sciences, which have always been most popular among women, our share of bachelor's degrees jumped from 28 percent to 42 percent, master's degrees from 31 percent to 37 percent, and Ph.D.s from 14 percent to 26 percent.

Altogether, women now earn more than a quarter of all doctoral degrees awarded in science and engineering, up from only 7 percent twenty years ago.

The statistics hide a disturbing truth, however. Young women entering college aren't really choosing science careers in greater proportions than previous generations did. The only reason there are more women earning science and engineering degrees today is that more women are getting college degrees, period. This is what Rand Corporation consultant Sue E. Berryman found in a recent study for the Rockefeller Foundation.

Throughout the decade of the 1970s, a fairly steady three out of every ten men getting bachelor's degrees chose to major in science, compared to one out of ten women. The percentage of both men and women graduate students who chose to earn their master's or doctoral degrees in science actually *declined.* (So did the percentage of women choosing to earn their professional degrees in scientifically based fields like medicine, dentistry, or pharmacy.)

As we saw in the last chapter, women undergraduates now outnumber men, and we're already earning half the bachelor's and master's degrees that colleges and universities award. We're still somewhat behind in doctoral programs, earning only a third of the Ph.D.s in all fields. But Berryman's projections show that if the current rates of increase continue, we should pull even with men our age by 1990 in the proportion of doctoral degrees we earn.

Since women are roughly half the population, about half the degrees is all we can probably expect to earn. I doubt we're going to see much larger proportions of women than men going off to college in the future. *So unless a greater share of our college-bound women choose to major in scientific fields, women may never make up more than a quarter of our scientists and engineers.*

And that's a career choice that can't wait until the summer before college, either. Berryman finds that you can go into the nation's schools by the ninth grade and identify the "talent pool" from which most of our scientists will ultimately come. It's not their special skills that set these students apart—by that age, most college-bound students have about the same math and verbal skills. What sets these youngsters apart is their strong interest in science careers. When they move on into high school, the children who don't already have such an interest—and this includes most girls—stop taking advanced math classes, drop back in their math achievement, and essentially close their options. Anyone who reaches the twelfth grade without developing strong math skills is very unlikely to show up in a science career ten years later, Berryman says, even if she finds in college that she's really interested in science.

I've already told you how I feel about the abominable condition of our schools in general. But it's the shameful neglect of science and math education that I find most distressing. Only a third of U.S. high school graduates take three years of math. And a mere 6 percent complete four years. Only a fifth of students get three years of science, and just 16 percent ever take physics. This scientific illiteracy is more than just a handicap for young people. *It seriously threatens America's position of leadership in an increasingly technological world.* Students in Japan and the Soviet Union emphasize technical expertise by taking *three* times as much math and science.

The issue of science illiteracy takes on an even greater urgency where it concerns women. Our educational system encourages girls to take subjects like home economics and art for beginners, while boys are pushed into physics and calculus. Only 25 percent of girls, compared with 40 percent of boys, take three or more years of high school math. And it's not because girls are born with less interest in these subjects. Rank discrimination, where it concerns teaching and counseling girls in math and science, is rampant in schools throughout the country. Our cultural stereotypes have created the imbalances that exist by perpetuating the myth that "science and math are for boys." Look how that message gets passed on to girls:

- *Girls and boys are given different toys to play with from the time they are born.* Boys' toys encourage them to take things apart and put them back together, which helps foster their curiosity about how things work. I'm hardly suggesting that parents should stop giving their daughters dolls for Christmas, but remember that a microscope or a space shuttle model to assemble are just as appropriate. (I remember only too well screaming when my brother's erector set was taken away from me although my mother, bless her, did buy me science books and encouraged my natural curiosity.)
- *Poor quality teaching may doubly handicap girls, especially if it is delivered by a female teacher.* Berryman points out that more than half of all third graders have positive attitudes toward science lessons, but by eighth grade only 20 percent do. She suggests that one "factor may be that the overwhelming majority of elementary school teachers are women, who themselves are less apt to like or be competent in science." I think young girls are bound to be influenced by these negative attitudes. (This also holds true when the female teacher is obviously timid and uncertain about having a computer in her classroom.)
- *Girls may get a similarly negative message about science from*

their mothers, their strongest female role models. I'm sure they can sense the same lack of interest that our survey revealed: that even though only 2 percent of you want to be secretaries, that's twice the number of you who want to be engineers. And interior design has as much career appeal to women as science, math, computer programming, and astronautics combined.

- *Somehow most young girls get the word that boys supposedly won't be interested in them if they like math and science.* And no matter how silly the notion is, it makes a strong impression on girls who are just beginning to turn "boy-crazy." Adolescents in particular have a real fear of being "different" and they need to know that even smart girls get dates. (Maybe it's the boys we need to work on. A national study of seventeen-year-olds conducted in 1982 found that 31 percent of the boys agreed with the statement "science is more for males than females." Only 12 percent of the girls agreed.)

- *School counselors have a notorious reputation for discouraging girls from taking math and science,* or even shop and drafting classes, where they could develop mechanical and spatial skills. Even counselors who don't actively discourage girls aren't likely to spend a lot of time encouraging them to take all the math and science that's offered.

- *Even parents who think they have equal aspirations for their sons and daughters can unconsciously limit their daughters' self-confidence.* This happens when they express pleasant surprise at her for bringing home good math grades, automatically assuming that it must be due to extra hard work rather than innate ability. (Women are well known for picking up this attitude toward themselves, and it shows up everywhere, particularly around men: "Don't be threatened by little old me. I only got the top prize because I struggled so hard, not because I'm as smart as/smarter than you.")

- *Most science material in schools is designed to appeal to boys.* I pointed out in the first two chapters how different the styles and sensibilities of the average boy are from those of the average girl. The research that went into developing the prize-winning Children's Television Workshop series called 3-2-1-CONTACT highlighted these differences. "Girls more than boys tend to prefer programs that involve warm human relationships, family themes, and female leads," Andrew R. Molnar of the National Science Foundation (NSF) recounts. "Boys tend to prefer programs that involve male leads, action, adventure, and competitive situations.

Technology and outer space are topics of more appeal to boys. Girls are not interested in these topics unless they directly involve human relationships and social activities. Using information of this type, writers were able to create programs that could attract and hold the attention of both boys and girls. For example, one program treated human relations and social activities in a space colony."

Designers of computer games and educational software have also found in their research that girls would rather see their on-screen "helicopters" dropping CARE packages than dropping bombs.

- *Girls get the misguided impression that a life in science or math is lonely and isolated, that scientists have to prefer "things rather than people," and that women in science must forgo marriage and children.* We do a very poor job of showing girls that science can fulfill female values.

I certainly second a suggestion Berryman and many others have made, that *we require high school students to take science and advanced math courses instead of offering these only as electives. "Removing choice during high school would preserve it after high school,"* she notes. I think we'll be doing our daughters a big favor if we refuse to let them limit and define their futures based on their fourteen-year-old views of the world.

You might be asking why we should bother. What difference does it make if only 13 percent or 25 percent of the nation's scientists and engineers are women? I think it makes a *big* difference, both for us and for the world of the future. Let me give you five reasons:

First, *science is an exciting career, and it taps an important part of our nature that finds no outlet in most traditional women's work*—our need for self-expression and our sense of wonder, curiosity, excitement, creativity, and passion. Some of us can express that side of our natures in dance or music or literature. Others find it in the lab.

I know what some of you are thinking: "That's crazy. Science is rational, cool, dispassionate, nonemotional." But it's not. One of my favorite scientists, Candace Pert, chief of the brain biochemistry section at the National Institute of Mental Health, wrote:

"Shouldn't every experiment be designed with dispassionate calmness? No! Real science—science at the forefront, where intuition meets reality —is a wildly passionate affair. Experiments either work or they don't work. Whoever said that every experiment should be designed to get an answer regardless of whether it supports the scientist's working hypothesis was a liar—or worse, a very boring scientist. It is indeed ironic that science draws upon a group composed (predominantly) of men who pride themselves on the ability to suppress, or even deny, an emotional involvement with the expected experimental results.

"The truth is that all scientific discovery begins purely in the realm of imagination, where daydreams and fantasies hold sway . . . To believe in an idea with no hard evidence for it goes against our notions about science. Yet that kind of strongly held, irrational attachment to an idea *before* it has been proved correct provides the driving energy to stay with it. Almost the same experiment—with just one or two things varied—must be repeated day after day to find the magic combination of variables to make it 'work.' Passion for the idea keeps the scientist going until that unforgettable moment when reality crystallizes out of fantasy."

Pert knows just the sort of eureka moment she's talking about, too. In 1973, when she was still a graduate student, she discovered opiate receptors in the human brain, a startling find that led to the isolation of endorphins, natural morphinelike chemicals in our body.

Vivian Gornick found a universal trait among the scientists she interviewed for her book *Women in Science*. "Each of them had wanted to know how the physical world worked, and each of them had found that discovering how things worked through the exercise of her own mental powers gave her an intensity of pleasure and purpose, a sense of reality nothing else could match." She adds later, "Science—like art, religion, political theory, or psychoanalysis—is work that holds out the promise of philosophic understanding, excites in us the belief that we can 'make sense of it all.' Such work strikes the deepest chords of responsiveness. To act on that responsiveness is to achieve expressive life."

Second, *jobs in science and engineering today are seldom lonely and isolated*, unless you choose to follow the lead of ethologists like Jane Goodall and Diane Fossi, who have spent years in the forests observing chimpanzees and gorillas. (And they seem to be delighted with their work and the outdoor lifestyle it has provided them.) In university, industry, and government labs, the problem is more often overcrowding than isolation. And scientists and engineers have more flexibility than most professionals to set their own schedules and direct their own work.

You'll still run across a myth that some scientists like to perpetuate— that research requires total, unwavering devotion, the kind that's incompatible with marriage and family. Pert and her three children would emphatically deny it, as would thousands of other women scientists who lead accomplished, well-rounded lives. The two things it takes—a supportive partner and a good enough salary to hire the help you need—are the same, whether a woman is a scientist or a corporate executive. (In other words, don't marry a fellow graduate student who expects you to serve as his research assistant and tend his house and lab while he earns tenure and prizes.)

Third, *science and high technology are where the best jobs are and will continue to be, and also where the narrowest salary gap between men and women exist.* According to the NSF, average annual salaries for women scientists and engineers are about 80 percent those of men (compared to 64 percent for working women in general). The gap partly reflects the fact that women are recent entrants into science, and we're younger and less experienced than men in the field. For instance, in 1982, 60 percent of female scientists and engineers were under thirty-five, and two-thirds had less than ten years' professional experience. Only a third of the men were under thirty-five or had that little experience.

When salary differences between younger men and women are compared, the gap drops considerably—and in engineering it disappears or is reversed. "According to the College Placement Council, *engineering is the only field in which average starting salaries for women are higher than those for men,*" Samuel Florman notes in *Blaming Technology.* And a higher proportion of women engineers than men graduate from the best schools and rank in the top third of their classes, a study by engineer Marilyn W. Bush, of the Jet Propulsion Laboratory, shows.

Women in technical and scientific fields have twice the unemployment rate of men—4.3 percent, compared to 2 percent. (The unemployment rate for women in general is 9.4 percent, and among female college graduates, 3.2 percent.) But the NSF says this sex gap occurs largely "because women are more likely to restrict their job search because of geographic location, family responsibilities, and desire for part-time employment." When men and women with these sorts of limitations are excluded "the unemployment rate is virtually identical for male and female scientists and engineers."

Unemployment isn't going to be something most people with scientific and technical educations have to worry about in the future as long as they stay on top of the rapidly expanding knowledge in their fields. Some of the social sciences and psychology are becoming crowded right now, but the demand for systems analysts, computer scientists, aeronautical engineers, industrial engineers, and many other specialties outstrips the supply. Don't forget that there's also a great need for people with strong math and science backgrounds to teach in our schools—and I hope we'll start paying the kinds of salaries that will attract such people.

I have to admit to you that women scientists, like other working women, still face some discrimination when it comes to career advancement, especially getting tenure at universities. Women there must feel about the same way middle-management women do when they look up the corporate ladders at all the post-middle-age males on whom their fates depend. But time and the law are on our side, as well as our growing numbers, and very few young women entering science today need get sidetracked into dead-end jobs like research associate the way women of their mothers' generation did.

By 1983, 19 percent of university faculty in this country were women. Half of them had tenure, compared with 70 percent of men. And women still tend to be clustered in the humanities and home economics. "More than half of college teachers in English, foreign languages, health specialties, and home economics are women, but they are less than 5 percent of the total in engineering and physics," the Scientific Manpower Commission reports.

Certainly, women today don't face the blatant men-only rules that were common just thirty years ago. One of the world's foremost observational astronomers, soft-spoken British-born Margaret Burbidge, found when she went to Caltech in 1955 that women weren't allowed to use the massive Palomar telescope. So her husband, Geoffrey, an eminent theoretical astronomer, had to apply for observing time in his name. Fortunately, the staff turned a blind eye when it was she who climbed into the observer's cage, something no single woman could have done without openly challenging the rules. (Burbidge, now director of the Center for Astrophysics and Space Sciences at the University of California, San Diego, actively challenges the system on behalf of other women today. And she's too respected in her field for anyone to want to deny her access to the right equipment. When the Space Telescope is launched in 1986, one of the five experiments aboard will come from her team.)

The obstacles women face today are attitudes, not rules. A geochemist who recently left a research fellowship at Caltech to take her first tenure-track job told us about the response of a male colleague when he heard she planned to apply for a faculty opening at Stanford. "You know they just hired two women there so the pressure's really off them to hire a woman," he told her. "Maybe you should apply somewhere else." She recalls: "It didn't even dawn on him how insulting that was. I told him, 'Well then, maybe they'll hire me because I'm right for the job.' " It was a concept he obviously hadn't considered. But the world changes, and dinosaurs don't live forever.

Fourth, *women can bring a fresh point of view and a different range of values and priorities to the sciences.* Don't expect to see too many changes when a lone woman physicist is appointed to a faculty or only one female is admitted to a corporate board. Remember, it's when you have groups of men and groups of women that differences in style, values, and sensibilities—not to mention *power*—become apparent. Physiologist Estelle Ramey, for instance, thinks the kind of biomedical research the National Institutes of Health (NIH) supports is colored by the fact that there are few women in decision-making roles there, and few chairing medical schools or basic science departments in universities.

"Priorities and choices in the selection of research projects are no more exempt from bias or emotion than any other choices in life," she writes. "The disfiguring radical mastectomy, for example, was retained as almost the only treatment for breast cancer long after data from many sources indicated that it was no better than less traumatic surgery. Male surgeons didn't want to mutilate patients. They wanted to save their lives, but inevitably they were less sensitive than women to the consequences of this assault on the woman's self-image. It is just one example of the great need to have both women and men involved in every phase of medical care and medical research."

Less than 2 percent of the NIH budget goes to support research on the reproductive biology of women, even though we make up half the population, Ramey points out. (And as we saw earlier, absolutely *nothing* is spent on test-tube fertilization or any other alternative birth technologies.) Other neglected areas are the disturbing increases in cesarean sections and hysterectomies, and the special health needs of elderly women (and I would add research on aging in general). "It is fortunate that women are so well endowed genetically," Ramey adds. "Otherwise they would be hard put at times to survive."

Other women in science see themselves as "less embedded and steeped in the prevailing view and in a position to be more critical and try a fresh approach." Less likely to become isolated and dehumanized by the technology they work with. (Women computer programmers, for instance, almost never end up as "nerds" or "hackers.") More likely to apply a social conscience to their research goals and lean away from "projects that are technologically sweet but potentially destructive."

A national study conducted by the University of Minnesota of schoolchildren at ages nine, thirteen, and seventeen found that boys "tend to have more positive attitudes toward science careers, science classes, and the field of science in general" while girls are more positive "toward their responsibility to use science to solve community and world problems."

"Having sat in on too many scientific meetings to enumerate, I find there's a fundamental difference between the way women scientists approach things and the way men do," Stanford psychologist Diane McGuinness told us. "Women tie their science back to the world of people, constantly seeking for avenues to make connections."

There are still people who think science requires a certain mind-set that women don't have. They cite the work of several investigators, starting in the 1950s, who have profiled the personality traits most common in scientists. Can you guess what they found? They found that the most characteristic traits were ones most frequently associated with men: "extremely strongly motivated . . . self-propelled . . . dominating others to gain his desired outcome . . . completely engrossed in his work to the exclusion of social and civic interests . . ."

I can't imagine what else these people expected to find when they set out to study a group that was almost exclusively male (and the few women in the fraternity had to be careful to act like "one of the boys"). I'm sure a study of Roman Catholic priests would come up with largely male traits, too. But *I reject the notion that there's only one personality type— object-oriented rather than people-oriented—fit to do science.* (And I know Candace Pert would put it more emphatically than I just did.) *We have to do a better job of letting young girls know that they don't have to copy the style and sensibilities of men to make a contribution in science, engineering, business, or any other field.*

There's another side to this, too. *Working Woman* editor-at-large, Kate Rand Lloyd, drew an almost unanimous show of hands from women who flocked to an employment options conference in Los Angeles in 1984 when she asked how many of them wanted to "work with people." But " 'working with people' is a code phrase that often means 'spare me the hard facts,' " she told them. Too many women "have been specializing in a limited number of areas of study which has helped to limit us to a few fields. We have not been keeping up with the trends of work." As a result, she told them, women are "playing into the hands of pay discrimination."

I have a fifth reason for believing it's important that more women consider science and engineering careers, and I've said it before: *Science and technology are the most powerful forces for change in the world today, and women who hope to have a hand in shaping a better future must participate in their advance.*

"I think that genius, and really highly creative intelligence, is rare," Ramey says. "It occurs just occasionally. We don't even know why. So if you take 50 percent of the population and make it impossible for that genius to be expressed, what you've done is slow down the rates of cure for heart disease, for cancer, the rates for solutions to social problems. What I'm saying is if you eliminate 50 percent of anybody, if you eliminate all those brains, you're cutting down on the possibility of solving some major problems."

o   o   o

We asked women which area of science they would prefer to study if we offered them a grant. Thirty percent said computers. That's a good choice, because hundreds of computer specialties are thriving now, and even women without strong math backgrounds can find a place. Anthropologists, psychologists, and social scientists with computer training are busy examining "human-machine interactions": the way computers alter social relationships in the office and home; the impact of computer video games on children; the features a computer system needs to have to be truly "user friendly" to novices.

Systems analysts and programmers are constantly devising better ways to make the machines do what we need them to do, and helping businesses, labs, hospitals, and government agencies put together the best combinations of computers and software to serve their specific needs.

Hardware engineers and scientists from dozens of fields are racing to design newer, smaller, more powerful chips and novel memory systems to provide the brain capacity for tomorrow's fifth-generation computers. Artificial-intelligence experts are studying how the human mind processes thoughts in order to devise ways to get computers to understand normal speech, recognize objects, draw conclusions, make decisions, and learn from experience. And software designers are already using what they've learned to teach computers to search for oil, to recommend who should get bank loans or insurance coverage, to decide how air traffic should be routed, and to diagnose disease.

Obviously, the challenges for computer scientists, engineers, technicians, programmers, and systems analysts are going to be around for a long time. In fact, they should still be exciting fields for Kelly and Nina's children.

The second most popular area women would choose to study is infertility and test-tube baby research, fourteen percent opted for this field. Interestingly, this is twice as popular among homemakers, at 18 percent, as among working mothers, at 9 percent. Shamefully, right now, the U.S. government isn't putting a cent into the new birth technologies for fear of having to deal with touchy issues like embryo research. I think this is going to have to change in the next few years as procedures like in vitro fertilization become socially acceptable, even commonplace, and infertile couples start to demand the service as part of their normal health insurance coverage. Some clinics already have waiting lists more than ten years long, with couples returning time after time to obtain that 20 percent chance of a pregnancy.

There is lots of room for improvement. Questions need to be answered about why some embryos implant and survive in the womb while most are lost; why so many spontaneously abort in the first three months; why some embryos are damaged when frozen; and why unfertilized eggs have resisted all attempts at cryopreservation.

The related fields of molecular biology and genetic engineering tied for third place, with 13 percent of women choosing each one as the field they would like to study. It was through basic research in molecular biology that the procedures we now call recombinant DNA, or genetic engineering, were developed. Scientists can now isolate single genes, splice novel combinations of genes together, and insert these "recombinant" molecules into bacteria, yeast, plants, or animals—even humans. And if the right genetic signals have been attached, these genes will do the same thing in these alien settings that they did in their natural one—order the production of a protein or enzyme.

Human genes for insulin and the antiviral protein interferon have already been inserted into bacteria, turning them into living factories for the production of much-needed drugs. Other "bugs" are being engineered to aid in biomining, the leaching of valuable metals from low-grade ores, and to enhance various industrial fermentation processes (like the one that gives us beer). Infusions of novel genes will one day give us superior crop plants that resist disease and insects, survive drought and salty soil, require no fertilizers, and contain enhanced supplies of nutrients. Gene transplants may do in a single generation what thousands of years of selective breeding of livestock couldn't, creating new strains of fast-growing, disease-free food animals. And scientists are already gearing up to use infusions of laboratory-grown genes to treat children with inherited diseases.

Genetic engineering, like computers, is no longer just a specialty unto itself. It's a process, a tool that virtually everyone in the chemical and biological sciences will use, whether they are probing the mysteries of human behavior or trying to develop faster-growing pine trees to reforest burned land. In fact, some computer scientists and genetic engineers are already exploring a possible merger of their skills to try to create an "organic computer," a "biochip" manufactured by specially engineered bacteria.

The biochip would work more like a synthetic brain than a machine, computing through molecular reactions rather than electronic circuits on silicon chips.

Eleven percent of women would choose to study astronomy. Among the younger age group and all the childless women we surveyed, astronomy ranks second behind computers as the most popular field. We know from crumbling solstice-markers and crude observatories at archaeological sites around the world that astronomy was the first science. Today, with powerful infrared and radio telescopes in place, the Space Telescope ready to go, and even larger optical telescopes in the works, scientists are studying strange phenomena, objects and worlds so faint and distant that even twenty years ago people couldn't have guessed at their existence.

Another 6 percent of women would prefer to study bionics, a field that's already produced artificial hearts, artificial pancreases to secrete insulin to diabetics, wearable artificial kidneys for dialysis patients, mechanical limbs driven by electrical signals from an amputee's own muscles, the first rudimentary artificial ears and eyes connected directly to the human brain, and computerized leg braces that allowed a person paralyzed by a spinal cord injury to walk unassisted. This field interests me particularly, since I suffered from the effects of polio as a child and know how devastating life can be when one's mobility is impaired.

Five percent of women say they would choose to study robotics, a field that, as I pointed out earlier, can do nothing but grow as faster, smarter computers give us the means to create truly useful mechanical servants and laborers.

I hope women will also become interested in developing new energy sources for the future, such as nuclear fusion, the reaction that powers our sun, and laser technologies that speed our telephone conversations and electronic mail along fiberoptic cables, etch volumes of data onto videodiscs, cut and drill in our factories, and aid in delicate eye surgery.

I'm not just expressing this challenge to women of Adrian and Nina's generation, either. Remember, the majority of American women tell us they expect to need more education or training to stay employable, and they are willing to go after it. Women over twenty-five already account for the biggest boost in college enrollments in the past decade. It's never too late for a woman to start to find a place for herself in any of these frontier fields. (Support groups have already been formed to help women in almost every field of science and engineering. You can get a free list by writing to the Office of Opportunities in Science, American Association for the Advancement of Science, 1776 Massachusetts Avenue N.W., Washington,

D.C., 20036. Ask for the booklet of "Associations and Committees of or for Women in Science, Engineering, Mathematics and Medicine" and the list of "Resources Relating to Women in Science." These should be useful to women in any country, if only to get ideas about the kinds of groups that exist and how to start them where you live. A list of free booklets that provide career information for women in various fields of science can be obtained from Box C, AAAS at the same address.)

The country needs scientists and engineers to improve life on earth and help expand into space. And to me, that's the grandest dream of all. *Space is a frontier that our generation has breached by conquering the most difficult first step: escaping the iron grip of earth's gravity. The next generation will be free to inherit the high frontier. For more and more women in the future, a career in science will be a ticket to the stars.*

o o o

When astronaut Sally Ride became the first American woman in orbit in 1983, *Newsweek* noted that her flight had come "22 years, 36 manned missions, and 57 astronauts after the first Mercury capsule splashed into the Atlantic . . ." That twenty-two year delay wasn't because of lack of interest on our part. In 1960, many scientists fully expected to see a woman orbit the earth in one of those Mercury capsules. A surprised NASA even found itself with thirteen qualified candidates. But in those days—and for many years thereafter—NASA was more worried about beating the Russians into space than about being fair to the "girls." Let me show you just how American women reached the high frontier:

The cover of *Look* magazine in February 1960 gave no hint of what was really going on in the astronaut test program that month. "Should a girl be first in space?" the headline queried. The photo showed "a girl"— thirty-three-year-old pilot and automobile test-driver Betty Skelton, fitted into a space suit and posing in front of an Atlas booster rocket. She was at Cape Canaveral as a reporter for the magazine, not as an astronaut candidate, although her story noted that "two thousand American women, mostly teenagers, have volunteered for space flight." Air Force Brigadier General Don Flickinger was quoted as saying that women wouldn't be seriously considered until the age of three-person space vehicles arrived.

But amid great secrecy, Flickinger and W. Randolph Lovelace II, the scientist responsible for medical screening of Project Mercury astronauts, had already decided to see if women were fit for spaceflight. In 1959—the same year seven military test pilots were selected as America's first astronauts—they'd quietly chosen a dozen of the top women pilots in the

United States to undergo the same screening tests. The same month that *Look* ran its article, the first candidate slipped into the Lovelace Foundation in Albuquerque, New Mexico, after telling co-woɪkers that she was off to visit her parents. She was Geraldyn "Jerrie" Cobb, twenty-nine, chief pilot for an Oklahoma aircraft company, a woman who had already logged more flight hours than any of the male astronauts and held world speed and altitude records for certain classes of aircraft. In 1959, she had been chosen U.S. aviation's Woman of the Year.

In August 1960, Lovelace let the secret slip at an international space symposium in Stockholm. Cobb had undergone "a brutal battery of seventy-five separate physical and psychological tests," *Time* magazine reported. "The result, according to Dr. Lovelace, was that [emphasis is mine] *she had qualified to 'live, observe and do optimal work in the environment of space, and return safely to earth.' Jerrie Cobb had become the first U.S. lady astronaut."*

Cobb had "demonstrated a point that many scientists have long believed: that women may be better equipped than men for existing in space," the magazine said. Lovelace explained that "women have lower body mass, need significantly less oxygen and less food, hence may be able to go up in lighter capsules, or exist longer than men on the same supplies. Since women's reproductive organs are internally located, they should be able to tolerate higher radiation levels."

Cobb was now facing an even more grueling series of tests: underwater isolation, explosive decompression, whirling centrifuge, and an oven-hot chamber. "If all goes well, perhaps in late 1962 Jerrie Cobb will don a formless pressure suit, tuck her pony-tail into a helmet and hop atop a rocket for the long, lonely trip into space," *Time* reported glibly. (Of course, no human being had yet done that. Just a Russian dog.)

But apparently no one in NASA expected her or any of the other women to pass the next stage of tests. They certainly weren't making any plans to deal with women in the program. (And even the press touted Cobb's achievements with that same smirking style reporters displayed twenty-three years later when they asked Ride whether she cried or wore a bra in space. Blond "Bachelor Girl Cobb," *Time* reported, measured "36-27-34.")

A month later, Flickinger put an end to the speculation caused by Lovelace's disclosure: *The tests had only been preliminary, he said. Cobb wasn't an official astronaut.* NASA didn't have any spacesuits "to accommodate their particular biological needs and functions."

Still, Cobb was sent on to stage two of astronaut testing at the Navy School of Aviation in Pensacola, Florida, and Lovelace started putting the other women through their paces. Apparently the space agency expected the problem to resolve itself when the women flunked their tests. But they, like Cobb, passed and were scheduled to follow her to Pensacola. *It looked as though NASA, much to its surprise, was going to end up with thirteen qualified women candidates and the embarrassment of public attention while it decided what to do with them. So in July 1961, NASA abruptly cancelled all testing of women.*

That might have been the end of the matter. The nation's attention was focused on the Russians. Soviet cosmonaut Yuri Gagarin had a few months earlier become the first human to orbit the earth. But the thirteenth woman in the program, a recent addition to the group, just happened to be helicopter pilot Jane Briggs Hart, wife of then-Senator Philip A. Hart of Michigan. By July 1962, she and Cobb had made enough noise to get a congressional subcommittee hearing convened.

Astronaut John Glenn, who earlier in 1962 had become the first American in orbit, was sent before the committee to explain why NASA wasn't training women. His answer: because astronauts have to be jet test pilots and engineers, and women aren't. And as for the qualifying tests: "They're such a minimum. As an analogy, my mother could probably pass the preseason physical examination given the Washington Redskins, but I don't think she could play many games." NASA official George M. Low told the congressmen that training women would be a waste, a luxury the nation couldn't afford if we were to get a man to the moon by 1970.

Almost a year after the hearings, the Russians beat America once again, sending female cosmonaut Valentina "Valya" Tereshkova to circle around the earth for three days in a space capsule. Not only was she not a jet pilot, she wasn't a pilot at all—just an amateur sky diver. (Some charged it was a publicity stunt on Moscow's part, not any real commitment to train women for space. And it *was* nearly twenty years before they sent another woman up—just in time to upstage Ride's first flight.)

A year later, in 1964, NASA announced a turnabout. The agency was beginning to recruit a new elite corps of scientist-astronauts for the upcoming Apollo and Skylab missions, and women were welcome to apply. Many did, but none were chosen. Not for another fourteen years.

By then the nation's space goals had shifted away from military-style plant-the-flag-and-come-home missions. Americans had begun to realize the great commercial and industrial potential of space, and work was focused on designing a reusable transportation system that would get us up and back easily.

It was the space shuttle that offered the first real opportunity of taking women into orbit. The shuttle was designed from the beginning to accommodate everybody—the diverse crew of pioneers America would need to establish her first permanent presence in space. It even had a $3 million zero-gravity toilet that could accommodate either sex. (Of course, when the first shuttle was being built in the 1970s, America's shortsighted leaders refused to set any goals for the space freighter, so all the thrill and excitement that the race to the moon generated was lost. I can't tell you how pleased I was when President Reagan in his 1984 State of the Union address pledged us to the challenge of building a permanent space station in earth orbit by the early 1990s.)

Knowing that a new generation of astronauts would be selected for the shuttle, NASA took up in 1973 where it had left off a dozen years before, *testing whether women could handle the physical and psychological rigors of space. The answer turned out to be a resounding yes, just as so many scientists of the late 1950s expected.* In 1973, a dozen Air Force flight nurses aged twenty-three to thirty-four spent weeks in bed to simulate the debilitating effects of weightlessness, and were then whirled in centrifuges to simulate the high gravity forces of reentry into the earth's atmosphere. NASA announced that they had performed as well as men who had undergone the tests.

Starting in 1977 and continuing for the next four years, NASA performed even more detailed tests on three groups of civilian women—composed of homemakers, secretaries, court reporters, teachers, nurses—ranging in age from thirty-five to sixty-five, and on similar groups of men. They were confined to bed for long periods, spun in centrifuges, dunked in tanks of water, had the lower halves of their bodies encased in vacuums, and exercised to the point of exhaustion. All the while they wore biobelts, electrodes, and rectal probes and gave frequent blood samples.

The results: *The women endured the physical hardships as well as the men, and the staff felt the women did a superior job psychologically.* The women formed tightly knit, supportive groups that helped them endure the boredom of bed rest and the trauma of testing better than the men did. And that's certainly a more important quality than muscular strength to have aboard a spacecraft or orbiting station, where small groups of people are confined together and depend on each other for support and survival. This is the age of team players in space and in science itself, not macho lone wolves.

Because of that, Dr. Harold Sandler, chief of NASA's Ames Biomedical Research Division, remarked, "In space, women are going to beat men."

NASA's astronaut recruiters, however, didn't even wait for the results of the tests. In 1978, Ride and five other women became America's first official female astronauts, part of the first group of new astronauts to be selected since the 1960s. Two more were added in 1980 and three in 1984, giving us *eleven women in today's astronaut corps of ninety-two.*

These women all applied not as pilots but as mission specialists, a job that requires no flight experience, just excellent health and a strong science or math background. By training they are physicians, astrophysicists, geologists, biochemists, and all types of engineers—electrical, ceramic, biomedical, civil, and environmental. Some of those selected in 1980 and 1984 were already working at NASA's Johnson Space Center, in Houston, as payload officers, flight simulation engineers, or medical officers when the call for new astronauts came out. (Besides the astronauts, there are other women preparing for eventual spaceflights as *payload specialists* who'll go aloft to tend their corporation's experiments.)

Some of the astronauts are married, and several have children. Except for their extensive experience in science and medicine, there are few generalities that fit all these women. Some have dreamed of space since Sputnik. Others never really thought about becoming astronauts until they saw NASA's recruitment announcements. In size, shape, muscular strength, personality, temperament, and interests they're very much individuals.

It's hard to imagine many more firsts by America's female astronauts for the press to celebrate: first American woman to go up, first to go up twice, first two to go up together, first to walk in space, first mother in space. The press even seems to have recovered from some of its obsessive fascination with the intimate details of their grooming and hygiene (yes, there are tampons aboard) and sleeping arrangements in space (they are "a lot like summer camp," with bodies floating in sleeping bags tethered to the cabin walls, Judith Resnik told reporters after her first flight.) Two years after Ride's first flight, the mere fact that another woman is hurtling into space is treated as unremarkable. We've rebounded quickly from two decades of neglect.

But America's space program is much bigger than the astronaut corps. For every person who is launched into space, thousands of support personnel are at work on the ground. (And in fact, astronauts spend years on the ground for every day in flight. They not only train but help with crew communications and scheduling during flights, preparation of payloads, and research and testing on items like the remote manipulator arm used to launch and return satellites to the shuttle's cargo bay.) NASA has had women technicians and engineers from the beginning, and they've been moving into higher visibility along with the women astronauts.

Lisabeth "Betsy" Cheshire, for instance, took her masters degree in math and went to work for NASA at the same time the first women astronauts did. In fact, she wanted to be an astronaut—and still does. But in the meantime she's made a different kind of mark as a data processing systems officer, becoming the first NASA female to work the "front room," the prime flight control room, during a shuttle mission. (The "back rooms" have even more women in support and secondary roles.) And her "coming out" was almost as tense a debut as Sally Ride's, with her boss and colleagues holding their breaths, praying nothing would go wrong. Nothing did.

Engineer Barbara N. Pearson is one of NASA's few women EECOM officers—electrical, environmental, consumables, and mechanical systems engineers. She, too, had dreams of being an astronaut. "I grew up with Star Trek, especially Scotty, who could fix anything," she recalls. "It's our inherent nature to push into space. It's not good to stop hoping for new things, to have to dwell on what we have." Now, like many young women in NASA, her sights have turned from astronaut to administrator.

The part of our space program where women are still in shortest supply is at the administrative and policy-making level, but that, too, is changing. At the highest rung is Carolyn S. Huntoon, an expert in space metabolism and biochemistry who has been with NASA since 1968 and served as advisor and mentor to the first women astronauts. In 1984, she was named associate director, third in command at the Johnson Space Center.

In the early 1970s, NASA management began recruiting young professional women into its formerly all male ranks, and they've been moving up slowly ever since, hoping to get into positions to influence the direction of America's space program. Lyn Gordon-Winkler arrived at Johnson Space Center in 1973 as a management intern, her bachelor's degree in English fresh in hand, and began to work her way up through the ranks of the contracting office, earning her master's and Ph.D. degrees on the side. Early in 1985, with NASA staffing up to meet President Reagan's mandate, Gordon-Winkler was named assistant for external affairs in the Space Station Program Office. Her job is to help set policies and bring private industry into partnership with NASA to build the orbiting station.

"There are other women who came to NASA when I did," she says. "They've put in their time, and they're ready. Unless there's some terribly blatant discrimination, you're bound to see more women in policy-making positions in the next few years."

And I can't imagine anything more important and exciting than the space policy decisions NASA, Congress, and the President are going to have to make during the next five to ten years. The space station is only our first step away from earth, an "industrial park" with as many as eight people at a time staffing it to begin with, and perhaps double that by 2000. They'll be assembling and launching communications and solar power satellites, tending space telescopes, conducting research for government and industry, including the manufacture of precious chemicals and medicines, ultra-pure crystals, and novel alloys for export to earth.

It's a marvelous first step, but it's just that. Washington policymakers and NASA-sponsored study groups are already debating what the next goal should be. (There are still only a handful of women scientists involved in these studies.) Do we concentrate our money on expanding the station, building up our space industries and research facilities and even tourism? Or should we return to the moon as soon as possible and establish permanent mining colonies. Or should we open up the twenty-first century in a truly spectacular fashion with a manned expedition to Mars? Better yet, if we were able to get industry and government from many nations working together, perhaps we could do it all.

There's an important reason I imagined the world looking heavenward to a festival like Earthlight 2000 as this century closes. I think we need the inspiration that the vision of a new frontier can bring. We're too crowded here, too steeped in ancient feuds and angers, too limited in our power to make sweeping changes without causing great pain. We'll leave the earth first for economic and commercial reasons, to bring back the bounty of other worlds. But in the end we'll stay and continue to explore simply because it's part of our nature to do so—just as we have explored every nook and cranny of our home planet.

Forty-six percent of American women say they would take a trip into space if they had the chance, and this includes 58 percent of the younger women, aged twenty-five to thirty-four. (Almost 80 percent of the Japanese women we talked to, 41 percent of the English, and 27 percent of the South Africans would go.) Why would they go? "To experience the feeling of newness." "It's new, exciting, unknown." "It would be an adventure." "It would be nice to see infinity."

And how many would stay? *Eighteen percent of American women find the idea of living in a space colony appealing,* and that goes up to 23 percent among childless women. *Fifteen percent would find life on another planet or moon appealing,* including 22 percent of working mothers. (Interestingly, the most popular alternative habitat among the Japanese and South African women we talked to would be an underwater city here on earth. Another planet or moon was the second choice, and a space colony third. The English would put another planet or moon first, an underwater city second, and a space colony third.)

The exploitation of space is already twenty years old and women can't afford to wait another generation to get involved at all levels. I truly believe some of the girls of Adrian and Nina's generation will raise their own children inside colonies in high earth orbit and settlements on the moon. They'll be the first to pioneer family life in space and to adapt the values, rituals, and cultural traditions of an earthbound people to novel, manmade worlds. These colonies will be too small and the challenges they face too great to permit the talents of any individual to be wasted. On the high frontier, the woman of tomorrow will truly be in her element.

12

BREAKING TRADITION

My dream for tomorrow's woman is not that she become like man but that she influence the future with her own intellect, values, and perceptions.
—Kathy Keeton

ook ahead with me again to 2025, when today's baby girls are approaching mid-life. I hope Kelly and Adrian and Nina seem familiar to you, because their hopes and dreams are much the same as ours. And so are their lives, a little bolder and perhaps more expressive than ours, less harried in some ways. Technology has not only allowed them to create more fulfilling careers but restored to them the leisure and family time so many working women find in short supply today.

I think the most unrealistic fear that people have of the future is that it will somehow be too orderly, cold, and mechanistic. Nothing could be further from the truth. *Women of tomorrow will not be "high-tech women," just ordinary women who have taken charge of the technology of their age and applied it to very human goals.* And the goals will be as diverse as the women themselves.

Kelly, for instance, with her love of art, uses all the rich magic of interactive video technology to take tomorrow's schoolchildren on entrancing "firsthand" tours of the world's great museums and galleries. She grew up as distant from the technology of her age as I did, but she's mustered the self-confidence to learn and to put the best tools to use in her teaching. (I hope our schools won't wait forty years to hire more people like her.)

She's also a mother who wants to be at home while her children are growing up, and the telephone/computer network that connects businesses, schools, and homes makes it easy for her to do that. Kelly's flexible hours and her husband's shorter workweek allow them to indulge their love of both art and travel, taking their children with them on jaunts to gallery openings and showings around the world. Their children aren't high-tech children, just because they live in a home with automated appliances. They still ride bicycles, jump rope, and, unfortunately, don't always pick up after themselves any better than the children of 1985.

Unlike Kelly, Adrian doesn't know much about how to produce the three-dimensional holographic images of homes she sells in her real estate business. They arrive on videodisc every week from the listing service, and she thinks of them as a sales tool, more effective than the brochures that came before them. But she's savvy enough to realize that they add a flare and drama to her presentations that she and her clients both enjoy. Besides, they save time that she can use doing what she really values.

Like many women of tomorrow, Adrian's avocation has become the real passion of her life. She and Mike devote as much time to their amateur theater company as they do to their jobs. (The word "hobby" hardly seems to apply in the twenty-first century. It's an industrial age concept that trivializes the things people do when they're not making a living. And after all, the bulk of people's time in 2025 is "spare time.")

Nina shares my special passion, a fascination with space, and she's chosen a career in microbiology, intensely exciting in its own right, as her ticket into orbit. For all her intellect and ambition, Nina is no steely technocrat either. She's a romantic, a poet who chose a life in science because of the rich promise of adventure and discovery. She's a woman as vulnerable to a broken love affair as any of us, and not immune to depression and a fleeting sense of failure when she learns she can't conceive a child without the help of technology. But she doesn't shrink from using the technology that's available to achieve her very human dream of having children.

These women of course, are products of my imagination. But *the educated imagination is where the future begins.* By anticipating tomorrow's possibilities, we and the women who follow us will be able to make wiser decisions about our own lives when the time for choice arrives. And I hope it has become clear to you as you've read this book that women of tomorrow will have plenty of choices to make.

On an individual level, we women are being called upon to take more responsibility for ourselves, economically, physically, intellectually, and emotionally. Our health and longevity depend increasingly on our own lifestyles. Our sex lives, childbearing decisions, and family patterns are no longer rigidly prescribed.

On a wider scale, we're coming into the workplace in force just as technology is breaking down the barriers that once kept us out of society's frontline jobs. We have, for the first time, the opportunity to provide half the values, the vitality, and the intellectual power to run the world.

If we women are to grasp this opportunity, I think *we're going to have to learn not to limit ourselves by shying away from at least a basic understanding of science and technology.*

For mothers of girls of Kelly's and Nina's generation, I think there are some specific things that need to be attended to right now, things that will have an impact on their spatial and math skills, self-confidence, and attitudes toward science and the future:

· Encourage your daughter's natural curiosity about how things work by giving her *toys and three-dimensional puzzles that can be taken apart and put back together again.* When she's older, get her a telescope or a book of science experiments that she can perform in the kitchen or garage with simple items like baking soda, soft drinks, and string. (Every child has her own idea about what's fun, but there are hundreds of toys, models, and kits on every subject to choose from in catalogs like Franklin Scientific from the Franklin Institute Science Museum, in Philadelphia, and in catalogs from companies that sell classroom aids to schools.)

· *Outdoor sports and games* can increase not only her fitness and coordination but her spatial skills as well—and that's apparently a plus when it comes to mechanical sense and mathematical reasoning. John Money points out that you get "geometry laid right out on the softball field." Just learning to throw and catch a ball requires well-developed spatial perception, so does anticipating a tennis shot and getting in position to return it. Kristina Hooper, a cognitive psychologist who directs Atari's computer research lab in California's Silicon Valley, told one interviewer that "sports gives you an intuitive feel for things like momentum, acceleration, pressure, velocity, and so on. Girls often get good at number manipulation only to find out in college that isn't what math is all about. It's more about the kinds of spatial relationships you can learn through athletics."

- Remember, too, the finding I cited before that *"cultures that allow independence to children tend to produce adults with higher spatial scores."* (An energetic little girl shouldn't be admonished constantly to "play quietly," "don't get dirty," and "be sweet." I certainly think I benefitted from my "tomboy" years and a tolerant mother.)

- *Your daughter will pick up whatever sense of comfort or discomfort you have about technology.* If there's a computer in your home, let her see you using it instead of just her father and brothers. If there isn't, I hope you'll get one by the time she's in kindergarten. Children have a delightful time at the keyboard learning to pick out letters and write their names or compose stories on the screen even before their little fingers are coordinated enough to hold a pencil. (I mentioned in Chapter 9 where to look for the best games and educational programs, for youngsters and for yourself.) Best of all, girls who get this early start never have the chance to become timid about computers or learn from their playmates that the machines are "for boys." All the studies to date show girls just aren't getting equal access to computers in the schools or in computer camps, and girls have an aversion to the male-dominated pool-hall atmosphere of video arcades, so home is the best hope to avoid creating another "gender gap." Don't think games are not important along with other computer skills. A Harvard study found that after five hours of playing video games, women who had first scored lower than men on spatial tests pulled even with them.

- *Assume your daughter has some natural competence.* Not everything she does well is accomplished because she's a "hard little worker." Girls on average are born with at least as great an intellect, sense of self-esteem, and achievement motivation as boys. A girl needs to be assured early that those are good, positive feminine traits and that the world is going to expect her to use them. It's not enough that she simply "be sweet" and "act like a lady."

- Stimulate her curiosity about science by giving her *books that tell about women scientists and engineers working on exciting projects and solving real human problems.* Remember, a girl isn't generally as interested in abstract subjects as a boy unless they can be tied into human needs and relationships. (You can't count on elementary school teachers to encourage your daughter *or* son's interest in science. As I mentioned before, half of third graders have positive attitudes about their science lessons, but that drops to 20 percent by eighth grade.)

- Make sure when she gets to high school that she takes *all the math, computer, and science classes that are available,* as well as all the English, foreign language, art, and history classes she can. This is no time for her to be taking home economics, study hall, and other "soft" classes.
- In *college,* for you or your daughter, *try not to specialize too narrowly,* even in a hot field like computer programming. A broad education is the best background for any specialty in today's fast-changing workplace, where even an engineer's knowledge is obsolete in five years. Scientists and professionals already have to count on a lifetime of learning, just as other workers should expect to need new training periodically. "Soon there will be work only for those who have the skills of speaking, listening, observing, and measuring, and the confidence to use their minds to analyze and solve problems," says James O'Toole, a University of Southern California management professor who writes extensively on the future of work. "Those who will succeed in the work force will be those who have learned how to learn—the unthinking jobs all will be done by machines . . ."

My purpose in making all these suggestions isn't to try to turn every young girl into a mathematician or scientist or engineer. I think most teenage girls simply have no idea what they want out of life. And I'd like to see them develop all their interests and abilities *so that twelve-year-old girls aren't foreclosing the options of twenty or thirty-year-old women.*

And on a larger scale, I think our nation desperately needs this kind of scientifically literate citizen if we're to make intelligent social and political decisions in the future. Science and technology are the greatest forces for change in our world. People who don't understand them too often fear and resent them. These are the people plagued by dark visions of a cold, sterile, doomed, and dehumanized society. And they're also the ones who feel too paralyzed and frustrated to do anything about it.

Women, more often than men, find themselves in this resentful and powerless role of "technopeasant," forced to choose among several unappealing options they had no hand in generating. *I have great hope that the women of Kelly and Nina's generation will put an end to our technological alienation.* Science and technology, after all, offer us our greatest, perhaps our only hope, of improving the human condition. *The truly degrading and dehumanizing forces in our world aren't computers and robots. They are poverty, disease, starvation, ignorance, oppression, and overcrowding.*

Humans are tool-building creatures. Tool-building is a trait as old as our humanity. We learned how to build fires and make baskets, stone knives, and wheels in order to ease the struggle to survive. We're building lasers and computers and genetically engineering our corn plants for the same reason. I can't imagine that handing our drudge work over to robots will diminish our humanity any more than loading burdens on ox carts did. A computer is more complex than a wheel, but no more unfathomable. *We women have to get back in touch with the tools of our age.*

o   o   o

I know from our survey that *the vast majority of you share my optimism about the future,* and you also think the world of tomorrow is going to be a better place. When I look ahead, I see before us a more relaxed, more fun, more richly diverse society. It won't be a perfect world, but it certainly won't be cold and sterile, either. After all, it will still be full of people, and we're the source of most of life's headaches, as well as its joys.

It will be, like today, a world in which our lives center on family and warm personal relationships. Although videophones, electronic mail, and satellite systems will allow us to communicate more easily with faraway friends, most of us aren't going to spend a large part of our time socializing that way. We're social animals, and we need to meet, mingle, talk, stroll, make love, and celebrate rituals together. And in the near future we're going to have more time to do these things.

Tomorrow's cities, like the best of today's, will be diverse, vital, unpredictable, and constantly in flux, celebrating our sociability as well as our individuality. Morton Hoppenfeld, chief architect of the 1960s "new town" of Columbia, Maryland, when asked what cities of the future would be like, pointed to the bustling old Lexington Market in Baltimore.

"If there aren't a hundred places for impromptu theater and celebration," Hoppenfield said, "it isn't a good city. When you're talking about cities, you're talking about life, not buildings. Architects are concerned with shape and form, which is largely irrelevant. To me, an architect's work is not complete until people flesh it out and fill it up." He'd make sure cities had plenty of choices in housing, education, and shopping and that they were full of trees, lakes and streams, markets, meandering lanes, and public gathering spots.

We're already beginning to humanize architecture, revitalizing the deserted downtowns of older cities with parks, theaters, shops, restaurants, and loft-apartments. The futurists of today, unlike those of the 1940s and 1950s, no longer envision moving our entire population into sterile two-hundred-story steel and glass towers with suspended highways arching between them. In fact, the planned "super city" of Brasília, which has never captured even a glimmer of Rio de Janeiro's vitality, is an example of why new cities can't be imposed on us from an architect's drawing board. Cities of the future will grow as today's great cities have, one building at a time, as people feel the need to come together at a certain spot for fun or commerce.

Tomorrow's communications systems and shortened workweek, of course, will give all of us a great deal more flexibility about where we live. Many more people will have two homes, spending three or four working days in a city and perhaps retreating to a beach or mountaintop the rest of the week. Or if a person's job permits telecommuting, she can spend all of her time at a rural or forest retreat. Technology eliminates the need for people to live in places they don't like just because company headquarters are located there. This is just one more area where we'll be able to express a lot of individuality in our future lifestyles.

New and old will blend within our homes, too, as we slide our VCRs and digital TVs into elegant walnut consoles next to grandmother's rocking chair. "High-tech dissonance results when you put your computer in an environment of minimalist furniture," *Megatrends* author John Naisbitt says. "The more computers in our houses, the more likely the other aspects of the environment, the furniture—say, the sofa, the curtains—will get softer, plumper, cuddlier, or whatever, in contrast."

We'll personalize our home robots when we get them, too—we are great humanizers of our tools—pressuring manufacturers to provide them in assorted colors and shapes, just as with our cars. And we'll undoubtedly try to impress one another with our robots' capabilities, just as we do with the horsepower, handling, and sleek lines of our cars. Everything we bring into our homes, no matter how alien and disquieting it seems at first, eventually accretes a moss of folklore and ritual.

This doesn't mean we *must* embrace every electronic gimmick on the market, filling our homes with gadgetry and applauding every new technology that emerges. Maybe you like grocery shopping in person instead of by computer, seeing the office gang every day instead of telecommuting, having your babies without the aid of high-tech medicine, or missing phone calls rather than using an answering machine. The choices about which technologies we invite into our lives and homes, and how they are used, will always be up to us. Even if your baby is conceived in a lab dish, you can deliver it in a home-style birthing center if you choose. But I think all of us should know enough about the technology of our age to make *wise* choices, not snap decisions based on timidity or fear.

I haven't said much about leisure time except that we're going to have more of it as the workweek inevitably shortens. How we spend it is a very individual choice. One thing I believe all of us are going to have to do in the near future, however, is to rethink what time means to us, and what's important in our lives. Too many Americans still treat the things they do in the gaps between job and household chores as "marking time" or "filling time." As I mentioned before, in the not-too-distant future our nonworking time will be the largest segment of our lives (assuming we don't opt for a second or third job).

Some cynics think most Americans will spend it in front of the TV, watching more football or soap operas. I'm sure some will (people our comedians have already dubbed "couch potatoes"). And once teletext and videotex link our homes, we're bound to see video gambling, transcontinental bingo and bridge tournaments, and a myriad of other on-line entertainments.

I don't think most of us are going to live in front of our screens, however. We'll want to get together, especially outdoors at sporting events, parks, zoos, and amusement parks. Some will camp and hike in the wilderness; others will lie on the beach. And we'll all travel more, on earth and eventually in space. (I hope to get at least as far as earth orbit in my lifetime. There's no telling what kinds of games and sports we'll invent in the weightlessness of space, but I can hardly wait to see! Pleasure and play are such important parts of human nature that we're bound to introduce a lot of fun into whatever space-based cultures we create.) Recreation is going to be one of tomorrow's fastest growing industries. For every pastime that requires equipment, from tennis racquets and skis to cameras, technology will bring us more and better.

(This goes for some more traditional pastimes, too. M. Granger Morgan, of Carnegie-Mellon University, foresees the application of computer-aided design to home sewing. "In the not very distant future, I can imagine my wife designing fancy stitches on our home computer with a 'mouse'-driven interactive graphics system and then downloading the results to the micro-processor in her next-generation sewing machine in order to produce intricate, perfectly executed, decorative borders.")

I'm most excited, however, by predictions of a renaissance in the arts—theater, dance, music, literature, poetry, and painting. Powerful new world-wide communications systems are being put in place, by satellite and fiber-optic cable. We can use these new media to explore our diverse cultural heritages, fulfill our psychic needs, and stimulate our minds and our imaginations. I have no doubt human creativity will grow and flourish in tomorrow's world.

I grow impatient with nostalgia, the romanticizing of a past that in reality was nothing we'd care to relive. The future is where we have to be, and it's the only part of our lives that we have the power to change. Sometimes we're so caught up in the present that we forget there's a future growing, taking shape from the decisions we're making now. I hope you'll focus your vision on tomorrow. Take a look at the possibilities I've outlined here and see which one fits your values and your dreams. Then work for it. Ambition and imagination are the keys to the future, for they'll prepare us to become what we've only dreamed of being.

LAST WORD

oin my imaginings once more and look ahead to our granddaughters' lives. The year is 2050. Women are making their mark in a world much larger than ours. Kelly's daughter Pamela has become a well-known artist who uses magnetized gases to paint images in the sky, ephemeral ballets of light and color that delight and inspire people all over earth and its orbiting colonies.

Adrian's daughter has followed her mother's footsteps, opening her own real estate business specializing in recreation homes. With earth and its moon so crowded now, she's concentrating on the growing market for ring-view cottages on the moons of Saturn.

Nina's daughter, born on earth but raised from earliest memory in the colonies, has inherited her mother's fascination with the adventure and challenge of space exploration. She'll be leaving the solar system soon, *captain of the* Athena, *earth's first starship bound for Alpha Centauri, the nearest star-group to our sun. With her scientist husband and the rest of the crew, she'll explore the planets around the star Proxima Centauri in search of brave new worlds to colonize.*

APPENDIX I

Sample Questionnaire from the Survey of Women in the United States

This study is being conducted to have women's perspective on life in the future—technology, home life, employment opportunities, family, and so on.

o   o   o

Hundreds of women across the country are being asked to participate in this opinion poll by completing this questionnaire. Your opinions are very important to the success of this project. Your answers, however, will never be linked to you personally, but rather tabulated with the answers of the other women who are being surveyed. Please do not sign your name on this booklet.

o   o   o

We are sure you will find the subjects covered in the questionnaire interesting and thought-provoking. As we mentioned to you over the telephone, the results of this study are to be published in a book in the fall of 1985. The book will examine, from a woman's point of view, the many options and challenges presented by our changing society and will explore the future roles and expectations of both sexes over the coming year.

INSTRUCTIONS

PLEASE ANSWER ALL QUESTIONS ON BOTH SIDES OF THE PAGES IN THE QUESTIONNAIRE. BE SURE TO READ EACH QUESTION CAREFULLY BEFORE ANSWERING. TO SELECT AN ANSWER, PLACE AN "X" IN THE BOX THAT MOST CLOSELY REPRESENTS YOUR SITUATION, FEELINGS, ETC. *IGNORE* THE NUMBERS NEXT TO EACH BOX. THEY ARE USED TO PROCESS ANSWERS ON A COMPUTER.

We personally guarantee that no one outside the Yankelovich, Skelly and White, Inc. organization will see your answers to this questionnaire. All completed questionnaires will be processed into a general report and then destroyed.

Florence R. Skelly
President
Yankelovich, Skelly and White, Inc.

SECTION I — ALTERNATIVE LIFESTYLES

1. In what type of environment do you expect to live most of your life?
   Urban neighborhood .... ☐ -1
   Suburb in commuting distance of a city .... ☐ -2
   Small town or village .... ☐ -3
   Rural area .... ☐ -4

2. If at sometime in the future, you were asked to live in a new type of environment, which of the following would appeal to you most?
   An underground community .... 6 ☐ -1
   An underwater community .... ☐ -2
   A colony somewhere out in space, like on a space ☐ -3
      station, satellite or ship ....
   Another planet or moon...................... ☐ -4

   Other: _____ ☐ -5
   (WRITE IN)

   None of these seem appealing at all .... ☐ -6

3. Which one or two of the following career choices is most appealing to you?
   Astronaut/pilot........................... 7 ☐ -1
   Athlete .... ☐ -2
   Business executive .... ☐ -3
   Combat soldier .... ☐ -4

   Computer programmer .... ☐ -5
   Engineer .... ☐ -6
   Fashion designer .... ☐ -7
   Fire fighter .... ☐ -8

   Interior designer .... ☐ -9
   Lawyer .... ☐ -0
   Mathematician .... ☐ -x
   Medical doctor .... ☐ -y

   Military officer .... 8 ☐ -1
   Nurse .... ☐ -2
   Policewoman .... ☐ -3
   Politician/stateswoman .... ☐ -4

   Scientist .... ☐ -5
   Secretary .... ☐ -6
   Teacher .... ☐ -7
   Mother .... ☐ -8
   Writer/editor .... ☐ -9

Other: _____   ☐ -0
(WRITE IN)

None of these ....   ☐ -x

4. Are there any jobs in this list that you think women are unsuited for, even with proper training? (PLACE AN "X" NEXT TO ANY THAT APPLY)
Astronaut/pilot   9   ☐ -1
Athlete ....   ☐ -2
Business executive ....   ☐ -3
Combat soldier ....   ☐ -4

Computer programmer ....   ☐ -5
Engineer ....   ☐ -6
Fashion designer ....   ☐ -7
Fire fighter ....   ☐ -8

Interior designer ....   ☐ -9
Lawyer ....   ☐ -0
Mathematician ....   ☐ -x
Medical doctor ....   ☐ -y

Military officer   10   ☐ -1
Nurse ....   ☐ -2
Policewoman ....   ☐ -3
Politician/stateswoman ....   ☐ -4

Scientist ....   ☐ -5
Secretary ....   ☐ -6
Teacher ....   ☐ -7
Writer/editor ....   ☐ -8

Other: _____   ☐ -9
(WRITE IN)

None of these ....   ☐ -0

5. Which one or two of these women do you think represents the best role model for young women today?
Margaret Thatcher (politician)   11   ☐ -1
Sally Ride (astronaut) ....   ☐ -2
Jane Fonda (actress) ....   ☐ -3
Mother Teresa (religious leader) ....   ☐ -4

Barbara Walters (news commentator) ......   ☐ -5
Ann Landers (advice columnist) ....   ☐ -6
Geraldine Ferraro (politician) ....   ☐ -7
Chris Evert Lloyd (athlete) ....   ☐ -8

Nancy Reagan (the President's wife) .... [ ]-9
Estee Lauder (businesswoman) .... [ ]-0
Sandra Day O'Connor (Supreme Court Justice) . [ ]-x
Helen Gurley Brown (publisher) .... [ ]-y

Lillian Hellman (writer) .... 12 [ ]-1
Jacqueline Onassis .... [ ]-2
Gloria Steinem (woman's advocate) .... [ ]-3
Christie Brinkley (model) .... [ ]-4

Other: _____ [ ]-5
(WRITE IN)

None of the above .... [ ]-6

SECTION II — TECHNOLOGY AND THE COMPUTER AGE

6a. With which of the following areas of science do you have any familiarity
at all? (PLACE AN "X" NEXT TO ALL THAT APPLY)
Computers .... 13 [ ]-1
Robotics (the design and construction of robots) . [ ]-2
Genetic engineering .... [ ]-3
Bionics (creation of artificial limbs and body parts) [ ]-4
....
Infertility and test-tube baby research .... [ ]-5
Molecular biology (medicine and biological re-
search) .... [ ]-6
Astronomy .... [ ]-7

None of above .... [ ]-8

b. Which of these areas of science would you like to learn more about?
(PLACE AN "X" NEXT TO ALL THAT APPLY)
Computers .... 14 [ ]-1
Robotics .... [ ]-2
Genetic engineering .... [ ]-3
Bionics .... [ ]-4
Infertility and test-tube baby research .... [ ]-5
Molecular biology .... [ ]-6
Astronomy .... [ ]-7

None of above .... [ ]-8

c. If you were offered an all-expense paid grant to study any of these areas
of science, which one, if any, would you choose?
Computers .... 15 [ ]-1

Robotics .... -2
Genetic engineering .... -3
Bionics .... -4
Infertility and test-tube baby research .... -5
Molecular biology .... -6
Astronomy .... -7

None of above .... -8

7. In which one or two of the following areas would a major technological
    breakthrough have the greatest positive effect on your life?
    Health 16   -1
    Energy .... -2
    Transportation .... -3
    Education .... -4

    Domestic environment .... -5
    Work environment .... -6
    Birth control/reproduction .... -7
    Weather .... -8

    Other: _____ -9
                        (WRITE IN)

Over the past few years, the media have been telling us that we are in
the dawning of a new age, the "Information Age," in which the computer
will play a major role in most people's households.

8a. Do you want to have a computer in your home?
     Yes, definitely 17   -1
     Yes, probably .... -2
     Maybe .... -3
     Probably not .... -4
     Definitely not .... -5

     Already have one .... -6

b. How would you use a home computer, if you had one?
    I'd write on it, like a word processor 18   -1
    I'd work at home, and use it to communicate with   -2
        the office ....
    I'd play video games and/or mental games on it   -3
    I'd use it with my children, both to teach them and   -4
        to learn with them ....

    I'd do family accounting and bookkeeping ..... -5
    I'd shop from home with it .... -6

I'd look up medical information, catalogs, directories, encyclopedia listings and other data using "databases" .... ☐-7

I'd file my own data on it—addresses, recipes, shopping lists, and so on .... ☐-8

Other: _____ ☐-9

(WRITE IN)

I wouldn't use one .... ☐-0

c. When do you plan to get a home computer, if you don't have one already?

This year .... 19 ☐-1
Within the next 2–3 years .... ☐-2
Within the next 4–5 years .... ☐-3
Not until more than 5 years from now .... ☐-4
Never .... ☐-5

Already have one .... ☐-6

One of the exciting new technologies being developed these days is robotics, and many people are predicting that robots will someday be widely available to do household chores.

9. In which of the following capacities would you be willing to let a household robot help you? (PLACE AN "X" NEXT TO ANY THAT APPLY)

Housecleaning .... 20 ☐-1
Cooking .... ☐-2
Gardening .... ☐-3
Teaching the children .... ☐-4

Acting as a burglar alarm .... ☐-5
Acting as a pet or companion .... ☐-6
Washing and changing the baby .... ☐-7
Planning personal finances (i.e., savings or investments) .... ☐-8
Doing laundry .... ☐-9

Other: _____ ☐-0
(WRITE IN)
None of the above .... ☐-x

SECTION III — WORKING OUTSIDE THE HOME — NOW AND IN THE FUTURE

10. Do you expect to work outside the home either part or full time for most of your adult life?

a. Yes. .... 21 ☐ -1

b. No .... ☐ -2

c. Not sure .... ☐ -3

11. *IF YOU ANSWERED "YES":* Why will you be working? (PLACE AN "X" NEXT TO ANY THAT APPLY)

Financial necessity .... 22 ☐ -1

To provide financial help for family, i.e., college tuition .... ☐ -2

For personal financial gains .... ☐ -3

To get out of the house and stay active .... ☐ -4

To get ahead in my chosen career .... ☐ -5

All of these reasons .... ☐ -6

Other: _____ ☐ -7

(WRITE IN)

12. Which of these jobs do you think will be made obsolete by new technologies? (PLACE AN "X" NEXT TO ANY THAT APPLY)

Bank teller .... 23 ☐ -1

Combat soldier .... ☐ -2

Draftsman .... ☐ -3

Factory foreman .... ☐ -4

Fast-food worker .... ☐ -5

File clerk .... ☐ -6

Fire fighter .... ☐ -7

Machinist .... ☐ -8

Miner .... ☐ -9

Secretary .... ☐ -0

Ticket agent .... ☐ -x

Welder .... ☐ -y

Other: _____ 24 ☐ -1

(WRITE IN)

All of the above .... ☐ -2

None of above .... ☐ -3

13. *IF YOU ARE PRESENTLY EMPLOYED:* How concerned are you about your job being made obsolete—within, say, the next 10–20 years?

Seriously concerned .... 25 ☐ -1
Moderately concerned .... ☐ -2
Not very concerned .... ☐ -3
Not at all concerned .... ☐ -4

14. If you had a job in which you had the choice of working in an office or doing the same work at home—communicating with the office by computer and telephone—which would you choose?

I'd work at the office .... 26 ☐ -1
I'd rather work at home .... ☐ -2
I'd want to spend some time working at home, but ☐ -3
  not all the time ....

15. *IF YOU ARE NOT EMPLOYED:* Would you be willing to go back to school or go through a training program in order to become more employable?

Yes .... 27 ☐ -1
No .... ☐ -2
Maybe .... ☐ -3
Already have done it/am doing it now .... ☐ -4

16. *IF YOU ARE EMPLOYED:* Do you think that you will need job retraining to remain employable over the coming years?

a. Yes .... 28 ☐ -1
b. No .... ☐ -2
c. Don't know .... ☐ -3
d. Already in retraining or going back to school . ☐ -4

SECTION IV — CHILDREN AND FAMILY

17. In your opinion, how many children should the ideal American family have?

None .... 29 ☐ -1
One .... ☐ -2
Two .... ☐ -3
Three .... ☐ -4
More than three .... ☐ -5

18. In China, the government already tries to restrict the number of children to one per family. Should the American government similarly use tax incentives and welfare payments to encourage smaller families?

Yes .... 30 ☐ -1

No .... -2
Don't know .... -3

19. What do you think the typical family of the future will be like?
A single woman with children .... 31 -1
A mother and father with children (traditional fam-
ily) .... -2
A mother and father with children, and grandpar-
ents or other close relatives living nearby (ex-
tended family) .... -3
Communal groups of couples with children who
share childcare and other tasks .... -4
A childless couple .... -5
Single adults without children .... -6

20. Does raising a family get in the way of a woman's career?
Yes, always .... 32 -1
Most of the time .... -2
Only sometimes .... -3
Never .... -4

21. Are the children of full-time homemakers generally better off than the
children of working mothers?
Yes, always .... 33 -1
Most of the time .... -2
Only sometimes .... -3
Never .... -4

22. What age would you want your child to be before you returned to work?

Less than 1 year .... 34 -1
1–2 years .... -2
3–4 years .... -3
5–6 years .... -4
7–8 years .... -5
9–10 years .... -6
11–12 years .... -7
13–15 years .... -8
Over 15 years .... -9
I wouldn't work .... -0

23. If you had the financial choice, would you prefer to stay at home while
your child was young?
Yes .... 35 -1

No .... -2
Maybe .... -3

24a. *IF YOU DO NOT HAVE ANY CHILDREN:* Would you consider remaining childless in order to concentrate on a career or other personal goals?
Yes, I'd consider it .... 36 -1
No, I'd never consider it .... -2
I've already decided to remain childless .... -3
I considered it and decided I wanted children .. -4

b. *IF YOU HAVE HAD A CHILD:* Do you feel that being a mother has prevented you from pursuing a career or other personal goals?
Yes, but given the choice I would have done things 37 -1
exactly the same all over again ....
Yes, but given the choice I would have tried to do -2
things differently ....
No .... -3
Don't know .... -4

25. If you were unmarried and had not yet had a child, how concerned would you be at the thought of getting old without having children?
Very concerned .... 38 -1
Moderately concerned .... -2
Slightly concerned .... -3
Not concerned at all .... -4

26. If you were unmarried and wanted children, would you consider getting pregnant and raising a child on your own?
Yes, definitely .... 39 -1
Maybe .... -2
Probably not .... -3
Definitely not .... -4

27a. In an ideal household, in which both partners work, which of these domestic responsibilities should be *shared equally* by the woman and her partner? (PLACE AN "X" NEXT TO ALL THAT APPLY)
Cleaning the house .... 40 -1
Paying the bills .... -2
Doing home repairs .... -3
Doing the laundry .... -4

Tutoring the children .... -5
Deciding how money is to be saved and invested -6

Planning the meals . . . . -7
Transporting the children . . . . -8

Grocery shopping . . . . -9
Deciding how money is to be spent -0
Raising the children . . . . -x
Yard work . . . . -y

Doing the cooking 41   -1
Planning social activities with friends/relatives . . -2
Washing the dishes . . . . -3

b. *IF YOU ARE MARRIED OR LIVE TOGETHER:* Which of these responsibilities are currently shared between your partner and yourself? (PLACE AN "X" NEXT TO ALL THAT APPLY)

Cleaning the house 42   -1
Paying the bills . . . . -2
Doing home repairs . . . . -3
Doing the laundry . . . . -4

Tutoring the children . . . . -5
Deciding how money is to be saved and Invested -6

Planning the meals . . . . -7
Transporting the children . . . . -8

Grocery shopping . . . . -9
Deciding how money is to be spent . . . . -0
Raising the children . . . . -x
Yard work . . . . -y

Doing the cooking 43   -1
Planning social activities with friends/relatives . . -2
Washing the dishes . . . . -3

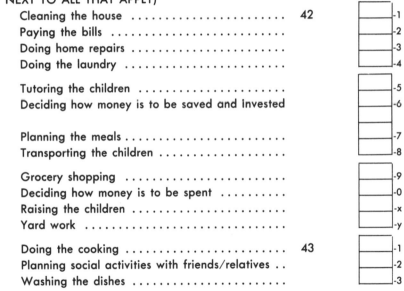

These are just a few more important questions to answer. Please know how much we appreciate your participation in this exciting and important research investigation. Your answers, and those of other survey participants, will lead to a better understanding of how American women really feel about some of the key issues of today—and tomorrow.

SECTION V — RISKS AND NEW OPTIONS FOR THE FUTURE

Many of the medical advances we've seen in the past fifteen years have been in the area of childbirth. One of the new procedures involves genetic testing of the unborn child to spot possible abnormalities before birth.

28. If you were pregnant, would you want to have a genetic test (amniocentesis) performed to check out possible defects in the fetus?

   Yes 44   ☐-1
   No ....   ☐-2
   Maybe ....   ☐-3

29. As genetic screening tests improve, which of these findings, if any, would lead you to consider aborting an unborn child? (PLACE AN "X" NEXT TO ANY THAT APPLY)

   Extremely serious illness such as: Down's syndrome 45   ☐-1
   (mongolism), mental retardation, schizophrenia, breakdown of the body's immune system ....
   Moderately serious illness such as: blindness, muscular dystrophy, risk of early heart disease ...   ☐-2
   Less serious illnesses such as: asthma, dyslexia, diabetes ....   ☐-3
   Other: _____   ☐-x
   (WRITE IN)
   None of the above—I wouldn't consider abortion   ☐-y

30. If the medical risks of pregnancy were the same at any age, what would you consider the ideal age to give birth?

   a. Under 20 years   46   ☐-1
   b. 21–25 years ....   ☐-2
   c. 26–30 years ....   ☐-3
   d. 31–35 years ....   ☐-4
   e. 36–40 years ....   ☐-5
   f. 41–45 years ....   ☐-6
   g. 46–50 years ....   ☐-7
   h. Over 50 years ....   ☐-8

31. One fascinating option for pregnant women that is being experimented with these days is *cryogenic freezing of the fetus,* in which the unborn child is removed from the womb and safely frozen by advanced scientific methods until the woman is ready to continue her pregnancy.

If the technique became safe and more widely available, would you consider having an embryo cryogenically frozen for reimplantation and birth later on in your life?

Yes .... 47 ___ -1
No .... ___ -2
Maybe .... ___ -3

32. If you could choose the sex of your first child, would you want a boy or a girl?

a. Boy 48 ___ -1
b. Girl ___ -2
c. Both (fraternal twins) .... ___ -3
d. Doesn't matter to me/I'd rather let nature take ___ -4
its course ....

33. If you could choose as the father of your child a man in any of the areas or professions shown below, which would be your first choice? Which would be your second choice? (ONE ANSWER ONLY)

	First Choice		Second Choice		
A politician or statesman	49	-1	51	___	-1
A scientist		-2		___	-2
An athlete		-3		___	-3
A lawyer		-4		___	-4
An actor		-5		___	-5
An entertainer		-6		___	-6
A writer......................		-7		___	-7
An artist		-8		___	-8
A musician		-9		___	-9
A scholar....................		-0		___	-0
A successful businessman		-x		___	-x
A religious leader		-y		___	-y
A teacher	50	-1	52	___	-1
Other: _____		-2		___	-2
(WRITE IN)					
None of these		-3	-3		

34. Which one or two of these famous men of the present and recent past is the best example of the kind of person you would find most desirable as the father of your child?

Neil Armstrong .... 53 ___ -1
Henry Kissinger .... ___ -2
Pablo Picasso .... ___ -3
Lee Iacocca .... ___ -4

Albert Einstein . . . .   [ ]-5
John D. Rockefeller . . . .   [ ]-6
Michael Jackson . . . .   [ ]-7
John McEnroe . . . .   [ ]-8

Billy Graham . . . .   [ ]-9
Leonard Bernstein . . . .   [ ]-0
John F. Kennedy . . . .   [ ]-x
Muhammad Ali . . . .   [ ]-y

Walter Cronkite 54   [ ]-1
Robert Redford . . . .   [ ]-2
Mahatma Gandhi . . . .   [ ]-3
John Lennon . . . .   [ ]-4
Johnny Carson . . . .   [ ]-5

Other: _____   [ ]-8
(WRITE IN)

None of these . . . .

35. If it were possible to change the genetic makeup of a child before birth, in which of the following categories would you consider making changes?

Physical characteristics (i.e., eye color, beauty, 55   [ ]-1
    strength, etc.) . . . .
Intelligence . . . .   [ ]-2
Personality/emotional characteristics . . . .   [ ]-3
Would not consider genetic changes for any reason   [ ]-4

Would only consider changes for health reasons,   [ ]-5
    such as to correct for handicaps, inherited dis-
    eases, etc. . . . .

In the past, a couple that could not conceive a child naturally had only two choices: they could adopt, or they could spend their lives without children. These days, many other options are either available now or will soon be, making it possible for infertile men and women to have children.

36a. If *you,* personally, were infertile and could not bear a child, and really wanted a child, which option would you prefer?
Adopt a child 56   [ ]-1
Hire a *surrogate mother* to carry and give birth to   [ ]-2
    your mate's child . . . .
Decide not to have children . . . .   [ ]-3
Other: _____   [ ]-4
(WRITE IN)

b. If you could *bear* a child, *but not conceive one,* which option would you prefer?

Adopt a child   57   ☐-1

Hire a surrogate mother to carry and give birth to your husband's child . . . .   ☐-2

Transplant to your womb another woman's embryo, fertilized scientifically (i.e., in a test tube) with your mate's sperm . . . .   ☐-3

Decide not to have children . . . .   ☐-4

Other: _____   ☐-5

(WRITE IN)

c. If your mate were infertile, which option would you prefer?

a. Adopt a child   58   ☐-1

b. Artificial insemination . . . .   ☐-2

c. Have no children at all . . . .   ☐-3

d. Find another mate . . . .   ☐-4

e. Decide not to have children . . . .   ☐-5

f. Other: _____   ☐-6

(WRITE IN)

37. If you and your mate were both fertile, but could not conceive a child in the natural way, would you consider *in vitro fertilization,* that is, the scientific fertilization in a "test tube" of your own embryo with your mate's sperm (i.e., "test-tube baby")?

Yes, I'd consider it   59   ☐-1

No, I wouldn't consider it . . . .   ☐-2

38a. If you were to undergo artificial insemination, would you want to know more than the age, race and the general health of the sperm donor?

a. Yes   60   ☐-1

b. No . . . .   ☐-2

b. *IF YOU SAID "YES" TO Q.38a:* Which of the following qualities would be most important to you in a sperm donor? (PLACE AN "X" NEXT TO ALL THAT APPLY)

High intelligence   61   ☐-1

Good looks . . . .   ☐-2

Athletic ability . . . .   ☐-3

Artistic talent . . . .   ☐-4

Financial success . . . .   ☐-5

Leadership qualities . . . .   ☐-6

Scientific ability . . . .   ☐-7

Emotional stability . . . .   ☐-8

Pleasant personality . . . .   -9
Other: _____   -0
(WRITE IN)

c. *IF YOU SAID "YES" TO Q.38a:* And which of these qualities would be least important to you in a sperm donor?

High intelligence 62   -1
Good looks . . . .   -2
Athletic ability . . . .   -3
Artistic talent . . . .   -4

Financial success . . . .   -5
Leadership qualities . . . .   -6
Scientific ability . . . .   -7
Emotional stability . . . .   -8
Pleasant personality . . . .   -9
Other: _____   -0
(WRITE IN)

39. How does it make you feel to know that women have so many new childbearing options?

a. Pleased 63   -1
b. Indifferent . . . .   -2
c. Uneasy . . . .   -3

40. Do you find these new childbearing options immoral?

Yes, all of them 64   -1
Yes, some of them . . . .   -2
None of them . . . .   -3
Not sure . . . .   -4

41. How do you think the new options for motherhood will affect the relationship between women and their children?

a. Children will be better planned, more wanted, 65   -1
    and more loved . . . .
b. Children will be ordered like consumer goods   -2
    and the relationship will be less personal . . . .
c. No change . . . .   -3
d. Other: _____   -4
(WRITE IN)

SECTION VI — DIET, EXERCISE, AND SEXUAL EXPRESSION

42a. Do you read the ingredient labels and nutrition information on the foods that you buy and eat?

All the time .... 66 ☐-1
Generally .... ☐-2
Only on items that I'm really concerned about .. ☐-3
Never .... ☐-4

b. Are you concerned about additives and preservatives in your food?

Yes, very concerned .... 67 ☐-1
Pretty concerned .... ☐-2
Not really concerned .... ☐-3
Not at all concerned .... ☐-4

c. How aware are you of the nutritional value in your daily diet?

Very aware of the nutritional value of the foods I 68 ☐-1
eat ....
Pretty aware of the nutritional value of the foods ☐-2
I eat ....
Not at all that aware of the nutritional value of the ☐-3
foods I eat ....

43. About how often during the year are you actively on a weight-loss diet?

Never .... 69 ☐-1
A few days during the year .... ☐-2
A total of 1 or 2 weeks during the year .... ☐-3
A total of 1 month during the year .... ☐-4

A total of 2–3 months during the year .... ☐-5
A total of 4–6 months during the year .... ☐-6
Most of the year .... ☐-7
Always—every single day .... ☐-8

44. Which of the following would you want to use if they were made available? (PLACE AN "X" NEXT TO ALL THAT APPLY)

Energy-boosting medicine .... 70 ☐-1
Memory-enhancing medicine .... ☐-2
Proven aphrodisiacs .... ☐-3
Intelligence-boosting medicine .... ☐-4
Life-extension drugs .... ☐-5
None of the above .... ☐-6

45a. Do you think that most men tend to feel more casual about their sexual relationships than women do?

Yes .... 71 ☐-1

No .... ☐-2

Not sure .... ☐-3

b. *IF YOU SAID "YES"*: Do you think it will always be this way? Or will
things equal out in the near future?

        Always be this way .... 72 ☐-1

        Things will be more equal in the future .... ☐-2

        Not sure .... ☐-3

SECTION VII — A LITTLE ABOUT YOU

The following questions are to be used only for classification
purposes. Your answers will give us the means to quantify
your opinions with those of the other respondents across the
country who are helping us with this study. Again, in no way
will your answers be tied to you personally.

A. In which of the following groups is your age?

        18–24 years .... 73 ☐-1

        25–29 years .... ☐-2

        30–34 years .... ☐-3

        35–39 years .... ☐-4

        40–44 years .... ☐-5

        45–54 years .... ☐-6

        55 years or over .... ☐-7

B. Are you married or single?

        Married .... 74 ☐-1

        Single .... ☐-2

        Divorced/separated .... ☐-3

        Widowed .... ☐-4

        Living as married (living together) .... ☐-5

C. Including yourself, how many people are there living in your household?

        1.. 75 ☐-1

        2.. ☐-2

        3.. ☐-3

        4.. ☐-4

        5 or more .... ☐-5

2. Do you have any children?

        Yes, living at home .... 76 ☐-1

        Yes, living away from home .... ☐-2

Yes, both living at home and away from home . [____]-3
No, I have no children . . . . [____]-4

3. *IF "YES":* What are their ages? (PLACE AN "X" NEXT TO ALL THAT APPLY)

Under 2 years old . . . . 77 [____]-1
2–5 years old . . . . [____]-2
6–9 years old . . . . [____]-3
10–14 years old . . . . [____]-4
15–17 years old . . . . [____]-5
Over 18 years old . . . . [____]-6

D. What is the highest level of education you have achieved?

High school graduate or less . . . . 78 [____]-1
1–3 years of college . . . . [____]-2
College graduate . . . . [____]-3
1–2 years of postgraduate education . . . . [____]-4
More than 2 years of postgraduate education . . [____]-5

E1. Are you currently employed?

Yes, full time . . . . 5 [____]-1
Yes, part time . . . . [____]-2
No, but will be getting a job in the near future . [____]-3
No, and will not be getting a job in the near future [____]-4

2. *IF "YES":* What is your occupation?

(PLEASE PRINT) Position: _____ [____]-6
[____]-7
Type of Industry: _____ [____]-8
[____]-9

F. *IF YOU ARE MARRIED OR LIVING AS MARRIED:* Does your partner work?

Yes, full time . . . . 10 [____]-1
Yes, part time . . . . [____]-2
No, but will be getting a job in the near future . [____]-3
No, and will not be getting a job in the near future [____]-4

G1. In which of these categories is your total *household income,* before taxes?

$14,999 a year or less . . . . 11 [____]-1
$15,000–24,999 a year . . . . [____]-2
$25,000–29,999 a year . . . . [____]-3

$30,000–34,999 a year .... -4
$35,000–39,999 a year .... -5
$40,000–49,999 a year .... -6
$50,000–74,999 a year .... -7
$75,000 or more a year .... -8

2. *IF WORKING:* And in which of these categories is your total *personal income,* before taxes?

$4,999 a year or less .... 12 -1
$5,000–9,999 a year -2
$10,000–14,999 a year .... -3
$15,000–19,999 a year .... -4

$20,000–24,999 a year .... -5
$25,000–29,999 a year .... -6
$30,000–34,999 a year .... -7
$35,000–39,999 a year .... -8
$40,000 or more a year .... -9

H. Which of these products do you or someone else in your household either own or plan to purchase in the next year?

Video cassette recorder .... 13 -1
Personal computer .... -2
Telephone answering machine .... -3
Video game player .... -4
Projection television .... -5
Cable TV/Pay TV .... -6
Component stereo equipment .... -7

11. What is your religion?

Catholic .... 14 -1
Protestant .... -2
Jewish .... -3
Greek Orthodox .... -4
Nondenominational .... -5

Other: _____ -6
(WRITE IN)
None .... -7

12. *IF YOU SAID PROTESTANT ABOVE:* What denomination?

Adventist .... 15 -1
Baptist .... -2
Congregationalist .... -3
Episcopalian .... -4

Lutheran .... □ -5
Methodist .... □ -6
Morman .... □ -7
Pentecostal .... □ -8

Presbyterian .... □ -9
Unitarian .... □ -0
United Church of Christ .... □ -x

Other: _____ □ -y
(WRITE IN)

None .... -16 □ -1

J. And what is your race?
White .... 17 □ -1
Black .... □ -2
Hispanic .... □ -3
Other _____ □ -4
(WRITE IN)

Thank you very much for your help in filling out this questionnaire.

APPENDIX II

Results of Woman of Tomorrow Survey in the U.S.

METHODOLOGY

The study was conducted in two stages:

- In the first stage, a national sample of women were contacted on the telephone via random digit dialing.
- The second stage involved a self-administered questionnaire, mailed to eligible respondents from the first stage who agreed to participate.

The universe investigated was defined as:

- Ages 25 to 44 years.
- At least some college (or educational equivalent).
- Household income of at least $15,000.

The response rate was very high for a study of this type.

- Over 90 percent of eligible respondents contacted in the first stage agreed to fill out the mail questionnaire.
- Of the 613 questionnaires mailed, 434 were returned by the cutoff date, yielding a response rate of 71 percent.

DESCRIPTIONS AND SIZES OF ANALYTIC SUBGROUPS

Age	Number in Group
25–34 years	178
35–44 years	229

Have Children (Either at Home or Away)	
Yes	344
No	89
Working mother (defined as having a child *under 10 years old* and being employed full or part time)	117

Household Income	
<50K ($15,000–49,999 per year)	228
50K+ ($50,000 or more per year)	183

Employment Status	
Yes (either full or part time)	296
No	136
Professional/managerial (employed full or part time in a professional or managerial position)	162

Have PC (Personal Computer)	
Yes (either respondent or other household member *has or will get in next year*)	154
No	270

FEELINGS ABOUT THE FUTURE

(Number in Group)	Total (434)
	%
Total	100*
Describe Self as:	
Generally optimistic	63
Generally pessimistic	3
Some place in between	34
Level of Interest	
Fascinated	38
Mildly intrigued	55
Basically indifferent	5
Not sure	2

Opinion on the World in the Year 2000	
A better place	65
Not a better place	18
Not sure	17

From Which Sources Obtain Most Impressions About the Future	
Newspapers	33
TV	30
Magazines	26
Books	21
Friends/relatives	10
Somewhere else	11

*Percentages add to more than 100% due to multiple response.

SPACE TRAVEL

(Number in Group)	Total (434)
	%
Total	100

If You Had the Chance, Would You Take a Trip into Space?	
Yes	46
No	49
Maybe	5

INTEREST IN SCIENCE

	Total		
(Number in Group)	(434)		
	%		
Total	100*		

Computers	
Have some familiarity	64
Want to learn more about	63

Robotics	
Have some familiarity	6
Want to learn more about	27

Genetic Engineering	
Have some familiarity	14
Want to learn more about	33

Bionics	
Have some familiarity	10
Want to learn more about	27

Infertility/Test-Tube Baby Research	
Have some familiarity	34
Want to learn more about	31

Molecular Biology	
Have some familiarity	18
Want to learn more about	28

Astronomy	
Have some familiarity	18
Want to learn more about	34
Not familiar with any of these	18
Don't want to learn more about any of these	4

If Offered a Grant to Study One of These, Which Would You Choose?	
Computers	30
Infertility/test-tube baby research	14
Molecular biology	13
Genetic engineering	13
Astronomy	11
Bionics	6
Robotics	5
None of the above	7
Not sure	1

*Percentages add to more than 100% due to multiple response.

BENEFITS OF TECHNOLOGY

	Total		
(Number in Group)	(434)		
	%		
Total	100*		

Area in Which a Major Technological Breakthrough Would Have the Greatest Positive Effect on Your Life	
Health	67
Energy	23
Education	20
Domestic environment	20
Work environment	9
Birth control/reproduction	7
Transportation	7
Weather	5

*Percentages add to more than 100% due to multiple response.

THE COMPUTER AGE

	Total		Total
(Number in Group)	(434)	Number in Group	(434)
	%		%
Total	100*	Total	100

Feelings About the Computer/Information Age		*Ways Would Use Home Computer*	
Excites me	86	Use with children—both to teach and learn with them	64
Makes me uneasy	41	Do family accounting/bookkeeping	61
Not sure/don't care	7	File personal data—e.g., addresses, recipes, shopping lists	58

Desire for Home Computer[1]			
Definitely want	50 }75%	Use databases—medical information, catalogs, directories, encyclopedias, etc.	49
Probably want	25		
Maybe want	18	Use as a word processor	44
Probably don't want	5	Play video/mental games	28
Definitely don't want	2	Shop at home with it	22
		Telecommute/work at home on it	16
	Total	Other	6
(Number in Group)	(316)	Wouldn't use	3
	%		
Total	100		

When Plan to Get a Home Computer[1]	
This year	11
Within 2–3 years	40
Within 4–5 years	27
Not until more than 5 years from now	13
Never	6
Not sure	3

*Percentages add to more than 100% due to multiple response.
[1]Based on those who do not own a PC already.

ROBOTICS

	Total	*Ways in Which Robot Could Help*	
(Number in Group)	(434)	Housecleaning	86
	%	Acting as burglar alarm	79
Total	100*	Doing laundry	69
		Gardening	51
Interest in Owning a Robot to Help in Household		Cooking	43
		Planning personal finances	30
Interested	70	Teaching the children	24
Not interested	28	Acting as a pet or companion	9
Not sure	2	Washing/changing baby	1
		Other	3
		None of the above	5

*Percentages add to more than 100% due to multiple response.

NUTRITION AND DIET

	Total
(Number in Group)	(434)
	%
Total	100

Read Labels/Nutritional
Information on Foods

All the time	18
Generally	44
Only on items concerned about	35
Never	3

Concerned About Additives/
Preservatives in Food

Very concerned	31
Pretty concerned	47
Not really concerned	21
Not at all concerned	1

Awareness of Nutritional
Value of Daily Diet

Very aware	33
Pretty aware	62
Not at all aware	5

Amount of Time During the
Year Actively on a Weight
Loss Diet

Never	19
A few days	11
A total of one or two weeks	13
A total of one month	14
A total of two to three months	15
A total of four to six months	5
Most of the year	18
Always—every single day	3
Not sure	2

FUTURE DRUGS

	Total
(Number in Group)	(434)
	%
Total	100*

Future Medicines Would
Use If Available

Energy-boosting medicine	50
Memory-enhancing medicine	44
Intelligence-boosting medicine	41
Life-extension drugs	33
Proven aphrodisiacs	12
None of the above	26
Not sure	2

*Percentages add to more than 100% due to multiple response.

SEX ROLES: AREAS OF PERCEIVED MALE SUPERIORITY

	Total
(Number in Group)	(434)
	%
Total	100

Which Sex Is More Competent in:

Sports Ability/Other Physical Skills

Men	55
Women	1
Both equal	44

High Self-Esteem

Men	46
Women	13
Both equal	41

Math Ability

Men	46
Women	6
Both equal	48

Professional Ambition/Motivation

Men	46
Women	6
Both equal	48

SEX ROLES: AREAS OF PERCEIVED FEMALE SUPERIORITY

	Total	Social Skills	
(Number in Group)	(434)	Women	57
	%	Men	2
Total	100	Both equal	41

Which Sex Is More Competent in:		Verbal/Communicative Skills	
Nurturing Ability		Women	41
		Men	5
Women	71	Both equal	54
Men	1		
Both equal	28		

FUTURE SEX ROLES

	Total	Who Do You Believe Is More Prepared for the Future?	
(Number in Group)	(434)		
	%		
Total	100	Men	25
		Women	38
		Both equal	36
		Not sure	1

MEN VERSUS WOMEN: SEXUAL RELATIONSHIPS

	Total	Believe That Men Tend to Feel More Casual in Their Sexual Relationships than Women	
(Number in Group)	(434)		59
	%		
Total	100	In future, believe things will be more equal	44
		Believe it will always be this way	32
		Not sure	24

WOMEN ROLE MODELS

	Total		
(Number in Group)	(434)	Barbara Walters	10
	%	Nancy Reagan	9
Total	100*	Estee Lauder	8
		Jane Fonda	8
Which of These Women Represents the Best Role Model for Young Women Today?		Chris Evert Lloyd	5
		Helen Gurley Brown	4
		Gloria Steinem	4
		Lillian Hellman	3
		Ann Landers	2
Geraldine Ferraro	34	Jacqueline Onassis	1
Sally Ride	30	Christie Brinkley	1
Sandra Day O'Connor	27	Other	3
Margaret Thatcher	20	None of the above	8
Mother Teresa	13		

*Percentages add to more than 100% due to multiple response.

THE FAMILY OF THE FUTURE

	Total	Mother and father with children and grandparents/other close relatives nearby (extended family)	17
(Number in Group)	(434)		
	%		
Total	100	Communal groups of couples with children who share childrearing and other tasks	7
Typical Family of the Future		Single woman with children	6
Mother and father with children	63	Childless couple	3
		Single adults without children	2
		Not sure	2

THE FAMILY OF TODAY

	Total	More than three	5
(Number in Group)	(434)	None	1
	%	Not sure (no answer)	3
Total	100		
		Should American Government Use Tax Incentives/Welfare Payments to Encourage Smaller Families?	
Number of Children Ideal American Family Should Have			
One	5	Yes	35
Two	66	No	55
Three	20	Not sure	10

HOME LIFE

	Total	*Household Responsibilities That Should Be Shared Equally by Couple*	
(Number in Group)	(434)		
	%		
Total	100	Raising the children	98
		Deciding on investments	96
Environment in Which Expect to Live Most of Life		Deciding on household budget	95
		Planning social activities	95
Urban neighborhood	22	Housecleaning	93
Suburb in commuting distance of a		Tutoring the children	92
city	61	Transporting the children	92
Small town or village	15	Washing dishes	87
Rural area	2	Yard work	83
		Grocery shopping	81
		Doing the cooking	80
Future Alternative Home Environments Considered Appealing		Paying bills	79
		Doing laundry	77
		Planning meals	73
Colony out in space—like on a		Doing home repairs	72
space station or ship	18		
Another planet or moon	15		Total
Underwater community	10		
Underground community	9	Number in Group	(372)
Other	2		%
None of above are appealing at all	46	Total	100*

HOME LIFE *(cont.)*

Household Responsibilities That Are
Currently Shared
Equally by Couple [1]

Deciding on household budget	84
Deciding on investments	82
Planning social activities	81
Raising the children[2]	85
Yard work	61
Tutoring the children[2]	64
Transporting the children[2]	59
Doing home repairs	46
Washing dishes	44
Paying the bills	43
Housecleaning	41
Grocery shopping	40
Doing the cooking	38
Doing the laundry	32
Planning meals	28

*Percentages add to more than 100% due to multiple response.
[1]Based on those who are married or living together.
[2]Based on those who are married/living together and have children living at home.

WORK IN THE FUTURE

	Total
(Number in Group)	(434)
	%
Total	100*

Jobs That Will Be Made Obsolete
by New Technologies

Bank teller	81
Ticket agent	73
File clerk	68
Fast-food worker	34
Machinist	29
Miner	28
Draftsman	27
Welder	21
Secretary	19
Factory foreman	13
Combat soldier	9
Fire fighter	2
Other	1
All of above	2
None of above	5

	Total
(Number in Group)	(296)
	%
Total	100

Concern That Job Will Be Made
Obsolete Within 10–20 Years [1]

Seriously concerned	2
Moderately concerned	12
Not very concerned	30
Not at all concerned	53
No answer	3

Job Training/Retraining [1]

Think will need job retraining to remain employable in future	43
Believe will not need retraining	25
Not sure	20
Already have/currently in retraining or going back to school	12

	Total
(Number in Group)	(136)
	%
Total	100

Job Training/Retraining [2]

Willing to go back to school/training program to become more employable	63
Not willing	4
Not sure	22
Already have/currently in training or going back to school	11

*Percentages add to more than 100% due to multiple response.
[1]Among those who are now employed outside the home.
[2]Among those who are not employed—small base sizes.

WORKING OUTSIDE THE HOME

	Total
(Number in Group)	(434)
	%
Total	100*
Expect to Be Working Outside the Home Most of Adult Life	74

Why Will Be Working

To get out of house and stay active	50
To provide financial help for family	47
For personal financial gains	39
To get ahead in a chosen career	34

Financial necessity	26
All of these reasons	26
Other reason	5

If Had the Choice of Working in an Office or Doing the Same Work at Home, Which Would Choose?

Office	19
Home	14
Want to spend some time working at home, but not all the time	66
Not sure	1

*Percentages add to more than 100% due to multiple response.

CAREERS

	Total
(Number in Group)	(434)
	%
Total	100*

Career Choices with Greatest Appeal

Motherhood	29
Business executive	24
Interior designer	21
Teacher	15
Writer/editor	14
Medical doctor	13
Fashion designer	10
Lawyer	8
Nurse	8
Astronaut/pilot	6
Scientist	6
Computer programmer	6
Politician/stateswoman	6
Athlete	6

Mathematician	3
Policewoman	2
Secretary	2
Engineer	1
Military officer	1
Combat soldier	—
Fire fighter	—
None of these	1

Careers for Which Women Are Considered Unsuited Even with Training[1]

Combat soldier	37
Fire fighter	13
Military officer	8
Policewoman	4
Politician/stateswoman	1
None of these	53

*Percentages add to more than 100% due to multiple response.
[1]Same list given as previous question—only those with incidence over 1% are reported here.

CAREER VERSUS MOTHERHOOD

	Total
(Number in Group)	(434)
	%
Total	100

Does Raising a Family Get in the Way of a Woman's Career?

Yes, always	7
Most of the time	34
Only sometimes	56
Never	2
Not sure	1

Are Children of Full-Time Homemakers Better Off Than Children of Working Mothers?

Yes, always	6
Most of the time	35
Only sometimes	53
Never	6
Not sure	—

	Total
(Number in Group)	(89)[a]
	%
Total	100

Would You Consider Remaining Childless to Concentrate on a Career or Other Personal Goals?

Yes	31
No	17
Already decided to have children	32
Already decided to remain childless	20
	Total
(Number in Group)	(344)
	%
Total	100

Among Those With Children

Do You Feel That Being a Mother Has Prevented You from Pursuing a Career or Other Personal Goals?

Yes, but given the choice would have done the same	45
Yes, and given the choice would have done things differently	12
No	40
Not sure	3

	Total
(Number in Group)	(434)
	%
Total	100

If You Had the Financial Choice, Would You Prefer to Stay Home While Your Child Was Young?

Yes	77
No	10
Maybe	13

What Age Would You Want Your Child to Be Before You Returned to Work?

Less than 1 year	12
1–2 years	9
3–4 years	11
5–6 years	29
7–8 years	15
9–15 years	11
Over 15 years	11
Wouldn't work	2

[a]Based on those who do not have children.

DESIRE FOR CHILDREN

	Total
(Number in Group)	(434)
	%
Total	100

If (Hypothetically)
Unmarried and Childless,
Concern Over Getting Old
Without Having Children

Very concerned	39
Moderately concerned	27
Slightly concerned	21
Not concerned at all	11
Not sure	2

If (Hypothetically)
Unmarried and Wanted
Children, Would You Consider
Getting Pregnant and Raising
a Child on Your Own?

Yes, definitely	16
Maybe	24
Probably not	28
Definitely not	30
No answer	2

OPTIONS IN CHILDBEARING

	Total
(Number in Group)	(434)
	%
Total	100

Ideal Age to Give Birth if
Medical Risks Were the Same
at Any Age

Under 25 years	21
26–30 years	52
31–35 years	21
Over 35 years	4
Not sure	2

Would You Consider Cryogenic
Freezing of Embryo for Later
Reimplantation/Birth?

Yes	11
No	70
Not sure	19

Desire for Amniocentesis if
Pregnant to Check Out
Possible Abnormality of Fetus

Would want	52
Would not want	15
Not sure	33

Findings That Would Lead to
Consideration of Abortion

Extremely serious illness (Down's syndrome, schizophrenia, mental retardation, immune system breakdown)	38
Moderately serious illness (blindness, muscular dystrophy, risk of early heart disease)	34
Less serious illnesses (asthma, dyslexia, diabetes)	4
Other	1
None—would not consider abortion	23

	Total
(Number in Group)	(434)
	%
Total	100*

Categories Would Consider
Making Genetic Changes in
Child if Possible

Intelligence	11
Personality/emotional characteristics	9
Physical characteristics	3

*Percentages add to more than 100% due to multiple response.

OPTIONS IN CHILDBEARING *(cont.)*

Would only consider changes for health reasons	83
Would not consider making genetic changes	7

	Total
(Number in Group)	(434)
	%
Total	100

Preferred Sex of First Child, If Could Choose

Boy	24
Girl	12
Both (twins)	4
Doesn't matter—rather let nature take its course	59
No answer	1

Preferred Option if Personally Infertile and Really Wanted a Child

Adoption	77
Hire surrogate mother to bear mate's child	11
Other	3
Decide not to have children	8
Not sure	1

Preferred Option if Could Bear a Child But Not Conceive One

Adoption	47
Transplant another woman's embryo to own womb, fertilized by mate	42
Other	2
Decide not to have children	8
Not sure	1

Preferred Option if Male Were Infertile

Adoption	50
Artificial insemination	38

Other	1
Decide not to have children	10
Not sure	1

If Both Fertile, But Could Not Conceive Naturally, Would Consider In Vitro Fertilization

Yes	88
No	12

	Total
(Number in Group)	(434)
	%

Would Want to Know More than Age, Race and General Health of Sperm Donor	82
	(100%)*

Qualities Most Important in a Sperm Donor

Emotional stability	94
High intelligence	84
Pleasant personality	64
Good looks	47
Leadership qualities	40
Athletic ability	34
Artistic talent	28
Scientific ability	17
Financial success	16
Other	6

	Total
(Number in Group)	(434)
	%
Total	100*

Profession Would Choose for Father of Next Child

Successful businessman	49
Lawyer	23
Scientist	22
Scholar	21
Athlete	12

*Percentages add to more than 100% due to multiple response.

OPTIONS IN CHILDBEARING *(cont.)*

Writer	12	*How Does It Make You Feel to Know That Women Have So Many New Childbearing Options?*	
Teacher	12		
Artist	7		
Musician	7		
Religious leader	6	Pleased	68
Politician or statesman	4	Indifferent	12
Entertainer	2	Uneasy	19
Actor	1	Not sure	1
Other	12		
None of these	7	*Do You Find These New Options Immoral?*	

Famous Man Would Find Most Desirable as Father of Next Child[1]

		Yes, all of them	2
		Some of them	30
		No, none of them	41
John F. Kennedy	16	Not sure	27
Walter Cronkite	16		
Robert Redford	13	*How New Options Will Affect Relationship Between Women and Their Children*	
Albert Einstein	12		
Lee J. Iacocca	10		
Neil Armstrong	8		
Mahatma Gandhi	6	Children will be better planned, more wanted and more loved	47
John D. Rockefeller	5		
Billy Graham	5	Children will be ordered like consumer goods, and relationship will be less personal	11
Leonard Bernstein	5		
Henry Kissinger	4		
Pablo Picasso	2		
John Lennon	2	See no changes	33
None of these	28	Other	6
		Not sure	3

	Total
(Number in Group)	(434)
	%
Total	100

[1]Mentions of less than 2% not shown.

SOURCE NOTES

We wish to thank all the scientists who spent time talking to us and provided most of the scientific information used in writing this book. Other sources of quoted material are listed below.

Chapter 1

7 Samuel Florman's comments come from pp. 123 and 130 of *Blaming Technology,* published in 1981 by St. Martin's Press.

Chapter 2

22 The quotes from Candace Pert are taken from an extensive interview with her that was published in the February 1982 issue of *Omni*.

24 Vivian Gornick quotes I.I. Rabi on p. 36 of *Women in Science*, published in 1983 by Simon and Schuster.

26 Howard Gardner's *Frames of Mind* was published in 1983 by Basic Books.

28 A detailed summary of the work on sex differences in animal behavior and brain organization, and the influences of early hormone exposures on male and female brains and behavior, can be found in Robert W. Goy and Bruce S. McEwen's *Sexual Differentiation of the Brain*, published in 1980 by The MIT Press.

32 John Money's description of adrenogenital girls comes from pp. 27–28 of *Love and Lovesickness: The Science of Sex, Gender Difference, and Pair-Bonding*, published in 1980 by Johns Hopkins University Press. This book, along with our interviews with Money and information from several of his scientific papers, provided much of the background for this chapter.

33 June Reinisch's comments can be found in an article by Jo Durden-Smith and Diane de Simone in the August 1984 issue of *Omni*.

35 Money's statements on homosexuality are drawn both from interviews and from his writings on "Endocrine Influences and Psychosexual Status Spanning the Life Cycle" in the *Handbook of Biological Psychiatry*, Part III, published in 1980 by Marcel Dekker, and "Gender-Transposition Theory and Homosexual Genesis" in the *Journal of Sex & Marital Therapy*, Vol. 10, No. 2, 1984.

36 Jerre Levy's comments can be found in an interview published in the January 1985 issue of *Omni*. For quick background on the split-brain work, and some of the simplistic myths that have grown up around it, see her article "Right Brain, Left Brain: Fact and Fiction" in the May 1985 issue of *Psychology Today*.

38 Polly Henninger's work is described in the November 1984 issue of Caltech's *Engineering & Science* bulletin.

Chapter 3

44 Eleanor Maccoby and Carol Jacklin's findings reported here are taken from p. 351 of their comprehensive book *The Psychology of Sex Differences*, published in 1974 by Stanford University Press, which pulled together all the work done in the field up to that time.

51 Diane McGuinness describes sex differences in learning and the psychology

of learning in general in her book *When Children Don't Learn,* published in 1985 by Basic Books.

52   These quotes from Maccoby and Jacklin also come from *The Psychology of Sex Differences,* pp. 130 and 362.

55   *The Psychology of Sex Differences,* p. 373.

57   Seattle's fire chief was quoted in the September 1984 *Vogue.*

58   The material on Amy and Jake and on Kohlberg's scale is from pp. 18 and 25–31 of Carol Gilligan's *In a Different Voice,* published in 1982 by Harvard University Press.

60   John Naisbitt's comments on the eleventh megatrend can be found in the May 1983 issue of *Esquire.*

Chapter 4

61   The quote from Irven DeVore and Owen Lovejoy that opens this chapter is from p. 18 of "The Natural Superiority of Women" in *The Physical and Mental Health of Aged Women,* published in 1985 by Springer.

63   Robert Butler's comments were reported in the May 15, 1984, *Los Angeles Times.*

68   DeVore and Lovejoy's comments can be found on p. 19 of "The Natural Superiority of Women."

70   Leonard Hayflick's statements are from a paper entitled "Programmed Theory of Aging," which he presented at the annual meeting of the American Association for the Advancement of Science (AAAS) January 4, 1981, in Toronto.

71   Morton Rothstein's comments are reported in the spring 1983 issue of the *Source* Research Digest of SUNY, Buffalo.

71   W. Donner Denckla's research was described in an interview in the November 1981 issue of *Omni.*

72   George A. Sacher's statements are from a paper entitled "Evolutionary Theory in Gerontology," which he presented at the annual meeting of the AAAS January 4, 1981 in Toronto.

73   Roy Walford detailed his theories of aging in a book called *Maximum Life Span,* published in 1983 by W. W. Norton and Co.

75   The free radical theory of aging gained a huge popular following when Durk Pearson and Sandy Shaw's best-seller *Life Extension* was published in 1982 by Warner Books.

76   Albert Rosenfeld's column ran in the February 1983 issue of *Omni.*

78   Lois M. Verbrugge presented her findings in a paper entitled *Women, Work, and Health* at the AAAS annual meeting May 27, 1984, in New York City.

79   The study on prominent women is reported in Metropolitan Life Insurance
      Co.'s *Statistical Bulletin*, Vol. 60, No. 1, for January-March 1979.

Chapter 5

85   One of the first books to popularize the set point theory was *The Dieter's
      Dilemma* by William Bennett and Joel Gurin, published in 1982 by Basic
      Books.
88   Rudolph Leibel's statements are from a paper on "Obesity and Nutrient
      Metabolism," presented May 26, 1984 at the annual meeting of the AAAS
      in New York City.
95   The glycemic index presented here was drawn from a chart David J. A.
      Jenkins and his colleagues published in the August 18, 1984, issue of *The
      Lancet.*
100   Michael Colgan's book *Your Personal Vitamin Profile* was published in 1982
      by William Morrow.
103   Robert Stauffer is quoted in an article called "Fighting Chance" in the
      November 1984 issue of *Omni.*
104   Billie Jean King's comments came from her article "Why I Believe That
      Women Must Enter the Crucible of Sports Competition with Men" in the
      April 1984 issue of *Glamour.*

Chapter 6

106   Shere Hite's quote at the head of this chapter is from her article "True Love
      and Great Sex . . . Having It All" in the November 1983 *Mademoiselle.*
109   Donald Symons' book *The Evolution of Human Sexuality* was published in
      1979 by Oxford University Press.
109   Martin Daly and Margo Wilson's statement comes from their article "Sex
      and Strategy" in *New Scientist* January 4, 1979.
110   Sarah Blaffer Hrdy's *The Woman That Never Evolved* was published in 1981
      by Harvard University Press.
110   Hite's quotes are from pp. 421–22 of *The Hite Report: A Nationwide Study
      of Female Sexuality,* published in 1976 by Macmillan.
111   *Parade* magazine's survey of sexual attitudes was published as "Sex in Amer-
      ica Today" in the October 28, 1984 issue.
111   Alfred Kinsey's findings are reported on pp. 681–82 of *Sexual Behavior in
      the Human Female,* published in 1953 by W. B. Saunders Co.

114 Kinsey's findings on individual variation in females are quoted from pp. 650 and 688 of *Sexual Behavior in the Human Female.*

115 The Dear Abby column quoted ran in newspapers nationwide on March 6, 1985.

116 One of the best accounts of Owen Lovejoy's theory can be found in *Lucy: The Beginnings of Humankind* by Donald Johanson and Maitland Edey, published in 1981 by Simon and Schuster.

118 Money's statements on the Inquisition are quoted from "Food, Fitness and Vital Fluids: Sexual Pleasure from Graham Crackers to Kellogg's Cornflakes" in the *British Journal of Sexual Medicine,* June/July 1984.

119 John Harvey Kellogg's *Plain Facts for Old and Young* is excerpted in an appendix to Money's paper on "The Genealogical Descent of Sexual Psychoneuroendocrinology from Sex and Health Theory: The Eighteenth to the Twentieth Centuries" in *Psychoneuroendocrinology,* Vol. 8, No. 4, 1983.

121 The figures on teenage pregnancy appeared in an article in *The New York Times* March 13, 1985.

122 A good collection of the so-called "utopian" sexual prophecies I refer to can be found in Robert T. and Anna K. Francoeur's *The Future of Sexual Relations,* published in 1974 by Prentice-Hall.

122 Lorna J. Sarrel's quotes are from "Adult Sexual Relationships" in the March 1984 issue of the *SIECUS Report.*

124 The *Psychology Today* reader survey cited ran in the July 1983 issue.

125 Money's quotes on loveblots come from his chapter "Pairbonding and Limerence," in the *International Encyclopedia of Psychiatry, Psychology, Psychoanalysis and Neurology, Progress Volume I,* published in 1983 by Aesculapius Publishers, and from pp. 67–68 of *Love and Lovesickness.*

126 Kinsey's quote is from p. 261 of *Sexual Behavior in the Human Male,* published in 1948 by W. B. Saunders Co.

127 The article on "Apartners" ran in the December 13, 1982, issue of *New York.*

Chapter 7

136 Alex Comfort's quote is from p. 57 of *The Future of Sexual Relations.*

140 Hisako Matsubara's quotes are taken from her "First Word" column in the June 1985 *Omni.*

140 The material on marriage styles comes from Catherine E. Ross, John Mirowsky, and Joan Huber's paper on "Dividing Work, Sharing Work, and In-Between: Marriage Patterns and Depression" in the *American Sociological Review,* Vol. 48, December 1983, and from Ross and Mirowsky's presen-

tation May 25, 1984, at the annual meeting of the AAAS in New York City.

143   The quotes from the *Wall Street Journal*/Gallup poll of women executives are from the newspaper's October 30, 1984, issue.

143   The Connecticut Mutual Life Insurance Co. survey is quoted in "The Partnership" in the June 1984 issue of *Esquire*.

144   *American Couples* by Pepper Schwartz and Philip Blumstein was published in 1983 by William Morrow.

148   The survey report "Attitudes of Pediatricians Toward Maternal Employment" was published by Marilyn Heins and her University of Arizona at Tucson associates in *Pediatrics*, Vol. 72, No. 3, September 1983.

149   Jacqueline Lerner's results were described in *Research/Penn State* in December 1984 and published as "The Infant's Developing Individuality and Family Change: The Longitudinal Effects of Maternal Employment" by Lerner and Nancy Galambos in *Advances in Infancy Research, Vol. 5*, issued in 1985 by Ablex-Hillsdale.

149   The interview with Sandra Scarr entitled "What's a Parent To Do" ran in the May 1984 issue of *Psychology Today*. Her book *Mother Care, Other Care* was published in 1984 by Basic Books.

152   T. Berry Brazelton was quoted in an article on "Advice and Comfort for the Working Mother" in the June 1984 *Esquire*.

Chapter 8

155   For a look at the legal and other dilemmas posed by the new birth technologies see Lori B. Andrews' *New Conceptions: A Consumer's Guide to the Newest Infertility Treatments Including In Vitro Fertilization, Artificial Insemination and Surrogate Motherhood*, published in 1984 by St. Martin's Press.

161   Atef Moawad's advice was quoted in a UPI story appearing in the February 10, 1984, *Los Angeles Times*.

174   A closer look at the frontiers of gene therapy is provided in Yvonne Baskin's *The Gene Doctors*, published in 1984 by William Morrow.

Chapter 9

180   Jan Zimmerman's quote comes from p. 4 of *The Technological Woman: Interfacing with Tomorrow*, edited by Zimmerman and published in 1983 by Praeger Publishers.

182   The quotes are from a poll reported in the December 31, 1984, issue of *USA Today*.

182   Joan Wallach Scott's comments are from her article "The Mechanization of Women's Work" in the September 1982 *Scientific American.*

182   Ruth S. Cowan's *More Work for Mother* was published in 1983 by Basic Books.

185   Alvin Toffler's *The Third Wave* was published in 1980 by William Morrow.

185   John Naisbitt's quotes are from pp. 35–36 of *Megatrends,* published in 1982 by Warner Books.

186   *The Omni Online Database Directory* was published in 1983 by Macmillan.

187   Richard Adler's statements are from an article titled "Computers Face Trouble in the Home" in the September 7, 1983, *Los Angeles Times.*

188   Marvin Cetron's comments are from a May 16, 1984, speech in New Orleans to the Wine and Spirits Wholesalers Association.

189   George Leonard's statements are from his article "The Great School Reform Hoax" in the April 1984 *Esquire.*

189   Gerard K. O'Neill's prediction can be found on p. 98 of *2081: A Hopeful View of the Human Future,* published in 1981 by Simon and Schuster.

191   Andrew Molnar's comment is from his article on "The Search for New Intellectual Technologies" in the September 1982 *T.H.E. Journal.* Molnar and Dorothy K. Deringer's quote is from their article " 'Edutainment': How to Laugh and Learn" in the June 1984 *IEEE Spectrum.*

193   Richard A. Bolt describes his work in "Conversing with Computers" in the February/March 1985 *Technology Review.*

Chapter 10

205   The quote is from "Women at Work" in the January 28, 1985, *Business Week.*

207   These comments are also from Scott's article in the September 1982 *Scientific American.*

211   Lester C. Thurow is quoted in "Wage Gap: Women Still the 2nd Sex" in the September 13, 1984, *Los Angeles Times.*

211   Naisbitt's quotes are from pp. 14 and 63 of *Megatrends.*

212   Cetron's remarks here are also from his 1984 speech to the Wine and Spirits Wholesalers Association.

213   Wassily Leontief's comments are from an interview in the July 1984 *Omni.*

214   Vincent Giuliano wrote this in his article on "The Mechanization of Office Work" in the September 1982 *Scientific American.*

218   Norman Feingold and Norma Reno Miller's book *Emerging Careers: New Occupations for the Year 2000 and Beyond* was published in 1983 by Garrett Park Press. Marvin Cetron's *Jobs of the Future* was published in 1984 by McGraw-Hill.

Chapter 11

222   Sue E. Berryman's findings are in *Who Will Do Science?*, a special report published in November 1983 by the Rockefeller Foundation.

224   Molnar's quotes are from his September 1982 *T.H.E. Journal* article.

225   Candace Pert's column appeared in the December 1984 *Omni*.

226   Gornick's quotes are from pp. 15 and 66 of *Women in Science*.

227   Florman's quote is from p. 121 of *Blaming Technology*.

227   The NSF statement is from the agency's January 1984 *Women and Minorities in Science and Engineering* report.

228   The Scientific Manpower Commission's figures are from its 1984 annual edition of *Professional Women and Minorities—A Manpower Data Resource*.

229   Estelle Ramey's comments are from her chapter on "The Natural Capacity for Health in Women" in *Women: A Developmental Perspective*, published in April 1982 by the U.S. Department of Health and Human Services as NIH Publication No. 82–2298.

229   The study of schoolchildren quoted was the 1981–1982 National Assessment in Science conducted by Wayne W. Welch and Steven J. Rakow of the University of Minnesota with funding from the NSF.

230   The quote on the personality traits of scientists is from J. A. Chambers' "Relating Personality and Biographical Factors to Scientific Creativity" in *Psychological Monographs: General and Applied*, Vol. 78, No. 7, 1964.

230   Kate Rand Lloyd's talk was reported in the April 30, 1984, *Los Angeles Times*.

234   For a closer look at the early efforts by women to become astronauts, look at articles in the February 2, 1960, *Look;* August 29, 1960, *Time;* August 29, 1960, *Life;* October 8, 1960, *Science News Letter;* July 30, 1962, *Newsweek;* August 4, 1962, *Science News Letter;* October 21, 1962, *New York Times Magazine;* June 28, 1963, *Time;* May 11, 1964, *Newsweek;* and March 1965 *Science Digest.*

237   Harold Sandler's comments on women in space were reported in "Housewives in Space" in the June 1982 *Omni*.

Chapter 12

244   Kristina Hooper's comments can be found in an article entitled "Building Bridges for the Brain" in the June 1984 issue of *Discover*.

246   James O'Toole wrote this advice in an article in the April 1, 1984, *San Diego Union*.

247 Morton Hoppenfeld's quotes can be found in "Future Metropolis" in the October 1984 *Omni*.

248 Naisbitt made these statements in an interview published in the October 1984 *Omni*.

249 M. Granger Morgan's quotes are from his article "Electronic Entertainment: Balancing the Diet" in the June 1984 *IEEE Spectrum*.

INDEX